The
LIFE-CHANGING
SCIENCE *of*
DETECTING
BULLSHIT

The
LIFE-CHANGING
SCIENCE of
DETECTING
BULLSHIT

John V. Petrocelli

ST. MARTIN'S PRESS
NEW YORK

Published in the United States by

St. Martin's Press, an imprint of St. Martin's Publishing Group

www.stmartins.com

Library of Congress Cataloging-in-Publication Data

Names: Petrocelli, John V., author.
Title: The life-changing science of detecting bullshit / John V. Petrocelli.
Description: First Edition. | New York : St. Martin's Press, 2021. |
    Includes bibliographical references and index.
Identifiers: LCCN 2021006890 | ISBN 9781250271624 (hardcover) |
    ISBN 9781250271631 (ebook) | ISBN 9781250280152 (international,
    sold outside the U.S., subject to rights availability)
Subjects: LCSH: Critical thinking. | Reasoning. | Decision making.
Classification: LCC BF441 .P486 2021 | DDC 153.4/2—dc23
LC record available at https://lccn.loc.gov/2021006890

Our books may be purchased in bulk for promotional, educational,
or business use. Please contact your local bookseller or the
Macmillan Corporate and Premium Sales Department at
1-800-221-7945, extension 5442, or by email at
MacmillanSpecialMarkets@macmillan.com.

First U.S. Edition: 2021
First international edition: 2021

10   9   8   7   6   5   4   3   2   1

To my dearest of bullshit detectors,
Chepkemoi and Chepchumba—for calling me
on my bullshit when I needed it most
and giving me grace when I deserved it least.

Back in '82, I used to be able to throw a pigskin a quarter mile. I'm dead serious. How much you want to make a bet I can throw a football over them mountains? Yeah. If coach would've put me in [the] fourth quarter, we'd have been state champions, no doubt. No doubt in my mind. You better believe things would have been different. I'd have gone pro in a heartbeat. I'd be makin' millions of dollars and livin' in a big ol' mansion somewhere. You know, soakin' it up in a hot tub with my soul mate.

—UNCLE RICO (*Napoleon Dynamite*)

The truth may be puzzling. It may take some work to grapple with. It may be counterintuitive. It may contradict deeply held prejudices. It may not be consonant with what we desperately want to be true. But our preferences do not determine what's true.

—CARL SAGAN

CONTENTS

The

LIFE-CHANGING
SCIENCE *of*
DETECTING
BULLSHIT

INTRODUCTION

What Is Bullshit?

bull·shit (bo͝ol'shit') *Vulgar Slang n.* **1.** Foolish, deceitful, or boastful language. **2.** Something worthless, deceptive, or insincere. **3.** Insolent talk or behavior. **bull·shit·ted, bull·shit·ting, bull·shits** *v.intr.* **1.** To speak foolishly or insolently. **2.** To engage in idle conversation. *v.tr.* To attempt to mislead or deceive by talking nonsense. **bull·shit·ter** *n.*[1]

In February 2017, just two days before the 2017 NBA All-Star Game, superstar Kyrie Irving made some interesting claims in a podcast that ended up receiving more attention than the game. He stated:

> This is not even a conspiracy theory. The Earth is flat. The Earth is flat. The Earth is flat. . . . What I've been taught is that the Earth is round. But if you really think about it from a landscape of the way we travel, the way we move and the fact that—can you really think of us rotating around the Sun and all planets aligned, rotating in specific dates, being perpendicular with what's

going on with these planets [finger quotation marks on *planets*]? Because everything that they send—or that they want to say they're sending—doesn't come back. . . . There is no concrete information except for the information that they're giving us. They're particularly putting you in the direction of what to believe and what not to believe. The truth is right there, you just got to go searching for it.[2]

Kyrie isn't the only one. When online surveyor YouGov conducted a survey asking over 8,000 US adults, "Do you believe that the Earth is round or flat?," only 84% of respondents felt certain that the Earth is round. A total of 5% expressed doubts, 2% affirmed a flat Earth, and 7% weren't sure.[3] Even more, over 226,000 Facebook followers of the Flat Earth Society dispute the Earth's curvature by promoting the false belief that the Earth is flat. However, when someone like Kyrie Irving, a world-famous basketball star with over 4 million Twitter followers, promotes these kinds of claims, they will gain a lot of attention.

But did Kyrie actually believe what he was saying, or was he merely *bullshitting*?

As a social scientist, I take Kyrie's claims very seriously. I don't take them seriously because I think Kyrie is correct—I know his claims make as much sense as arguing that the Moon is made of cheese. I take them seriously because, as a researcher who studies bullshit, Kyrie's claims fit a pattern of behavior I see deployed over and over again. A belief in a flat Earth would make sense if there was genuine evidence of a worldwide conspiracy to fake decades of space exploration, a denial of many branches of science, or discoveries of new forces and laws of nature. But it doesn't really take any of this—all it takes is a mindset that completely disregards truth and genuine evidence. In other words, all it takes is bullshit.

Kyrie encourages us to seek the truth by finding concrete information and "doing some research."[4] That is a classic bullshitter move—ignore the overwhelming and convincing evidence by implying the real answer is not based on commonly accepted evidence or is actually unknown.[5] Although I won't pretend to know what Kyrie meant by "research," had he actually approached the question of the Earth's shape scientifically, he would have determined that the answer is certainly not "flat."

If Kyrie wanted to approach this question scientifically, he might have taken a glance at readily available scientific evidence on the issue. Scientists love using this method of analysis because critically evaluating a bunch of studies is much easier (less costly and time-consuming) than conducting their own experiments. There is well-documented evidence: of the Earth's shadow on the Moon when the Earth passes between the Moon and Sun (i.e., lunar eclipse), the fact that sunrise and sunset do not happen at the same time all over the world, our perspective at sunset, the shapes of other planets, and the fact that worldwide space research programs have gathered massive collections of satellite images—all supporting the belief that the Earth is not flat. As a *critical thinker* employing *evidence-based methods of reasoning*, I feel confident that the Earth is spherical. Why? Because multiple, independent sources of inquiry converge—with evidence—on the same conclusion that the planet we live on is shaped much more like a basketball than a hockey puck.

If historical records don't satisfy Earth-shape skeptics like Kyrie, there is always value in experimental replication (an essential piece of the scientific method). One very simple demonstration was conducted over 2,000 years ago by the Greek scholar Eratosthenes. Eratosthenes determined the shape of the Earth by putting a stick in the ground and doing a bit of math. He was aware that in Syene, the Sun was directly overhead on the first day of summer (June 21), casting no shadows at noon. Eratosthenes was in Alexandria, nearly 500 miles north from Syene. He planted a stick directly in the ground in Alexandria and waited to see if a shadow would be cast at noon. Sure enough, the angle of the stick's shadow measured about 7 degrees. Now, if the Sun's rays are coming in at the same angle at the same time of day, and a stick in Alexandria is casting a shadow while a stick in Syene is not, it must mean that the Earth's surface is curved.[6] Of course, Earth-shape skeptics could also try out Portuguese explorer Ferdinand Magellan and Spaniard Juan Sebastián Elcano's route of circumnavigating the globe. Magellan and Elcano set sail from Seville on September 20, 1519, sailed across the Atlantic, passed the southern tip of South America, sailed into the Pacific and Indian Oceans, around the southern tip of Africa, and returned to Seville on September 6, 1522.[7] If you don't have three years to circumnavigate the Earth, you might take Dick Rutan and Jeana Yeager's route by air—they were the first to do so—which they completed in nine days. In short, there are many routes to get to the same conclusion.

Kyrie isn't alone in believing something that isn't true. Many people still believe you can see the Great Wall of China from the Moon, despite the fact that Apollo astronauts confirmed that you cannot.[8] Many people believe that one human year is equivalent to seven dog years, although dog age actually depends on the size and breed of the dog (after 7 years, a Saint Bernard is 54, but a Maltese is only 44).[9] It's often said that you lose your body heat fastest through your head, despite the fact experts have shown humans to be just as cold if they went without wearing pants as if they went without wearing a hat.[10] People continue to insist that giving children sugar makes them hyperactive, despite the fact that virtually all tests show that sugar does not cause hyperactivity.[11] And many people still believe that vitamin C is an effective treatment for a cold, despite the fact that experts have demonstrated little to no evidence that this is true.[12]

Yet, sharing these facts often don't persuade people who never believed in science in the first place. If someone believes that it is more likely that thousands of scientists, worldwide, are colluding in a conspiracy to hide the true shape of the Earth, then explaining otherwise won't get you very far. Despite the public criticism Kyrie received for his flat-Earth theory, he stood firm and remained unconvinced, saying in 2018, "I don't know. I really don't," and added that people should "do [their] own research for what [they] want to believe in" because "our educational system is flawed."[13] It is one thing to suggest people do their research and another thing to make claims about things one clearly knows nothing about—but something tells me Kyrie hasn't really cared to look at genuine research evidence.

I'm not interested in insulting Kyrie. But as a scientist who happens to study the insidious consequences of bullshit, I am invested in the value of genuine evidence and the blind spots in our reasoning. We should believe the Earth is spherical because that is where compelling evidence, from multiple independent sources, leads us. Flat Earthers, like Kyrie, assume the Earth is flat and chase evidence in support of their claim. But no one has a vested interest in the Earth being round or flat, only in the shape offered by evidence-based methods of reasoning. This is why, as a scientist, I would have absolutely no problem accepting that the Earth is flat if this conclusion were supported by genuine and convincing evidence.

Like many people, Kyrie uses scientific terms without properly employing the scientific method. If he had been more sensitive to the method than the terms, he may have arrived at a very different conclusion. That is because the scientific method isn't employed to support what one desires to believe. The scientific method is a systematic way of collecting and recording objective observations in the hopes of making objective conclusions about our world. Scientists use the method because they desire to know the truth.

How does the scientific method work? First, scientists *observe* things and develop theories and testable explanations for what they see. These are called *hypotheses*. Scientists are concerned with *genuine evidence* relevant to their hypotheses. Genuine evidence is information that reasonably indicates

Experiments using scientific method

whether a claim, belief, or proposition is valid. A commonly employed alternative, not to be confused with evidence, is that of *mere argument*, which is a justification for a claim. The difference is important because evidence can sometimes provide overwhelming reasons to believe that a theory is true (or at least approximately true) or false. For instance, suppose that after eating several plates of spaghetti, we developed a preference for an extra pinch of salt in the sauce. If we approach the question scientifically, we will state that salt is our proposed mechanism for better-tasting spaghetti sauce. This is our hypothesis that must be tested by further investigation—and at this point, the hypothesis is neither right nor wrong.

To keep from fooling themselves into assuming their theories are correct, scientists don't stop at what they think and hope to be true.[14] Rather, they make *predictions* based on their hypotheses and *test them with fair experiments* that are designed to put their hypotheses to the most stringent tests possible. Scientists don't just seek evidence to confirm their hypotheses; rather, they bend over backward to seek evidence that might refute their hypotheses. When a hypothesis has survived very stringent tests of this type—carried out by the proposer and by other, independent scientists—then, and only then, can we draw the tentative conclusion that the hypothesis is probably approximately true. Likewise, we wouldn't stop at simply stating or predicting that spaghetti sauce tastes better with an extra pinch of salt—for a prediction with such important implications, we better determine if there is any evidence at all for or against it.

To test our spaghetti sauce example, we could run a

controlled study. We would first make two large, identical batches of sauce. Then we would add a pinch of salt into one batch and not the other. Then we would randomly assign thousands of people to taste one of the spaghetti sauces and rate their experience using the same scale. We would be careful to put the spaghetti sauces in the same types of pots so that neither we, nor the taste testers, could detect any differences between the sauces before they were tasted. Importantly, both the taste testers and we (as the experimenters) would remain blind to which sauce contained extra salt, with that revealed only after the taste ratings are obtained.

If and only if the salty spaghetti sauce is rated significantly better than the nonsalty spaghetti sauce does the evidence support the conclusion that extra salt makes a positive difference. Any other pattern of data would show that our hypothesis was wrong and that spaghetti sauce preference may be more complex than we first thought.

We would also need to replicate our results through additional experiments (sometimes hundreds and thousands) before our claims about extra salt in spaghetti sauce would be accepted by the greater scientific community. In this way, scientific conclusions can be dynamic—new ideas and methods are invented and old ones are abandoned.[15] It is perfectly normal for scientists to change their conclusions and opinions after learning new information. This is not a sign of weakness; it is, in fact, an essential feature of the scientific method.

When scientists later publicize their experiment-based conclusions, you can be sure that they will be scrutinized. Dozens, if not hundreds, of qualified experts will ask: Are the premises true? Are the conclusions supported by all of the data? Are the arguments and conclusions logically strong? Were *all* relevant factors considered? It is this often-forgotten stage of critical scrutiny that fortifies the strength of the scientific process. If we were to publish a paper that claims spaghetti sauce tastes better with an extra pinch of salt, you can be sure the scientific community would have its way with the claim—and if the claim was found to be wrong, the community would be the very first to revel in letting us know. This is what makes scientific judgment unique. Making one's claims subject to the scientific method is like putting one's claims on trial, and in that trial, all parties get to ask tough questions. The jury makes the final call. But the jurors are not common citizens; the jurors are qualified experts with the specialized training required to evaluate technical claims. This is why scientists do not own facts. As in cooking, no one owns the fact that a pinch of salt helps to intensify the flavor of food. It's been tested and unanimously agreed that it improves the flavor of food. It's why salt is so ubiquitous in the world's cuisine. And the same can be said of the Earth's shape.

Of course, scientists are human beings and the process of science is a social enterprise not immune to error—there are times when it's wrong. After all, it took thousands of years for people to begin to accept that the Earth was spherical. Despite all the clever demonstrations since the time of Eratosthenes—and there were many—it wasn't until after confirmed reports that Magellan and Elcano completed a circumnavigation of the globe from 1519 to 1522 that the true shape of the Earth was commonly accepted. Only after convincing evidence, provided by explorers who physically tested the idea, did the consensus shift.

Yet we now live in a world that pays increasingly more attention to fake news, social media opinion pieces, and intriguing but unsupported theories, and less attention to science, skepticism, and good old-fashioned critical thinking. Take, for instance, the Pizzagate conspiracy. In March of 2016, the personal e-mail account of John Podesta, Hillary Clinton's presidential campaign chairman, was hacked. By November, just before the presidential election, WikiLeaks published some of Podesta's e-mails. Conspiracy theorists were quick to spread the news online that the e-mails of high-ranking Democratic Party officials, including Clinton, contained coded messages connecting them with a human trafficking and child sex–ring through pizzerias in Washington, DC.

Conspiracies like Pizzagate sound like they may be bullshit, but how can we really know for sure? There must be better ways of evaluating information. Just ask Edgar Welch. If only Welch had better bullshit detection skills he wouldn't have responded to Pizzagate by shooting up the Comet Ping Pong pizzeria in Washington, DC, with a lightweight semi-automatic rifle. And he wouldn't have been sentenced to four years in prison for doing it. Welch was passionate—he wanted to save the kids—but genuine evidence would have led him to see that, in fact, no kids were being harmed at that pizzeria. A public without basic bullshit detection and disposal skills cannot defend itself against the many unwanted effects of bullshit. Better information doesn't always result in better decision-making, but better decision-making almost always requires better information.

Scientific reasoning and critical thinking are the very best tools we have for finding truth and gaining wisdom and fundamental understanding. After all, science has harnessed electrical energy, eradicated smallpox, engineered genome editing, developed X-rays, built telescopes capable of seeing galaxies trillions of miles away, discovered electromagnetic induction, and created a supercomputer that can do 200 quadrillion calculations per second. Science can free us from dogma, superstition, and bullshit, which are goals I think we should all aspire to. *I agree.*

I am a professor of experimental social psychology, and I study bullshit and bullshitting for a living. Like nearly everyone, all my life I have been surrounded by bullshitters, though I didn't call anyone that until I read analytical philosopher Harry Frankfurt's dandy of a 20-page article-turned-book titled *On Bullshit*. With over 100,000 copies sold, it is one of the best-selling philosophy books of all time and easily my favorite book.[16] Frankfurt argued,

> One of the most salient features of our culture is that there is so much bullshit. Everyone knows this. Each of us contributes his share. But we tend to take the situation for granted. Most people are rather confident of their ability to recognize bullshit and to avoid being

taken in by it. So the phenomenon has not aroused much deliberate concern, or attracted much sustained inquiry. In consequence, we have no clear understanding of what bullshit is, why there is so much of it, or what functions it serves. And we lack a conscientiously developed appreciation of what it means to us.

My research has been about trying to find scientific answers to Frankfurt's claims. I study the causes of bullshit, its potential benefits to individuals, its consequences to society, and how people can better detect and dispose of its unwanted effects—basically, what this book is all about.

WHAT IS BULLSHIT?

According to Frankfurt, bullshitting involves intentionally or unintentionally, consciously or unconsciously, communicating with little to no regard or concern for truth, genuine evidence, and/or established knowledge. Bullshitting is often characterized by, but not limited to, using rhetorical strategies designed to disregard truth, evidence, and/or established knowledge, such as exaggerating or embellishing one's knowledge, competence, or skills in a particular area or talking about things of which one knows nothing about in order to impress, fit in with, influence, or persuade others.[17] The degree to which something qualifies as bullshit is inversely proportional to the degree to which the claim is based on truth, genuine evidence, and/or established knowledge.

BS has no truth or logic in experimented knowledge.

Philosophers and scientists generally agree that there are four types of established knowledge. Established knowledge may be considered *semantic*, like the things found in dictionaries. For example, a dictionary describes a tree as a woody, perennial plant, typically having a single trunk growing to a considerable height and bearing lateral branches at some distance from the ground. When we communicate using definitions from dictionaries, our claims are warranted. Knowledge may be considered established if it is justified by the rules of *logic*: if A > B and B > C, then A > C. When we follow the rules of logic, our claim is warranted. Knowledge may be considered established if it is justified by a *system* of information, such as 30 + 11 = 41. When we follow the rules of math, consistent with the definitions and processes, our claims are warranted. Finally, knowledge may be considered established if it is supported by *empirical* information found with evidence that comes through our senses, such as "there is a book in front of you right now." A more common term to describe empirical information is data. When we use all of the relevant data to interpret the world around us, our claims are warranted.

You might be confused by the scientific definition of bullshit because the word itself is so widespread. For instance, when you think you've been ripped off by someone or something, you might say, "Hey, that's bullshit!" We often use the word to describe casual conversations: "Why yes, we were just bullshitting about the weather." We might also use the word to express frustration or disdain: "He is so full of bullshit!" But these cases are not, by my standards, bullshit. I'm not concerned with the content of communication. Rather,

I'm interested in *how* people communicate—their underlying concern for evidence or established knowledge and the manner in which they promote and defend claims. If I tell you, "People out there are saying Pluto isn't a planet, but I really don't care what astrophysicists say about Pluto's status—gosh darn it, Pluto is a planet in our solar system," and I care little about the definition of a planet and whether any readily available evidence supports or refutes my claim, I am bullshitting. In essence, the bullshitter is a relatively careless thinker who plays fast and loose with ideas and information.[18]

no data to back up claim = b.s.

Obviously, it is impossible to have an informed, evidence-based opinion about absolutely everything. When my friends or colleagues are talking at length about something like cars or the latest smartphone apps, I feel like a fish out of water. It compels me to talk about things I really know nothing about—and what usually comes out is bullshit. In other words, we all bullshit to some degree—it's an inevitable consequence of life. Nonetheless, I will guide us through how bullshit occurs, and why, which is useful at a time when evidence-based reasoning and rational judgment are failing to keep up with the bullshit generated in this era of mass and rapid communication.

Bullshitting Isn't Lying

Suppose you are in the market for a used car. You visit a used-car dealership. The dealer shows you a car. He tells you all about the features of the car—it appears to be in great shape, it only has 15,000 miles on the engine, and it seems like a steal of a great deal. Did you just happen to stumble on a car that the dealership is practically giving away, or is there some sort of catch? You are already in love with the car, but you are concerned about its history and why the price looks too good to be true. The dealer tells you, "The previous owner also loved this car and took great care of it, but because of financial hardship, she had to sell it at a loss. So you're getting a great deal here." But you're skeptical about the dealer's claims. Not only does the dealer's livelihood depend on selling you cars, but he appears just as excited for you to make the purchase as you are. Is the dealer lying to you or is he bullshitting?

A quick look at an official data report like Carfax (which lists the service history of the vehicle and any reported collision incidents or water damage from a flood) and the highly recommended pre-purchase inspection may clarify it isn't really a deal. The only way to determine if the used-car dealer was bullshitting or lying to you is to discover his level of concern with the truth. It isn't the content of a claim that determines its status as a lie or bullshit, but rather what the used-car dealer actually knows about the truth and his degree of concern about it. If the dealer knew the truth, but communicated something other than the truth, then he lied to you, but if he didn't care at all about the truth, he was bullshitting. If after reviewing the Carfax report, you ask the dealer about the collision incident you found on the report, and he tells you, "Oh, we didn't look at the vehicle's detailed history," or he says that the previous owner reported to him that the vehicle had a minor dent repaired but it "did not have" any frame damage, the "deal" is probably a hot rock that should be dropped immediately. Because, the truth is, the used-car dealer has no way of knowing the finer details of any collisions listed on a Carfax report. Furthermore, if he admits that he hasn't looked at the vehicle's detailed history, he isn't any more likely to have paid $350 for the pre-purchase inspection that would have revealed any potential frame damage to the vehicle. Frame damage is used as a warning, signaling that something major, like the vehicle's transmission or expensive engine parts, should be treated with caution. If the used-car dealer doesn't care enough to investigate such things about a vehicle for sale, he's not necessarily lying, but he is most certainly bullshitting you.

The important distinction between bullshitters and liars has to do with their motivations. In fact, bullshitters and liars may say the very same things. When the used-car dealer says something false about the car, and he actually knows and cares about the fact that it isn't true, he is lying. But when the used-car dealer communicates the same falsity without any regard for truth or any evidence in support of what he believes, hopes, or wishes to be true, he is bullshitting. Unlike the liar, it is also possible for the bullshitter to communicate something that is actually true, but the bullshitter wouldn't know it because he isn't paying attention to the truth of his claims or that they can and should be substantiated by readily available evidence and/or existing knowledge. It is true the bullshitter and liar are both deceptive in that they *appear* to be genuinely concerned with the truth. By definition, the liar does whatever he can to hide the truth—to do it successfully, the liar distorts his portrayal of reality and tries to remember the lie. The bullshitter doesn't have these burdens because most often he actually believes his own bullshit. Think of how much easier it would be to lie if you didn't have the burden of knowing the truth or remembering that something you said was false. It wouldn't feel like lying at all.

The fact that people differentiate between bullshitting and lying can be seen in our typical emotional reactions toward them. When people lie, those who are lied to usually feel anger and there can be severe consequences for lying. On the other hand, when people bullshit, those bullshitted usually turn a blind eye and assume that it has no effect. The motives of the liar and bullshitter are distinctly different, and people readily recognize this difference. Lies are intentional distortions or concealments of the truth, whereas bullshit claims are made without any attention to truth at all—and they may even be correct. Lies can get you fired. But bullshit might get you promoted to CEO—you might even become president!

SURROUNDED BY BULLSHITTERS

We've come to expect that political leaders and media personalities will bullshit us, and it seems likely that a few big bullshitters will always be among us. Yet there are many more little bullshitters—people who share their bullshit with us personally—who have the greatest unwanted impact on our thinking and reasoning. If political analysts on the evening news tell us something, that is one thing—they are paid to have something interesting or provoking to say, even if it is bullshit. But if the people we actually know, interact with, and trust are saying the very same thing, it tends to have more influence.[19]

Because bullshit is all around us it can feel overwhelming. However, it's important to recognize that not all bullshit is the same. That is why I've devised a useful key to think about the different types of bullshit we will encounter—I call it the *Bullshit Flies Index*. Depending on the severity of bullshit, a grade of one to three flies is given. As you'll see, the more bullshit there is, the more flies it attracts. Likewise, if you've ever been to a farm, safari, or dog park, you may be keenly aware that the potency of animal droppings is a determining factor of the number of flies they attract. The more potent the bullshit, the greater the severity of the potential unwanted consequences.

Using the Bullshit Flies Index is easy—all you have to do is ask yourself the following question when you suspect you may be exposed to bullshit: *If what I am hearing turns out to be false, what is the worst that can happen?* Some bullshit is *harmless* and leads to little more than expressions of belief or disbelief, embarrassment, or the proverbial eye-rolling of listeners, perhaps attracting one fly on the Bullshit Flies Index. Other bullshit can be *bad* because it leads to undesirable behaviors and deserves two flies. Bullshit can also be *dangerous* if it leads to false beliefs and destructive decisions, such as when it negatively affects the lives of others, attracting three flies. What determines the number of flies that bullshit attracts is the potential harm that the bullshit causes when it is wrong.

For example, consider the implications of using bullshit to *control the narrative*. Controlling the narrative occurs when

[handwritten margin notes: "Not all BS is the same"; "For instance, the game! BS bears little to no consequence"]

BULLSHIT FLIES INDEX

Flies	Type	Definition	Example
✳	HARMLESS	innocuous, mildly offensive, unlikely to cause harm	making up the weather
✳ ✳	BAD	harmful potential by failing to conform to standards of moral virtue or acceptable conduct, unpleasant, unwelcome	making up numbers
✳ ✳ ✳	DANGEROUS	able and likely to cause harm, injury, or problems with adverse consequences	lethal advice

you influence what other people think about a situation by the way you explain what is going on. The way a story is told matters—by emphasizing details, or your perceptions of them, you can influence how people think about the situation. Like him or not, President Donald Trump is masterful at controlling the narrative with bullshit and provides examples of all three levels of harm along the Bullshit Flies Index. It isn't Trump's political stance or opinions that make him a brilliant bullshitter, but rather, the way he speaks and makes conclusions about things.

In January 2017, Trump spoke about the weather during his inauguration speech: "I said, it was almost raining, the rain should have scared them away, but God looked down and he said, we're not going to let it rain on your speech. In fact, when I first started, I said, oh, no. The first line, I got hit by a couple of drops. And I said, oh, this is too bad, but we'll go right through it. But the truth is that it stopped immediately. It was amazing. And then it became really sunny. And then I walked off and it poured right after I left. It poured."[20] Of course, it isn't worth wasting the time to fact-check the validity of Trump's claim that God looked down and stopped the rain, but none of the other claims are based on fact. Trump was bullshitting because he was more concerned with portraying a consecrated inauguration than he was with perceiving and reporting the weather accurately. In fact, the rain did not stop immediately, and the sky remained cloudy during his speech.[21] Although it will likely produce some eye-rolling from the audience, this bullshit is relatively harmless—and thereby warrants but one fly on the Bullshit Flies Index.

Perhaps to embellish his status, within days of that speech, Trump bragged about the attendance at his inauguration. "Honestly, it looked like a million and a half people. Whatever it was, it was. But it went all the way back to the Washington Monument."[22] "In terms of a total audience including television and everything else that you have we had supposedly the biggest crowd in history. . . . They say I had the biggest crowd in the history of inaugural speeches."[23] One might assume that such statements represent a subjective opinion.[24] But, in fact, Trump's claims can be easily tested objectively. Of course, "They" could mean anyone, but there are still no experts declaring that Trump had the largest inauguration crowd in history. More importantly, all of the evidence leads to the contrary of Trump's claim. President Barack Obama's first inauguration in 2009 drew far more people in person and in television viewership.[25] The reason this sort of bullshit is bad is that it discourages factual accuracy while promoting misleading claims in the face of overwhelming evidence to the contrary. It also mischaracterizes reality and elevates opinions and "alternative facts" to fact status—thereby, it warrants two flies on the index.

Finally, there is bullshit that is dangerous, as when Trump spoke about finding a cure for COVID-19, but managed to suggest something that could actually injure people. In an April 23, 2020, briefing, Trump said, "And then I see the disinfectant, where it knocks it out in a minute. One minute. And is there a way we can do something like that, by injection inside or almost a cleaning? Because you see it gets in the lungs and it does a tremendous number on the lungs. So it would be interesting to check that. So, that, you're going to have to use medical doctors with. But it sounds—it sounds interesting to me."[26] Sodium hypochlorite, in the form of laundry bleach and other readily available household cleaning supplies, has a pH level of 12 and a high level of alkalinity that makes it corrosive. Ingesting such disinfectants will cause severe burns to the stomach and esophagus. Depending on how much is ingested, it can result in death unless medical attention is sought immediately. If the president of the United States suggests that people might consider ingesting Lysol, Clorox, or laundry detergent, people take it seriously, and they may act upon the advice. That is why almost immediately after Trump's suggestions, poison control centers, life insurance providers, city health commissioners, and makers of disinfectant products issued statements urging the public, in no uncertain terms, not to consume disinfectant products. Yet, many poison control centers reported sharp increases in the number of calls from people claiming to have ingested bleach products, and some medical experts believe that many people died by following the misinformation.[27] After receiving universal condemnation for his suggestion, Trump unconvincingly argued that he was being sarcastic.[28] Even if that were true, leaders with great influence like the president of the United States must be responsible brokers of information—they can put people in danger with sarcastic bullshit. No matter one's political stance, evidence should guide all principles—bad things can happen when it doesn't. That is why I give this sort of bullshit three flies. It is dangerous bullshit because it can cause direct harm and has the potential to promote flippant attitudes toward science and medicine and advocate pseudoscience and alternative medicine, both of which have dire consequences for society writ large.

TOOTHBRUSHING BULLSHIT

Of all the many things that people believe in, I can't think of a more universally agreed upon belief than the benefits of toothbrushing. What we believe about toothbrushing is an example of a *cultural truism.* Cultural truisms are beliefs that most members of a society accept uncritically and have never so much as considered defending—they are so widely shared within the social environment that people have not heard them attacked or even considered an attack possible.

Nonetheless, a study conducted by a team of social psychologists, led by Michael Ross at the University of Waterloo, demonstrated just how vulnerable unexamined beliefs about toothbrushing actually are.[29] In one experiment, Ross and his colleagues had some participants listen to a recording that was either favorable or unfavorable toward toothbrushing (and some participants who did not listen to any recording). The positive recording described how frequent brushing strengthened tooth enamel and protected the teeth and gums against disease. The negative recording described the dangers of frequent brushing, including how abrasive toothpastes can cause erosion of the enamel, that gum damage leads to infection and tooth loss, and emphasized that flossing was much superior to toothbrushing. After listening to the recording, participants returned to a waiting area to participate in a second "unrelated" study. Participants then completed a questionnaire allegedly designed to assess the relationship between personality type and lifestyle. Embedded within the questionnaire were questions asking them to estimate the frequency with which they had engaged in various activities during the past two weeks. Among many other health-related items was "How many times have you brushed your teeth in the past two weeks?" They also responded to whether brushing their teeth after every meal was unimportant or important, unhealthy or healthy, and harmful or beneficial on a 9-point scale.

What Ross and his colleagues found was nothing short of amazing. As you would expect, participants who listened to the positive message about toothbrushing and participants who received no message reported positive attitudes about toothbrushing at the very top of the scale (9 and 8.5 on average, respectively). They also "recalled" brushing their teeth on average 35.85 and 32.80 times, respectively, over the course of the previous two weeks. Conversely, participants who listened to the negative message about toothbrushing reported relatively neutral attitudes about toothbrushing on average (near the midpoint of the scale at 4.75) and recalled brushing their teeth only 28.62 times on average over the course of the previous two weeks (18% less often than their positive message and no message counterparts). Apparently, bullshit-based reasoning can lead to incorrectly recalling one's own hygienic behaviors.

For more than six decades now, social psychologists have known that a person's resistance to persuasive attacks on their cultural truisms, like toothbrushing, is only effective to the extent they are motivated to defend their beliefs and have some practice doing so.[30] People are unpracticed because they have rarely, if ever, been called upon to defend their beliefs, and they are unmotivated to start because they regard their beliefs as irrefutable.

That's what this book is all about—getting you to recognize that it is to your distinct advantage to seek evidence and truth rather than permitting people to continue bullshitting you, leading you to buy into belief systems of which the centers do not hold. By the end of this book, if you can honestly say that you ask yourself and others important critical-thinking questions that you wouldn't have asked otherwise, then I will have accomplished my primary goal.

In each chapter of this book, I will lead you through examples of common everyday bullshit. Then I will show you how this bullshit may be beneficial to the bullshitter but affect everyone else in very negative ways. I will also show you how current social psychological research speaks to these particular examples. You don't need to be a scientist to better understand bullshit, but you can better understand bullshit by understanding how it works.

1

COSTS OF BULLSHIT

Wine, Bullshit Markups, and the Myers-Briggs

Facts are stubborn things; and whatever may be our wishes, our inclinations, or the dictates of our passions, they cannot alter the state of facts and evidence.—JOHN ADAMS

Consider the following scenario: You want to buy Merlot for a special occasion. You narrow it down to two selections and read the reviews of each on winemag.com:

The third reserve by this producer made of this variety, this is 100% estate and varietal. It unfurls in fireplace smoke, red and black berry, leather and tobacco, with an edginess of cedar and herb. The texture is soft and integrated around a full-bodied concentration of flavor. Rating: 93 points.[1]

The merest hint of dark chocolate and a touch of graphite play alongside the juicy ripe cherry notes on the nose. The palate is fresh and is held by a fine gauze of soft tannins on its medium body. This is an elegant, understated red that is evolving beautifully and will evolve further. Lovely now. Drink by 2030. Rating: 93 points.[2]

Which wine will you purchase? The first review is for the Jarvis 2012 Estate Grown Cave Fermented Reserve Merlot (Napa Valley), and it sells for $200 a bottle. The second is for the Pleil 2015 Ried Gerichtsberg Merlot (Niederösterreich), and it sells for $19 a bottle. Do the descriptions betray the stark difference in price?

In the multibillion-dollar wine business, such language is commonplace. Most wine labels describe a wine's aroma or bouquet to characterize its scent. They mention the body or weight to describe a wine's alcohol attributes. References are made to crispness or smoothness to describe how refreshing or acidic its flavor. A wine might also be described as juicy, chewy, angular, laser-like, oaked, or my personal favorite, intellectually satisfying. Who doesn't want to drink something reminiscent of a cozy cottage fireplace in the middle of a frigid winter? But are these descriptions accurate and useful? To better understand how wine is packaged and sold, I spent time researching the industry and speaking with people on the front lines of production and sales.

Robert Hodgson is a retired professor of statistics at Humboldt State University and the proprietor of Fieldbrook Winery in northwestern California. Founded in 1976, Fieldbrook is a small operation, selling 1,500 cases of wine each year, with no shortage of wine competition awards. In the wine world, awards bring much more than prestige. Awards can boost reputation and sales—wines bearing gold, silver, or bronze foil stickers can sell up to seven times as many bottles as the same wine with no sticker.[3]

Wondering how his wines could win a gold medal at one competition, yet fail miserably in others, Hodgson decided to get his hands on the competition data. When he analyzed it, Hodgson found that medals appeared to be awarded at random, with each wine having a 9% chance of winning a gold medal in any given competition.

In one of Hodgson's own experiments, he blindfolded wine experts and offered each of them three glasses of wine to taste.[4] The blindfold was necessary because Hodgson didn't want the experts to evaluate the wines based on their labels or the 36 unique color states of wine. The experts then graded each sample according to the industry's standard rating scale running from "good," a solid, well-made wine (80–84); to "very good," a wine with special qualities (85–89); to "outstanding," a wine of superior character and style (90–94); to "classic," a great wine (95–100).

On average, the judges' ratings of the wines varied by 4 points (plus or minus). But here was the catch—all three glasses were poured from the same bottle. Nonetheless, a wine rated 92 by one expert in her first trial would be rated an 88 or 96 by the same expert in subsequent trials. Some of the judges did much worse. Only one in ten judges regularly rated the same wine within a range of ±2 points. Hodgson later found that judges in the California State Fair wine competition (the oldest and most prestigious in North America), whose ratings were the most consistent in any given year, landed in the middle of the pack in other years, suggesting that a "consistent" performance in any particular year was simply chance. Furthermore, less than 10% of the judges were able to replicate their scores within a single medal group. Another 10% scored the same wine a gold that they had earlier scored a bronze.

Hodgson's results weren't unique. Researcher Frédéric Brochet wanted to know if wine critics' taste buds can reliably distinguish between red and white wines. Brochet had 54 wine experts report their opinions on two glasses of wine, one "red" and the other white. In actuality, the two wines were identical white wines—the "red" wine had been dyed with food coloring. Sure enough, the so-called experts tended to describe Brochet's "red" wine in language typically reserved for characterizing reds, referring to it as "jammy" or containing "flavors imparted by its crushed red fruit." Not one of the 54 experts surveyed detected that the red wine was, in fact, a white.[5]

What are we to make of this? Wine critics and competition judges are experts in the field. If they are inconsistent in their ratings and so easily duped by red dye, what about the rest of us? We can hardly expect a subjective thing like wine tasting to be an exact science, but it doesn't make much sense to put confidence in wine awards and professional reviews if there are no systematic, quantifiable standards. A scientific approach requires test cases and a verifiable set of standards that everyone adheres to. If wine experts don't use these things and can't reliably differentiate between a Clos Pegase Merlot and a Cannonball Merlot, it seems likely that professional wine descriptions will continue to proliferate bullshit.

Aside from reading the descriptions, people often assume that the quality of a wine is positively correlated with its price.[6] This is why marketers only need to make a wine sound expensive. Like many commodities, wine is a Veblen good. Veblen goods are luxury goods whose prices do not follow the typical laws of supply and demand. They are in demand because they are expensive. Marketers are well aware that people use price as a rule of thumb. When purchasing a bottle of wine for a special occasion, people might choose an $80 bottle over a $25 bottle because they assume the pricier bottle will taste better.

Massachusetts Institute of Technology behavioral economist Coco Krumme took a closer look at the relationship between professional wine reviews and the price of wine. She studied the words used to describe 3,000 different wines—ranging in price from $5 to $200—from an online aggregator of professional reviews.[7] Using text analysis, Krumme determined how frequently single words and unique combinations of words appeared in the reviews. She found that cheap and expensive wine words are used differently. Cheap wine words (for example, *juicy*, *fruity*, *tasty*) were used more frequently across descriptions, whereas top-end wine words tended to be used relatively infrequently, and sometimes reviews created a new vocabulary all together. Cheap wines tended to be described as *pleasing*, *refreshing*, and *enjoyable* and recommended with cheaper dishes such as chicken and pizza. Expensive wines tended to be described with darker words (for example, *intense*, *supple*), single-flavor words (for example, *tobacco*, *chocolate*), and exclusive-sounding words (for example, *elegant*, *cuvée*) and recommended with more expensive dishes like shellfish and chateaubriand steak. Based on her analysis, Krumme offered the following description of an expensive wine: "A velvety chocolate texture and enticingly layered, yet creamy nose, this wine abounds with focused cassis and a silky ruby finish. Lush, elegant, and nuanced. Pair with pork and shellfish."

It is easy for wine marketers to pass bullshit for something valid because most consumers know very little about wine. If you are like most people, you believe that wine gets better with age. You might be surprised to learn that most wines are intended to be drunk now. Those wines are not going to get better over time—they are more than likely to get worse. There are only a few wines bottled for aging, and they are prohibitively expensive for all but the most avid enthusiasts. If you happen to be saving affordable wine, it is safe to assume that the taste will not be improved by your decision to keep it unopened.

After reviewing the data, there are two reasonable conclusions to reach: Wine selling is much more about *selling* than it is about wine. And with a total US market size of over $70 billion and a global market of over $350 billion, wine bullshit is good for wine sellers and bad for our wallets. The good news is that you no longer have to feel guilty about buying cheap wine!

We will get a much better understanding of what we prefer by collecting relevant data than we will from experts' wine bullshit. Discovering what wines you like requires tasting a lot of wine. If the head waiter suggests a Screaming Eagle Cabernet Sauvignon with your meal, you might find the wine very pleasing, but it doesn't mean there aren't dozens of other wines out there you would like even better. The only way you discover that is by approaching wine like a scientist would and trying the wines yourself. Wine retailers do this by applying two rules when selecting their own wine. Rule number 1: Drink what tastes good. Rule number 2: Drink what you can afford. Both rules are very sensible. Combine the two rules and you've got a serious wine decision strategy.

Wine can be B.S. - pay attention!

BULLSHIT MARKUPS

Given the subjective nature of wine value and price, I began thinking more broadly about the price of goods—or, more accurately, the marked-up prices of goods. A markup is the ratio between the cost of the good or service and its selling price. For instance, a retail markup is calculated as the difference between the wholesale price (the price charged by producers to retailers) and retail price (the price charged by retailers to consumers).[8] Most goods and services are marked up to a degree, and this is necessary, as turning a profit is ultimately the goal of any business. *markup = profit*

As a bullshit analyst, however, I am interested in whether a markup is applied reasonably. To determine this, we need a baseline to serve as a standard of comparison. My reference point is the fact that the accepted retail markup for most items is between 50 and 100%. That means the price of a good/service usually costs the consumer twice that it costs a retailer to provide or deliver. A 50–100% markup is reasonable for the investments and risks the retailer is willing to take—I have no problem paying it. However, we would be naive to believe all retail markups are 50–100%.[9] Purchasing wine at a restaurant will come with a markup of about 400%. As a result, some people opt for soda instead, believing they are saving money. Yet the markup of restaurant soda is outrageously high, at over 1,000%. *Soda markup*

Most any good or service comes with a markup built into its price. When the markup is beyond that which covers the costs of doing business and a reasonable profit, it is a *bullshit markup*. *beyond reasonable profit = bs markup* For example, it is common for car buyers to negotiate the fake sticker price of a new car because they know that car dealers have added a high markup with the expectation that buyers will negotiate the price down to a more reasonable level. It's a win-win because even if buyers manage to cut a $5,000 markup in half, the dealer is still making $2,500 on the sale. What is more, the moment a car buyer wishes to add any unnecessary but costly add-ons, like extended warranties, anti-theft window etching, racing-style seats, brake caliper covers, or moisture-sensing window wipers, the markup can quickly skyrocket back to $5,000 and beyond. From a salesperson's perspective, bullshit markups are either the icing on the cake or their bread and butter. From a consumer's perspective, paying bullshit markups makes no sense at all.

Bullshit markups in the form of confidence tricks cost consumers in the United States over $800 million per year, with the average loss per person lodging a complaint at over $6,000. Confidence tricks are attempts to defraud people by first gaining their trust and then exploiting them by taking

Confidence tricks

advantage of their credulity. The most common types involve dating and romance, gambling, and investment schemes, with over 80% delivered via phone or e-mail.[10] Many confidence tricks are pure lies intended to lure victims. The reason that many confidence tricks are bullshit markups is that they survive by establishing trust and offering promises to consumers that, upon further reflection, could not possibly be delivered. Consumers invest in fortune-telling services for $3.95 per minute, on average, but they receive no actual goods or services in return.[11] Many tarot card readers, crystal ball fortune-tellers, and horse racing handicappers who sell their betting tips rarely think of their confidence tricks as tricks because they actually believe in their methods of foretelling the future. They appear to believe their own bullshit. But their services come at a great markup—the chances that you will gain actual value from the information they sell you are no greater than the chances of receiving a large sum of money on the condition you help someone overseas transfer money out of their country using your bank account details.

Why People Pay for Bullshit Markups

Psychological research suggests that there are at least three good reasons why people tend to neglect the better voices of critical thinking and fork over good money for bullshit markups: a *preference for bullshit over the truth, hearing is believing,* and *the power of intuition.*

A Preference for Bullshit Over the Truth

Sometimes it is easier to accept bullshit than to fight it. Pre-ferring bullshit over the truth is especially likely to occur when the bullshit aligns with our views of the world or the way we want or hope things to be. We like what we like—and some-times what we like doesn't correspond with the truth or the available evidence. It is not uncommon for people to prefer to believe the bullshit that global warming is a hoax than to accept the facts that icebergs are melting, floods and droughts are increasing, the Amazon rain forest is disappearing, and dan-gerous methane gases are bubbling up from the ocean floor all because global temperatures are rising.

When my daughter, Sydney, was eight years old, I signed her up for a one-week golf camp for kids. For only $85, she received 15 hours of instruction from two golf pros—what a great deal! By the end of the week, I was asked by the pros if I would be interested in registering my daughter for the junior golf club. The pros expressed to me that not all kids were in-vited to participate, but because of her exceptional athleticism and talent, she was being recruited. They gave me a pamphlet explaining what was involved in the junior golf club, which cost $200 for 12 hours of instruction per month. The next day I received a follow-up call from the golf pros who reminded me that thousands of college scholarships go unclaimed each year in women's golf and that they could see great potential in my daughter. They depicted it as a win-win situation. Their claims about Sydney's golf skill and potential were entirely unsubstan-tiated. Not only did I see how miserable she was at golf, but Sydney was ten times better at tennis than golf. When she was four, we began playing tennis and we both had dreams of her becoming the next Venus Williams. The problem was, Sydney didn't want to play tennis; she wanted to play golf. It would have been very easy for me to pretend my daughter had great potential in golf. Though it would have been easier for me to believe the golf pros' bullshit, which would have allowed me to justify paying for my daughter's golfing habits, I *chose not to prefer bullshit over the truth*. I continued paying for golf lessons because that is what she wanted to do. I want my daughter to be happy, not moneyball her chances to be a professional athlete. The real win-win was in Sydney's decision to participate in the activity she found most enjoyable and rewarding and my continued grip on the truth.

Hearing Is Believing

First proposed by philosophers and more recently supported by experimental psychologists, we now have considerable evidence showing that if we hear something, we assume it to be true.[12] When people are presented with a new idea, they accept that idea as true—at least temporarily—to aid their comprehension of the idea. This human tendency is sometimes referred to as *truth-default theory*. When people communicate with each other, they tend to passively presume that another person's communication is honest and true, independent of its actual truth. This presumption enables efficient communication and frequently leads to correct beliefs. However, the presumption of honesty and truth also makes people vulnerable to forms of deception.

Multiple experiments conducted by social psychologist

Daniel Gilbert and his colleagues demonstrate that accepting new information as true aids comprehension.[13] If the information is false, it can be rejected only after further reflection. Because further reflection requires mental effort and attention, it may be derailed by simple distractions. In one of Gilbert's experiments, participants read statements about two equally serious robberies and were asked to recommend the robber's jail sentence. Participants were informed that not all of the statements they would read were true—all the true statements would be displayed in green, while the false ones would be displayed in red. The statements were read one at a time and false statements varied in such a way that made one of the crimes seem worse (for example, "the robber had a gun") and the other crime appear less serious (for example, "the robber had starving children to feed"). Half of the participants were also given distractions in the form of irrelevant information and the other half were not. It was assumed that participants given distractions would have fewer mental resources to correct the misleading information's unwanted influence on their judgments. Gilbert's participants who were not distracted as they received information about the robberies recommended the same prison sentence for the perpetrators of the "seemingly" serious and less serious crimes (about 6.50 years). Presumably, because these participants were not distracted they had the mental resources to correct for the false information they had initially accepted as true. However, Gilbert's participants who were distracted as they received false information recommended almost twice the prison sentence for the "serious" crime (11.15 years) as they did for the "less serious" crime (5.83 years).

Unfortunately, after we accept something to be true, we have a hard time unlearning it if it turns out to be false. Rejecting the idea that someone had a gun is more mentally effortful than initially accepting the idea. Rejection of an idea only comes after the idea is accepted and comprehended. Only after careful examination can an idea be rejected as false. Yet even when people do think more carefully and examine new information, they tend to do so in a very biased way. Rather than considering why something may be wrong, answering *disconfirming questions*, we have a much stronger tendency to think of reasons for why it is correct, answering *confirming questions*.

Suppose we encountered the four cards displayed below. Each card has a number on one side and a letter on the other. I tell you, "If a card has a vowel on one side, it has an even number on the other side." Which cards would it be necessary to turn over to test my claim?

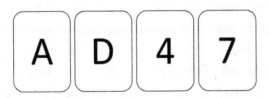

Most people would choose to turn over the A and 4 cards. If there is an even number on the other side of the A card, then my claim is at least partially confirmed. If there is an odd number on the other side of the A card, then my claim is falsified. However, many people incorrectly select the 4 card too. The 4 card is often treated as if it represents another confirmatory test, but the 4 card cannot disconfirm the statement. Finding a card with a consonant on one side and an even number on the other does not falsify my claim. My claim does not state that *only* vowels have even numbers on the other side. Likewise, turning over the D card reveals nothing special, even if an even number is found on the other side. The other necessary card to turn over is the 7 card. The 7 card represents a disconfirmatory test. In order for my claim to be true, there must be a consonant on the other side. Finding a vowel would falsify the claim. Despite its simplicity, the 4-card problem is difficult for many people. In a study conducted by the late psychologist Robyn Dawes, four of five "highly regarded" mathematical psychologists (psychologists whose approach to psychology is based on mathematical modeling of perceptual, thought, cognitive, and motor processes) could not solve the problem correctly.[14] Most of us neglect the 7 card because we are consistently biased toward confirming our existing beliefs by interpreting, seeking, or attending to information that confirms our preconceived notions while ignoring or explaining away anything that would provide disconfirming evidence. Not only are people biased to confirm their hypotheses, but the fact that people often incorrectly think the 4 card needs to be examined suggests that people incorrectly assume that the reverse of a statement (if even number, then vowel) must also be true. That is, when people are informed that cards with a vowel on one side have an even number on the other side, they assume that cards with an even number on one side have a vowel on the other.[15] In psychology, this tendency is one aspect of what is known as *confirmation bias*.

An obvious problem with truth-default and confirmation biases is that they can lead to accepting and retaining information that is not true. The process of rejecting something that you believe to be true requires more mental effort. When we lack the *cognitive resources* or *motivation* to critically assess new information, we may accept and retain falsehoods as truths.[16] *[handwritten: tend to believe falsehood]* In other words, our characteristic ways of mentally processing new information can lead us to pay for bullshit markups because we fail to see things for what they really are.

The Power of Intuition

Social psychological evidence suggests that people find it difficult to explain why they feel what they feel or how they reached a judgment, even though they frequently make up explanations anyway.[17] For instance, consider the following case I've surveyed in my research lab:

> Norman is a soft-spoken and shy young man who lives with Mother in a large house and runs the family motel. From time to time, he wears a woman's wig and dresses in his mother's clothes. For whatever reason, Norman never gave his mother a proper burial when she died ten years ago. Instead, he leaves her corpse sitting in a chair in the cellar of the home. Norman sometimes "speaks" to Mother and simulates her voice in response. No harm befalls Norman, nor anyone else. Norman keeps the fact that his mother's corpse is in the cellar a secret between he and Mother. What do you think about that? Is it okay for Norman to keep his mother's corpse in the cellar?

[handwritten: NO]

As demonstrated in morality research conducted by social psychologist Jonathan Haidt, people usually express that Norman putting his dead mother in the cellar is wrong.[18] However, their response as to why it is wrong is usually full of intuitive, emotion-based reasons rather than evidence-based reasons. People say that it is creepy for Norman to keep his mother's corpse in the cellar and then begin searching for reasons why it is wrong. Eventually, many people say something like, "I don't know. I can't explain it. I just know it's wrong." Participants' responses to Norman's story are examples of how a person can know that something is wrong without knowing or being able to articulate why. Usually people think of their judgments and decisions as being the result of reason, but often it is the other way around. Intuitions and feelings can shape judgments and decisions, and reasoning comes afterward to support those judgments and decisions.

Using a less creepy example, cognitive scientists Steven Sloman and Philip Fernbach have shown the same tendency for people to rely on intuition over evidence-based reasoning.[19] In their studies, they ask people to report how much they know about how everyday devices work, like a zipper, piano key, flushing toilet, cylinder lock, quartz watch, or sewing machine. At first, people think they know how these things work because they rely on their intuition. However, when asked to write detailed, step-by-step explanations of how the devices work, they demonstrate they actually know very little. Intuition often does not align with evidence-based reasoning that may come later.

intuition
—————
evidence-based

The principle of acting on intuitions and feelings first and thinking second was demonstrated in a set of famous studies conducted by Richard Nisbett and Timothy Wilson.[20] In one study, participants were asked to view a brief documentary film. Some participants had to watch the film while a loud power saw was running just outside the viewing room. Other participants viewed the film without any distractions. Everyone then rated the film on how interesting they thought it was, how much they thought other people would be affected by it, and how sympathetic they found the main character to be. The experimenters asked the group who had to watch the film while hearing the loud power saw noise whether the noise affected how they rated the film. Fifty-five percent of the power saw group thought that the noise had negatively affected their ratings—but their intuitions were wrong; their ratings of the film did not significantly differ from their counterparts not subjected to the noise. If people make erroneous conclusions about the effects of distractions on their reactions to films, it is reasonable to expect them to make the same sorts of errors with more complex events.

It is well established that people hold beliefs about the world and apply them as reasons for why they feel the way they do.[21] The intuitive way of thinking is often favored because relative to a more formal reasoning system, it is faster, takes less effort, and can draw on context. By definition, intuitions and feelings are not precise, and therefore, not rational. In fact, when offering reasons for why they feel the way they do, people often rely on what they find easiest to verbalize.[22] The problem is, what people find easiest to verbalize does

Ppl do what is easiest!

not always align with the real reasons for one's feelings and judgments—and what comes out is bullshit.

According to the Myers–Briggs Type Indicator (MBTI) personality test, I have an introverted, sensing, thinking, and judging (ISTJ) personality type. I am supposed to be "sensible and reliable and pay attention to detail." My strengths would be characterized as "dependable and systematic." I am supposed to "enjoy working within clear systems [and be] traditional, task-oriented and decisive." People are likely to view me as "typically thorough, conscientious, realistic but also systematic and reserved." As for areas in which I can improve, I am supposed to stop being so set in my ways, rigid, and impersonal. As a worker, I am supposed to favor "clear goals and realistic deadlines" and have preferences for working with "factual data to solve problems and monitor progress."[23]   *HA HA*

I am INFJ

Grazed

I actually like the sound of my MBTI feedback and would agree with most of it. But is the feedback accurate? Can the MBTI predict my behavior in various situations? Let's take a closer look at the evidence.

The MBTI purports to offer a psychological breakdown of how respondents perceive the world and make decisions. Respondents are asked to choose one of two possible answers to each of 93 questions. Based on their answers, respondents' personalities are described by a four-letter code that represents four areas: whether one is outwardly (*Extraverted*) or inwardly (*Introverted*) focused; if one prefers to take in information through *Sensing* or *INtuition*; if one prefers to make

Thinking- or *Feeling*-based decisions; and if one prefers to live one's outer life as *Judging* (preference for conformity to an established structure, neat and orderly) or *Perceiving* (preference for a flexible, spontaneous, and adaptable lifestyle). Someone who is deemed an ISTP would be described as an action-oriented, logical, analytical, spontaneous, reserved, and independent person who enjoys adventure and is skilled at understanding how mechanical things work.

The MBTI is perhaps the most famous personality test in the world. It is completed by more than 2.5 million people a year and is used in personnel decisions by 89 Fortune 100 companies. But what would you think if I told you that the MBTI was originally created not by psychologists but as a parlor game? The MBTI was first developed by Katharine Cook Briggs and her daughter, Isabel Briggs Myers, in the 1940s as a game loosely based upon a conceptual theory by Swiss psychiatrist Carl Jung. Importantly, Jung did not base his theory on systematic data. Jung speculated that people experience the world using four principal psychological functions, including sensation, intuition, feeling, and thinking. Presumably, these functions are modified by two personality types (extroversion and introversion), and individuals tend to rely on one dominant function over the others. Basically, because the theory was not based on systematic observations with clear and observable standards, the theory was bullshit. Worse news for the parlor game was that Jung didn't actually view any single person as being 100% of any of those types. Rather, Jung viewed the functions as spectrums. A person would fall somewhere between the two extremes, without being fixed at any particular point. So if you understand that Briggs and Myers got this particular part of Jung's theories wrong, it's difficult to see how the MBTI is anything other than an amusing parlor trick that you ought to forget right after you've finished getting your results.

Among the thousands of psychologists who have criticized the MBTI, psychologist and professor at the Wharton School of the University of Pennsylvania Adam Grant takes issue with the MBTI's reliability. Grant claims that the first time he completed the MBTI he was told that he was an INTJ.[24]

MBTI = bullshit?

> Although I spend much of my time teaching and speaking on stage, I am more of an introvert—I've always preferred a good book to a wild party. . . . But when I took the test a few months later, I was an ESFP. Suddenly, I had become the life of the party, the guy who follows his heart and throws caution to the wind. Had my personality changed, or is this test not all it's cracked up to be?

If you've ever completed the MBTI, you may remember being amazed that the feedback accurately described you. "This thing really hits the nail right on the head." But I'm not impressed with the results. Of course the measure describes you well. Why wouldn't it? By answering 93 questions about how you think about yourself you provided the assessment with enough information about how you think about yourself to tell you how you think about yourself. Who wouldn't agree with oneself? No one. A self-reported personality assessment is nothing more than applying a scoring and summarization algorithm to transform the information you provide about yourself into more eloquent language. If you responded true to questions that asked you about your tendency to eat fruits and vegetables and affirmed your joy of running and lifting weights, you shouldn't be surprised to find your personality summary describes you as a wise and health-conscious person.

The MBTI is also notoriously unreliable when examined *unreliable* under the controlled light of science. The fact that the same person can take the test multiple times and get different personality types is a clear indicator that something isn't right. Why, you might ask, does psychology research refrain from using the MBTI despite its great popularity in the corporate world? The main reason is that the predictive validity of MBTI hasn't been proven in a controlled study. Furthermore, using the MBTI to predict how someone is likely to perform in a job completely ignores a critically important component of performance—the job! As any psychologist knows, a person's behavior in a certain situation is best predicted not only by a person's personality but by the situation and context in which they perform.[25]

A powerful demonstration of the importance of context is found in a study conducted by Varda Liberman and her colleagues.[26] In their study, participants who were identified by others as either highly cooperative or highly competitive were recruited and asked to play rounds of a modified prisoner's dilemma game. The game involves multiple rounds with two players. In each round, players choose to cooperate or defect, either remaining silent or implicating the other player in a crime. If both players cooperate, they both receive a moderate reward for cooperating. If both players defect, they both receive nothing or lose points. If one player defects while the other cooperates, then the player who defected receives a "temptation payoff" in greater points, while the other player receives a "sucker's payoff" in nothing or a loss of points.

Despite it being in their best interest to cooperate, participants in the prisoner's dilemma often behave irrationally and choose not to cooperate. In Liberman's study, participants played the prisoner's dilemma under the title the "Community Game" or the "Wall Street Game." When the game was called the Community Game, everyone tended to cooperate, regardless of whether they had been identified by their peers as most likely to cooperate or compete. But when the game was called the Wall Street Game, everyone tended to compete, regardless of whether they had been identified by their peers as most likely to cooperate or compete. The participants' personalities, as assessed by their peers, didn't matter much at all. It was the context that mattered.

marketing

Behavior and performance are very complex things that require both an understanding of the person and his or her situation. Personality tests alone cannot explain behavior and performance. Two people who have the same personality type may vary greatly in their behaviors depending on the context. Likewise, an individual may fail miserably in one setting but thrive in another.

Advocates of the MBTI tend to believe that a person's score indicates something about that person's abilities and adamantly list a number of people to whom they ascribe those same qualities. However, if we were to test successful people in a particular field where MBTI adherents say that a particular personality type would predominate, I suspect we would find that the personality types of successful people in that field run the gamut. However, I am not aware of a study that has done this.

Nonetheless, without evidence one way or the other to prove predictive validity, the estimated money spent completing the annual 2.5 million MBTIs is $125 million—and that's not counting the hundreds of bullshit spin-offs that borrow the same approach as the MBTI or the thousands of consultants and coaches who charge companies and human resource departments upward of $10,000 to do training workshops. I can only imagine the trillions of dollars lost to the bad hiring or promotion decisions supported by the results of bullshit tests like these. I can only imagine the negative effects on people *OPCD* who used the test to see what kind of careers they should pursue. *tells us* How many great CEOs, directors, doctors, nurses, lawyers, *to do this test!* judges, and baseball managers did we miss?

The great success of the MBTI has led to dozens of spin-offs, including the audaciously titled Predictive Index, for which the copyright holders have offered no empirical evidence that it can be used to predict anything beyond dollars for them, and the Riso-Hudson Enneagram Type Indicator, which loosely uses the seven deadly sins as the basis for their personality types. Why do personality tests remain so popular in spite of the fact that they're bullshit? *→ Good question!*

Science journalist Annie Murphy Paul, who has long studied how personality tests are used in hiring and promotion decisions, argues that people cling to the MBTI and other tests for unwarranted reasons.[27] One is obvious—sunk costs. Thousands of people have invested time and money in becoming

MBTI-certified trainers and coaches. The second reason is the "aha" moment that people experience when the test affirms things they've long suspected about themselves. "Those who love type," Paul writes, "have been seduced by an image of their own ideal self." You can't necessarily blame anyone for that—it's seductive!

↳ Ppl want confirmation!

PSYCHOLOGICAL COSTS OF BULLSHIT

Perhaps the greatest practical cost of bullshit is the fact that the time and effort required to undo its unwanted effects can be exponentially greater than the time and effort needed to produce it. Bullshit can be produced in a matter of seconds, yet refuting it may take years. Filling the airwaves with bullshit effectively shapes and maintains beliefs and attitudes because it takes considerably more time and effort to find out if those claims your favorite radio host made are true than to believe without further thought a source you trust. During Barack Obama's campaign for president of the United States in 2008, opponents started the hyperbolic "birther movement," questioning the legitimacy of Obama's birth certificate and his eligibility to serve as president. Not only were major resources expended on both sides of the political spectrum to address Obama's legitimacy, but the controversy lingered throughout his presidency (and helped catapult his successor into office). This is why I believe that before we dismiss bullshit as harmless, we must understand the toll it takes on us psychologically.[28] The effects of bullshit have a devastating impact on our *memories*, our *attitudes/beliefs*, and our *decisions*.

Costs to Memory

Sydney is the capital city of Australia. Styrofoam was invented in Norway. The United States is storing weapons of mass destruction in Freedonia. Each of the above statements is false. However, you are more likely to misremember each statement as true simply because I have suggested it to you. A team of cognitive psychologists led by Vanderbilt University professor Lisa Fazio conclusively showed that this is true.[29]

For a long time, cognitive psychologists believed that people determined the truth or falsity of a statement, such as "the Atlantic Ocean is the largest ocean on Earth," by relying on their memory. Instead, psychologists have found that the ease with which one recalls a fact determines how "true" something feels.

We encounter false claims in abundance in consumer advertisements, political propaganda, rumors, and the like. Repeated exposure to false claims is one way that insidious misconceptions become "truths." But the real kicker of Fazio's research is that our level of knowledge does not protect us from developing illusions of truth. Although it was assumed that repeated exposure to the statement "Bette Davis is the name of the actress who received the best actress award for the movie *Mary Poppins*" would not make people who know better believe it, Fazio's research showed otherwise. In fact, research suggests that people rely on the subjective experience of ease or difficulty in recalling something instead of their actual knowledge.

In one study, research participants first reported how interesting they found several statements to be, such as "Venice is a city in Italy that is known for its canals." Some of the statements were true, but others were entirely false. Later, participants were asked to determine if these statements and several new statements were true. Importantly, Fazio and her colleagues knew from knowledge checks whether participants were actually knowledgeable of the content of the statements. Surprisingly, even when participants had demonstrated they had domain-specific knowledge, they were more likely to believe a false statement was true if it had been shown just once prior. This tendency is known as the *illusory truth effect*—the tendency to believe false information is correct after repeated exposure. For example, when a political candidate repeats something that couldn't possibly be true over and over again (and it is echoed by mainstream and social media), voters begin to believe it's true.

Information that we believe to be true and store in memory has critical effects on what we subsequently perceive, how we process new information, and the decisions we make. Bullshit, at least half of which is false simply by chance, can have a devastating influence on thinking.

Costs to Beliefs and Attitudes

What we believe to be true and our feelings about those "truths" fundamentally affect how we make decisions. Our beliefs and attitudes serve as moral compasses, guide our relationships with others, and motivate our behaviors in affairs large and small. It is because of our attitudes and beliefs that we shower using soap or we don't. We brush our teeth or we don't. We eat breakfast or we don't bother. We drive a Honda or a Ford. We vote for one political candidate or another. We adhere to our doctors' prescribed treatments or choose home remedies.[30]

Bullshit can impact both our beliefs and attitudes. I know this because of research conducted in our Bullshit Studies Lab that has tested bullshit's effect on beliefs and attitudes.

In one such study, we subjected participants to bullshit or lies using a *sleeper effect* procedure. The sleeper effect is a delayed impact of persuasion on a person's attitude toward something. For instance, when people are given only positive information about something (for example, a new restaurant), they tend to form positive attitudes about it. Later, if they learn something bad about the source of the initial message, which causes them to question the truth of that message (for example, an advertisement containing lies), they often adjust their attitudes immediately downward, reporting less positive attitudes. However, as time passes (for example, two weeks), the initial attitude returns, and people report a relatively positive attitude. In fact, sometimes the attitude is even more positive than when the attitude was first formed.[31]

In our experiment, participants were given a print advertisement detailing the great flavor and health benefits of a fictitious gluten-free pizza.[32] Participants were then told that parts of the advertisement contained inaccuracies. Importantly, we framed the inaccuracies as downright lies or bullshit. Attitudes toward the pizza were measured immediately after participants were told about the inaccuracies as well as 14 days later. How did our characterization of the inaccuracies, as lies or bullshit, affect participants' attitudes toward the pizza?

As with most sleeper effect demonstrations, attitudes about the pizza were more positive when assessed two weeks later, as compared to immediately after participants were told about the inaccuracies in the advertisement. However, whether the inaccuracies were characterized as bullshit or as lies mattered. After two weeks, attitudes were significantly more positive among participants who thought they had been bullshitted than participants who thought they had been lied to. Also, both participants who had been bullshitted and lied to generally failed to recall important details of the source that discounted the positive information about the pizza, suggesting that bullshit is just as easy to forget as are lies. Our experiment is important because it demonstrates (reliably) that bullshit results in a more pronounced sleeper effect than lies do.

My Bullshit Studies Lab also became interested in whether bullshit may have advantages relative to evidence-based arguments. We reasoned that because bullshit signals a lack of concern for truth, bullshit should activate *low levels of thinking*—an unsophisticated form of thinking characterized by a focus on peripheral aspects of the bullshitter, such as the number of arguments made or the attractiveness of the individual.[33] Because evidence-based communication signals a concern for truth, evidence-based arguments should activate *high levels of thinking*—a sophisticated form of thinking characterized by a focus on the core aspects and strengths of the arguments.

To test these ideas, our participants were provided with background information about a new mandatory comprehensive exam policy ostensibly under consideration at their university.[34] Under the policy, students would be required to pass a comprehensive exam in their area of study in order to graduate (students usually hate this idea). But just before reporting their attitude regarding the policy, participants reviewed either weak arguments (for example, "Duke University is doing it") or strong arguments in favor of the policy (for example, "Students who graduate from schools with comprehensive exams earn better salaries in their first jobs") framed in bullshit or with an obvious concern for evidence. Bullshit frames displayed the arguments prefaced with comments suggesting little to no interest in available and genuine evidence (for example, "I believe there is some research on this issue, but I'm not really concerned with the evidence concerning it"). Evidence-based frames included the very same arguments prefaced with comments suggesting considerable interest in available and genuine evidence (for example, "I'm really concerned with the evidence concerning this issue").

As we expected, analysis of attitudes toward the comprehensive exam policy revealed that strong arguments were more persuasive than weak arguments when the arguments were paired with an evidence-based frame. The same effect was nonexistent among participants exposed to bullshit. That is, strong arguments were no more effective than weak arguments when the arguments had been framed in bullshit.

strong = weak → BS

strong > weak → evidence-based frame

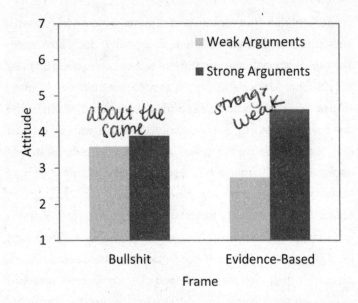

about the same (handwritten annotation over Bullshit bars)

strong > weak (handwritten annotation over Evidence-Based bars)

· Use weak when bsing
· Do not use strong when bsing (handwritten annotation in left margin)

Interestingly, while bullshit frames appear to weaken the potency of strong arguments, they strengthen the potency of weak arguments. When armed only with weak arguments it may be to the persuader's advantage to bullshit, but when armed with strong arguments it is to the persuader's disadvantage to sound as if he is bullshitting. As information consumers, our beliefs and attitudes are not things that we should permit to be based on bullshit because faulty beliefs and unwarranted attitudes can have dire consequences.

Costs to Decision-Making

Many of the decisions people make are based on perceptions and beliefs heavily saturated by bullshit. These decisions reach well beyond the wine, food, diamonds, or cars we buy. Bullshit is the foundation of contaminated thinking and bad decisions that lead to negative health consequences, financial losses, legal ramifications, broken relationships, and wasted time and resources.

Between 1958 and 1962, bullshit resulted in a death toll roughly six times that of the Holocaust, and you've probably never heard of it.[35] The event stands as the most extreme consequence of bullshit in the twentieth century.

Mao Zedong, affectionately known as Chairman Mao, was a Chinese communist revolutionary who ruled as the chairman of the Chinese Communist Party (CCP) from its establishment in 1949 until his death in 1976. In 1958, he instituted the Great Leap Forward, an economic and social campaign led by the CCP.[36] The idea was to transform China from an agrarian economy into a communist society through the formation of communes. One of Mao's plans was to increase agricultural yields and bring industry to the impoverished countryside. Although some officials doubted China's ability to stockpile grains, no one dared to challenge him.

In addition to outlawing private farming, Mao declared war on four pests blamed for inadequate grain yields. Through the Four Pests Campaign, four nuisance pests were to be eliminated—rats, flies, mosquitoes, and sparrows. At first, the idea sounded great. In order to protect grain fields, citizens were called on to destroy sparrows and other wild birds that ate crop seeds. It was believed that sparrows pecked away at supplies in warehouses and in paddy fields, with estimates of each sparrow accounting for a loss of four pounds of grain per

pests were not rly the problem

year. However, blaming the four pests was bullshit because no one really knew if they were the primary source of the problem, and preferred to believe that the solution was as easy as eliminating them.

The extermination of sparrows was also known as the Smash Sparrows Campaign. Millions of Chinese—civil servants and schoolchildren—quietly deployed in farms and streets carrying pots and pans, ladles, and kitchenware to wage war on the lowly sparrow. By May of 1958, an estimated 4,310,000 sparrows had been exterminated throughout China. A 16-year-old named Yang Seh-mun was deemed a national hero for killing 20,000 sparrows by sneaking around, locating sparrow nests, and strangling them with his bare hands.[37]

But, of course, sparrows and other pest birds eat locusts and other crop-eating insects in addition to grains. Without the sparrows around to stop them, the crop-eating vermin populations exploded. The devastation to grain fields by crop-eating insects was so palpable that by April of 1960, Mao ended the Smash Sparrows Campaign, redirecting the fourth focus to bedbugs. But the problem wasn't over. By 1962, the ecological imbalance resulting from the decimation of sparrows in part caused the Great Chinese Famine. The Great Leap Forward was a devastating slip backward for China, as some 36 million Chinese men, women, and children starved to death. It caused the largest famine and man-made disaster in human history.

WOAH! crazy how no one talks about this!

Mao's aim was to transform agriculture in China, but instead he landed his country in peril. Smashing sparrows wasn't based on existing knowledge and genuine evidence. And everyone was in on it. Not only was there widespread ignorance and denial of basic food-chain science and pervasive endorsement of the unsubstantiated claim that the average sparrow consumes four pounds of grain per year, but Chinese national officials contributed their share of bullshit as well—no one dared report the economic disasters caused by Mao's Great Leap Forward. Instead of facing reality, reports show that officials blamed the decline in food output on bad weather, ultimately taking no action.

blamed everything except for the problem itself

When the dark clouds of bullshit finally cleared, the Chinese government made peace with sparrows, importing 250,000 specimens from the Soviet Union.[38] The sparrows were given a chance, their numbers increased, they returned to eating up great numbers of crop-eating insects, fields of grains flourished, there was food again, and people stopped starving to death.

import of Sparrows

We are bullshitting ourselves if we think we are immune to bullshit today and things like the Great Chinese Famine cannot happen to us—because they most assuredly can. And this is why we really don't need bullshit.

A person's deeply held beliefs drive their decisions. That is why trust and bullshit-free exchanges are critical. Throughout history, our decision leaders' beliefs (for example, those of presidents) have led us into war, delayed peace, alienated allies, and appeased enemies. At other times, decision leaders' beliefs have led us to conquer new territory, enslave people, free slaves, declare the Earth flat, and sent us to the Moon. All of these events occur because decision leaders possess firmly held, strong beliefs—some of which are based in bullshit. As responsible citizens, it is vital that we know what our decision

Based on leaders' beliefs

leaders believe, but it is also critical that we know how and why they believe what they do—free of bullshit. We are in major trouble when our decision leaders obscure the what, how, and why of their beliefs.

Although it is an unfortunate reality, many of our memories, beliefs, attitudes, and decisions are based on bullshit rather than evidence-based reasoning. This is why a deeper understanding of bullshit might be one of the single most important intellectual and social issues that we face.

★ It's up to us to determine and learn a(b)
what our decision leaders believe!

2

BULLIBILITY

Bernard and His Bullible Gang

There are two ways to be fooled. One is to believe what isn't true; the other is to refuse to believe what is true.

—SØREN KIERKEGAARD

Founded in 1960, Bernard L. Madoff Investment Securities, LLC (BLMIS), operated as a securities broker-dealer in the United States and abroad, providing stock market executions for banks, broker-dealers, financial institutions, and wealthy investors. By 1989, the company had become one of the largest independent trading operations in the securities industry; by 2005, it was handling 5% of the trading volume on the NYSE. But in December of 2008, BLMIS was liquidated. One of the most esteemed men in the financial industry, former NASDAQ chairman, manager of three successful companies, and founder of BLMIS—Bernard Madoff—was accused of, convicted of, and sentenced to 150 years in prison for perpetuating the largest fraud in US history. Instead of running a

Bernard Maddoff → fraud

legitimate investment fund, Madoff was operating the nation's longest-running Ponzi scheme.

Named for con artist Charles Ponzi, who himself cost investors $20 million in 1920 (approximately $200 million today), a Ponzi scheme is an investment scheme that lures in new investors by guaranteeing unusually high returns. Ponzi himself promised 50% returns on investments in only 90 days. Ponzi operators lure in new investors and use their money to pay off the promised returns to those who invested at an earlier stage. As long as new investors continue to join the fund, the operation will appear profitable and legitimate, even though no actual investments and profits are being made.

Ponzi:
lure &
high
return

To avoid a complete collapse of the fund resulting from too many investors reclaiming their profits, Ponzi operators encourage their investors to keep their money in the game to earn even more money. When operators are questioned by investors, they describe the investment strategies in vague or mysterious ways, all the while claiming to protect their business with such secrecy. A scheme can be further protected by the fact that investors are willing to accept nonsensical explanations for profits and investment strategies as long as the returns keep coming in. Provided that the Ponzi operator can periodically report to investors how much money they are making, without actually producing any real returns, the operator can continue to pocket a share of the money or use it to continue developing the scheme.

always fail

The question isn't if a Ponzi scheme will collapse, but when. Schemes usually fall apart for one of three reasons: the Ponzi operator escapes detection and runs off with the remaining investment money, the flow of incoming money dies out as a result of failing to find new investors, or as in both Ponzi and Madoff's cases, too many investors simultaneously begin to pull out of the fund and request their returns. Ponzi's scheme began to collapse when financial journalists began asking hard questions about his investment strategy, and Madoff's scheme began to deteriorate when his investors requested a total of $7 billion back in returns when he only had $300 million left in the bank to give back.

How did Madoff manage to fly under the radar for so many years? Why did so many smart investors, with more than enough data to identify a possible scam, fail to see that it was impossible for BLMIS to perform consistently well for so long?

Madoff certainly had all of the hallmarks of credibility. He [*appears to be credible*] had been a familiar and active member of the financial indus-try since the 1960s and was a former NASDAQ chairman. Madoff also served as an advisor to the Securities and Exchange Commission (SEC). He claimed to use a legitimate-sounding strategy and was careful to make sure his returns were high but not outlandish. Investors were made to feel special as part of the chosen fellowship of exclusive investors with BLMIS. Most any investor would assume that the respectable, 70-year-old industry veteran who looked like he knew what he was doing could actually do what he was doing—as long as no one looked at the scoreboard. If it hadn't been for investors wanting more of their money than his fund could provide, Madoff might still be running his scheme.

From a social psychological perspective, I don't believe that Madoff's deceptive success was the result of supernatural persuasive skills that gave him extraordinary powers to dupe investors into giving him their money. In fact, the great majority of Madoff's investors never so much as met or spoke to him. I believe that Madoff succeeded because he had a lot of help from over 4,800 investors who, just like everyone else, are naturally *bullible.*

I've combined the words *bull* and *gullible* to get at aspects of thinking that *gullible* fails to fully capture.[1] Although some people repeatedly fall for deceptive influences, most everyone behaves in a gullible fashion on occasion. More generally, research suggests that many people suffer from bullshit blindness, or bullibility (bōoˈl/əˈbilədē)—accepting bullshit as fact by failing to infer from available social cues that the bullshitter has a disregard for the truth or has failed to take reasonable action to find truth.[2] A gullible individual may believe something despite signs of dishonesty, but the bullible individual is a relatively lazy thinker who doesn't even care about signs of dishonesty.

The inevitable bullibility of others is one reason why anyone can launch a successful Ponzi scheme. It doesn't take a stock market wizard to generate nonsensical explanations for performance growth and to persuade masses of people to give them large sums of money when they can demonstrate—at least temporarily—that they can capitalize on their investments. And that's all a successful Ponzi operator really needs.

The rest of the successful Ponzi scheme equation has nothing at all to do with the Ponzi operator and everything to do with the collective thinking of investors in the scheme. Most of BLMIS's private investors were smart and sophisticated people—people you wouldn't expect to find caught up in a major scam with bullshit written all over it. No one would accuse BLMIS investors like Jerome Fisher of lacking intelligence. Fisher was most well-known for founding the successful Nine West women's shoe company that imitates designer styles at affordable prices. A savvy businessman, Fisher, like many of his fellow investors, probably thought he was immune to investment fraud.

Another BLMIS investor was Robert Chew. In 2003, he and his wife decided to sell their home. It felt like the right time, and the stock market was doing well. They collected every dollar they could find and, with a bit of apprehension, handed over their life savings to Stanley Chais, a Los Angeles network organizer who worked for Madoff. It looked like a can't-miss opportunity for Robert and his family. After all, Robert's in-laws belonged to Madoff's investment fund for years and lived well on stock returns, which ranged from 15 to 22% annually. Everything appeared to be on the up-and-up for the Chews.

Of all the unlikely people to get mixed up with Madoff's Ponzi scheme, Stephen Greenspan is the type of person you'd expect to be immune to investment fraud. With advanced degrees from Johns Hopkins University, he spent his career as a clinical professor of psychiatry at the University of Colorado studying social incompetence and gullibility. At the time of his retirement, Greenspan had published nearly 100 scientific papers and was well-known in psychology for his book *Annals of Gullibility*. With interest and expertise in the science of gullibility, shouldn't Greenspan have recognized that

[handwritten margin note: ppl who were duped by Madoff BLMIS]

Madoff's firm was a scam? Yet he too was one of BLMIS's private investors.

While Fisher, the Chews, and Greenspan were receiving wake-up calls, Harry Markopolos received a very different kind of call. Markopolos was on to Madoff and had been trying to call attention to Madoff's bullshit for nine years prior to the big bust. Working as a securities industry executive and independent forensic accountant, Markopolos discovered evidence of fraud as early as 1999, and again in 2000, 2001, and 2005, Markopolos alerted the SEC that Madoff was likely running a Ponzi scheme.

When Markopolos testified before Congress in 2009, he stated,

> The SEC was never capable of catching Mr. Madoff. He could have gone to $100 billion. It took me about five minutes to figure out he was a fraud.
>
> I glanced at the numbers. And I knew immediately that the numbers made no sense. I just knew it. Numbers exist in relationships. . . . It was clear something was out of whack. I began shaking my head. I knew what a split-strike strategy was capable of producing, but this particular one was so poorly designed and contained so many glaring errors that I didn't see how it could be functional, much less profitable. At the bottom of the page, a chart of Madoff's return stream rose steadily at a 45-degree angle, which simply doesn't exist in finance. Within five minutes I told Frank, "There's no way this is real. This is bogus." As I continued ex-

amining the numbers, the problems with them began popping out as clearly as a red wagon in a field of snow.

If investors and the SEC had been paying just a bit of attention to the truth, they would have been wise to the Ponzi scheme that had been going on for over a decade. Unfortunately, as explained in Markopolos's book *No One Would Listen*, no one was listening. The SEC dismissed Markopolos and instead believed Madoff's accounts of his own investing proficiency.[3]

What did Markopolos see that everyone else was failing to notice? First, Markopolos made sure that he clearly understood Madoff's explanations for his extraordinary returns. Madoff claimed to achieve his returns by using a split-strike conversion strategy. This involved purchasing blue-chip stock shares of companies listed within the S&P 100 or S&P 500 (that is, large corporations listed on stock exchanges in the United States with a reputation for quality, reliability, and profitability in good and bad markets) and then insuring the stocks with put options, which gave him the right to sell at a specified price by a specified date. By allegedly purchasing put options, Madoff could further obscure his operation by making it harder to determine at what prices he was allegedly selling his stock shares. Madoff could hide the footprints of his alleged stock trades in this way because he wouldn't be expected to explain how his hedge funds consistently outperformed all the others on the basis of published stock prices. And it worked. But Markopolos wasn't buying it. Looking at Madoff's alleged strategy in combination with his "performance records," Markopolos discovered more red flags than there are in the Soviet Union. There were three major red flags among them that should have been salient to most investors. The first red flag was that somehow Madoff continued racking up steady returns of 1% a month, with a consistent average return of 12% a year, no matter how the S&P 100 and S&P 500 market indices moved. Madoff claimed that his returns were market-driven. But it is nearly impossible for one to have been making market-driven decisions, all within the S&P 100 and S&P 500, if one's performance corresponds to only 6% of the market fluctuations. This should have been blatantly obvious to anyone watching the markets. It is even easier to see this reality when the data are plotted on a graph.

So should it have been following the S&P 100 the entire time?

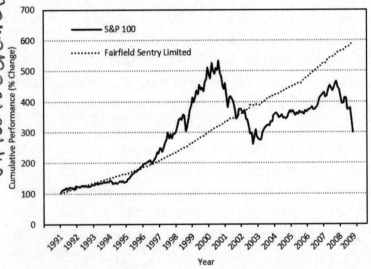

One of BLMIS's investment management firms was Fairfield Sentry Ltd.[4] Looking at the percentage of cumulative performance changes every month, it is easy to see that Madoff's performance (dotted line) with Fairfield Sentry Ltd. could not possibly be derived from making market decisions. If it had, Madoff's returns would look much like that of the market (solid line). All investors know that the market is volatile. Yet somehow, this principle didn't apply to Madoff's returns, because he was reporting a consistent 45-degree rise in returns every month while the S&P 100 showed its usual volatility and fluctuations.

The second red flag came when Markopolos tried to replicate Madoff's results. Like any good critical thinker open to empirical validation, he attempted to duplicate Madoff's results using Madoff's purported strategy. And why not? If someone tells you that a bowling ball can be balanced on the tip of a needle, and it is true, it should be easy enough to demonstrate yourself. Although Madoff's strategy was simple to understand and employ, Markopolos wasn't able to reproduce the same outcomes.

Another red flag was that there simply weren't enough put options in the market for Madoff to be doing what he claimed to be doing. Markopolos found you could realistically purchase only $1 billion of put options for blue-chip stocks. At various times, Madoff would have needed $3 billion to $65 billion of these options to protect his investments—far more than existed in the system.

These and other aspects of Madoff's returns and "strategy" are all things that should have been red flags for investors employing a bit of due diligence. Yet Madoff was so powerful and famous on Wall Street that investors paid little attention to what he was actually doing with their money, instead blindly trusting BLMIS. Besides, it all appeared to be making a lot of people a lot of money. And who wouldn't be thrilled with a 12% annual return on investment?

People like Greenspan, Fisher, and the Chews were never directly persuaded by Bernard Madoff. All they needed was something that looked like a great opportunity. They set up investments with people like Chais and other network organizers. It worked the same way for almost everyone. Investors were invited to think that they were special, that everything was private, and that they were among the select few being given the opportunity to invest in the ultra-successful BLMIS. All the while, Madoff's investors remained more concerned about their returns than they were with the evidence that those returns allegedly rested upon. They became bullible.

By the time the scheme was exposed as a house of cards, over 4,800 clients lost approximately $18 billion in investments— over $3.5 million on average and about 90 times what investors lost to Charles Ponzi's scheme.[5] This alone elevates Madoff's bullshit to three flies on the Bullshit Flies Index. Greenspan invested large sums of his retirement fund after learning that his sister and her friends had already invested in the Rye Prime Bond Fund (a major Madoff feeder fund). Greenspan summed up his detection failure: "In my own case, the decision to invest in the Rye fund reflected both my profound ignorance of finance, and my somewhat lazy unwillingness to remedy that ignorance. . . . In fact, I am not certain if Mr. Madoff's name was even mentioned (and certainly, I would not have recognized it) when I was considering investing in the 3 billion dollar Rye fund."[6]

Fisher was no stranger to SEC matters. His Nine West shoe business was once flagged by the SEC in the late 1990s for accounting irregularities, though no further action was taken. Shouldn't Fisher have recognized the fund's suspicious success before investing $150 million?

Before learning that he and his wife were wiped out of their life savings of $1.2 million, Robert Chew denied that his money was invested in a Ponzi scheme. Robert admitted, "I think everyone knew the call would come one day. We all hoped, but we knew deep down it was too good to be true, right? We deluded ourselves into thinking we were all smarter than the others."[7]

There are few areas where protecting oneself from bullshit is more important than how one invests one's money. Due diligence—seeking reality and truth—isn't the stuff of bullshitters or bullible investors, yet it is one of the most important processes to protect oneself from bullshit. A straightforward examination of relevant evidence (for example, financial statements) would have indicated that Madoff's claims were pure fabrications. Unbelievably positive and consistent returns despite market downturns, lack of oversight of his performance and operations by independent auditors, the opaqueness of his claims about his investment strategy, and the secrecy he insisted on from third parties were all signals of fraud. Yet banks, investment firms, institutions, pension funds, and hedge funds, with highly educated and sophisticated people managing them, were duped by Madoff and his financial advisors. Rather than by the artistry of their lies and bullshit, Ponzi scheme artists like Madoff attract investors with their own bullibility.

Everyone is Susceptible!

I want you to consider something you may have never considered before. You're probably not going to believe this, but you are just as susceptible to bullshit as anyone else. It's critical that you accept this, because a major reason bullshit is so destructive is that everyone believes they can sense it, despite research clearly demonstrating that bullshit is not easily detected. Bullshit is not limited to psychics who speak with the dead or Ouija board enthusiasts. It's everywhere, including spaces you wouldn't think to consider.

We want to believe we know things we don't. We want to believe we've made the right decisions—the car we bought, the career we pursued, the person we decided to marry, the school we send our children to, the candidate we voted for. There is a sense of security in thinking we are right. But there is a liability in pretending we know things that we really do not—however much we may want them to be true. It is easy to be drawn into the irrational and unexamined when the rational and informative approach leads to an unwelcome truth. When we give preference to what we wish is true over truth, we allow bullshit to flourish.

THE PSYCHOLOGY OF BULLIBILITY

Why is it that people are so bullible? The empirical science known as bullshit studies is still in its infancy. There isn't much empirical research to inform our understanding of what bullibility is, how it develops, and why there is so much of it. On the other hand, there is quite a bit of psychological research that speaks to the foundations of this question. I have divided this research into personal, contextual, cognitive, emotional, and motivational components. All of these components contribute to our tendency toward bullibility.

Personal Bullibility: Who We Are

Determining if someone is more bullible than others is the domain of personality psychology. A person's personality is their enduring and consistent ways of thinking, feeling, and behaving. To say that someone is an exceptionally bullible person would mean that, relative to others, that person tends to uncritically accept information, displays a great readiness to believe things, demonstrates an insensitivity to cues of untrustworthiness or a lack of concern for the truth, and shows a willingness to accept false premises even when the cues to untrustworthiness/lack of concern for truth are blatantly obvious.

In 1949, psychologist Bertram Forer conducted a study that demonstrates just how pervasive the bullible personality trait is.[8] In his study, Forer first had his participants complete a "Diagnostic Interest Blank" questionnaire, which asked participants about their hobbies, reading materials, personal characteristics, job duties, and secret hopes and ambitions for being their ideal selves. Participants were told the questionnaire would be scored and interpreted qualitatively to infer personality traits. One week after completing the questionnaire, participants were given a typed personality sketch with their names written on it. The personality sketch looked authentic, but in reality was completely contrived—nothing had actually been scored. For every participant, the sketch included the very same 13 statements, most of which were taken from a newsstand astrology book. The statements included "You have a great need for other people to like and admire you," "You have a tendency to be critical of yourself," "You have a great deal of unused capacity which you have not turned to your advantage," and "While you have some personality weaknesses, you are generally able to compensate for them."

Forer was interested in how his students rated the Diagnostic Interest Blank's ability to reveal their personalities. Remarkably, nearly every student found the Diagnostic Interest Blank accurate. Despite the fact that the personality sketches were bogus, nearly every student felt the sketch described their personality almost perfectly. In fact, only one of the 39 participants in Forer's study did not find that eight or more of the 13 statements were true. Forer's outcome has become known as the "Barnum effect," in reference to P. T. Barnum's apocryphal claim "There's a sucker born every minute."[9]

In 2009, American television personality John Stossel demonstrated a version of Forer's study in his "Give Me a Break!" segment for *20/20*. Once again, participants who completed the bogus personality questionnaire appeared shocked at how accurate their personality sketches appeared to be. Participants expressed that the sketch accurately captured their personalities, only to learn from Stossel that the personality sketch they had been given actually belonged to a mass murderer.

Forer's personality sketch prank demonstrates how easy it

is to get people to believe things about their own personalities, even when they have no connection whatsoever to the information they might provide about themselves. It suggests that anyone, no matter their personality, can be bullible. There aren't unique personality characteristics that make individuals especially bullible. Everyone is bullible.

But the Barnum effect doesn't stop at *beliefs* about oneself. Thirty years after Forer's work was first published, Richard Petty (the social psychologist, not the racecar driver) and Timothy Brock took the Barnum effect a step further. They were interested in the possibility that Barnum effect–based beliefs about oneself would lead people to behave in ways consistent with those beliefs. Before giving their students a homework assignment to list their thoughts about some campus proposals, Petty and Brock randomly assigned the students to one of four conditions. Some participants were provided with Barnum characterizations of themselves—as either open- or close-minded—and others were given straightforward instructions to behave open-mindedly or close-mindedly while completing the assignment. Interestingly, the students provided with Barnum characterizations that described them as open-minded people were subsequently more balanced in their thoughts, by listing an equal number of thoughts for and against the campus proposals, than their counterparts who were led to believe they were close-minded people. Furthermore, the differences found between students with the open- and close-minded Barnum conditions were almost identical to the differences between students who had been instructed to behave in open- or close-minded ways. The effects of Barnum inductions on subsequent behavior were just as powerful as direct behavioral instructions.[10]

Are any personality traits particularly vulnerable to bullshit? One possibility is high agreeableness. Agreeableness is one of the Big Five personality traits, along with extraversion, openness, conscientiousness, and neuroticism. A person high in agreeableness is often described by others as warm, friendly, tactful, helpful, selfless, sympathetic, kind, considerate, and trusting. They tend to hold optimistic views of human nature and get along well with others. One of my favorite highly agreeable characters is Forrest Gump (portrayed by Tom Hanks in *Forrest Gump*). His kindness and curiosity enabled him to do all sorts of extraordinary things, but left him vulnerable to others' influence. A good example of an individual low in agreeableness is Gordon Gekko, the greedy and ruthless corporate raider portrayed by Michael Douglas in *Wall Street*.

Highly agreeable people tend toward conformity, avoid violating social norms, eschew upsetting other people, and comply with social expectations. Agreeable people tend to see others through rose-colored glasses, trying to find the positive side in everyone.[11] By definition, agreeable people often have trouble saying no.

What happens when a highly agreeable person encounters bullshit? A study conducted by Laurent Bègue and his colleagues at the Université Grenoble Alpes, France, speaks to this very question.[12] Within the context of a fake television game show, Bègue replicated Stanley Milgram's famous studies of obedience to authority using perhaps the greatest line of bullshit in the history of social psychological experiments: "It is absolutely essential that you continue."[13]

Milgram's studies helped us understand the influence that authority figures have on behavior. In his studies, participants were led to believe they were delivering increasingly painful electric shocks to another study participant who was actually cooperating with the experimenters (that is, a confederate). Although the participants could not see the confederate, they could hear them, and it was made clear that the confederate "experienced pain" with each shock. As the study progressed, the shock intensities increased. If the participant began to hesitate or expressed any refusal to continue, the experimenter intervened by giving prods urging the participant to continue—"Please go on," "The experiment requires that you continue," "It is absolutely essential that you continue," and "You have no other choice, you must go on." This was bullshit. There was no need for the participant to continue. In fact, Milgram's participants could stop the study at any point they wished, without suffering any penalty for withdrawing. The question was, how far would participants go when the only influence was an authority figure's instruction to continue?

What would you do? How long would you continue to deliver painful electric shocks to another person? Most people are surprised to find that the majority of Milgram's participants continued to the very end of the study. Despite screams from the confederate and alleged shocks of over 400 volts, participants tended to obey the authority figure.

In replicating Milgram's procedures, Bègue included a

Big Five measure of personality. As expected, those highest in agreeableness were the most likely to continue delivering painful electric shocks at the prods of the game-show host. Being pleasant, warm, and nice, as highly agreeable people tend to be, conflicts with an ability to critically analyze and discard bullshit. This is why the techniques employed by bullshitters should be particularly effective with agreeable people. Agreeable individuals may be more likely to conform to bullshit by endorsing the bullshit publicly and obeying suggestions more readily than others.

What about highly trusting people? You might think that low-trusting people would be better at detecting bullshit than highly trusting people, but existing literature on this question suggests the opposite.[14] Japanese social psychologists Toshio Yamagishi and his colleagues have provided intriguing evidence suggesting that highly trusting people are less easily duped.[15] Yamagishi and his colleagues had study participants complete multiple questionnaires to identify how trusting they were of others in general. High- and low-trusting participants were then presented with vignettes, which contained either a brief positive or negative description of a character in a particular situation or no additional information about the character. When there was no additional information supplied about the character, high trusters were more likely than low trusters to say that the character would act in a trustworthy manner. However, when negative information about the central character was presented, high trusters changed their opinion of the character's trustworthiness more quickly than low trusters. Thus, high trusters may be more, rather than less, sensitive to overt negative cues than low trusters. And this is partly what bullshit detection is all about—being sensitive to bullshit cues when they are made available. A bullible person is not simply overly trusting. Rather, being bullible involves a failure to detect bullshit cues or act on those cues appropriately.

[handwritten margin note: Bullible—failure to detect BS cues]

Contextual Bullibility: The Situations We Face

In 1971, a team of psychologists led by Philip Zimbardo decided that it would be a good idea to convert their psychology lab into a mock prison.[16] Private cubicles were turned into prison cells, and college students were recruited to fill the prison and were randomly assigned to play the roles of prisoner or prison guard. After making it clear that cruelty on the part of the guards was part of their identity and necessary for the advancement of prison correction, Zimbardo and his colleagues watched what happened.[17] What they saw was healthy and normal functioning college students turn into prisoners who suffered such intense emotional stress reactions that the mock prison began to look like the real thing. Many prisoners acted like zombies, obeying the demeaning orders of other college students who transformed into ruthless and dehumanizing prison guards. So intense and unexpected were the transformations that the experiment—planned to last two weeks—was terminated by the sixth day. The research, now known as the Stanford Prison Experiment, is an example of what occurs when one group of people is encouraged to take total power over a group of derogated others in a dehumanizing environment such as a prison. The study demonstrated

situation can influence your attitudes and beliefs

the powerful effect that a situation can have on an individual's attitudes, values, and behavior.

The situation surrounding one's behavior influences one's thinking, feeling, and behaving. Yet the role context plays in behavior is often ignored or forgotten.[18] I may wish to believe that those popcorn and candy commercials at the movie theater don't influence my cravings and tendency to fork over cash for overpriced snacks, but my wishing doesn't change the reality that they most certainly do. The same is true of bullshit. Context is part of what makes people bullible.

A striking example of the power of context was provided by Harvard university psychologist Ellen Langer and her colleagues.[19] They studied people waiting in line at a library copy machine. While incognito, an experimenter would try to cut the line to use the machine. As they did so, the experimenter would ask the bystander they cut in front of one of three questions. Sometimes they would make a request and provide no reason: "Excuse me, I have five pages. May I use the Xerox machine?" Other times they would make a request with a real reason: "Excuse me, I have five pages. May I use the Xerox machine, because I'm in a rush?" And other times the experimenter would make a request using a placebic reason that provided no real information: "Excuse me, I have five pages. May I use the Xerox machine, because I have to make copies?" Imagine if you were patiently waiting in line and someone you don't even know tells you one of these excuses. What would you do?

When Langer and her colleagues made a request with no apparent reason, people in the copy line complied by letting the experimenter cut in line 60% of the time. However, when the experimenters made the request with real and placebic reasons, compliance increased to 94% and 93%, respectively! These compliance results were much less likely when the favor was relatively large (for example, 20 pages to copy led to 24–42% compliance)—but still, a 93% compliance rate is incredible after providing only a placebic reason. An equally absurd finding was reported by social psychologist Robert Cialdini. He gave his participants a fixed amount of time to collect as much money as they could from complete strangers (without entertaining them) on the streets of a large city.[20] The most successful money collectors used the key word *because*. Incredibly, it didn't matter what came after the word *because.* The only thing that mattered to success was how frequently the word *because* was used.

Sometimes context can influence bullibility because the domain of judgment and available options shape the standard of comparison. That is, when perceiving something accurately is difficult because reference points activated by the situation shape perception. Restaurant owners and chefs know this trick well. For instance, you might see Chilean sea bass on the menu of a restaurant rather than its actual name, the Antarctic toothfish. Chilean sea bass is closer to anyone's reference point for tasty fish than is Antarctic toothfish. In fact, Chilean sea bass isn't even a bass at all—it's a sea cod. In domains such as art, food, or real estate, which are characterized by subjectivity and uncertainty, it is relatively easy to persuade people of one's competence. On the other hand, it would probably be very difficult for me to convince you that I am a world-class sprinter capable of dethroning Usain Bolt of his world records because it is easy enough for you to time me in the 100m dash—and my time of 14 seconds is five seconds too slow. The important underlying ingredient is the degree of certainty. Persuasion and influence always work best under conditions of uncertainty because uncertain people are looking for answers and clarity, and frankly, they usually don't know enough to detect bullshit.

BS uncertain ppl!

Cognitive Bullibility: How We Think

How do the ways in which we think play a role in our own bullibility? Perhaps the most critical thinking–based error that makes us more bullible is confusing argument with evidence. An *argument* is a reason or theory provided for a claim. Arguments help us understand how or why something occurs, but they don't demonstrate or verify that the something occurs for those reasons. *Evidence,* on the other hand, is the available body of information and facts supporting a belief or proposition as true or valid. When considering evidence, one is interested in proof, confirmation, and verification. Evidence requires making observations in a systematic way using observable, objectively measured variables. It also requires us to define demonstrable criteria. If I were to claim that airplanes fly, I must clearly define what is meant by flight. How high must an airplane be from the ground to say it flies? And for how long? Under the most ideal of circumstances, we might conduct diagnostic tests to determine if airplanes can fly.

I find it comforting to believe an airplane will take flight and safely take me where I need to go. Is my belief based on mere argument or genuine evidence? I could explain that an airplane can be used to fly from New York to London because that's what airplanes do. Or I could go beyond the wings, engine, fuel, and pilot and talk about the finer details of the physics of flight—but my arguments do not serve as evidence. All of the arguments for the possibility of flight weren't enough to get the earliest passengers to risk their lives in structures that flight experimenters believed could and should take flight. Only after the Wright brothers cracked the code of flight and provided visual evidence that airplanes could fly were people willing to put their trust in airplanes.

Although evidence can be interpreted in multiple ways, evidence is *always* better and more compelling than mere argument. Being grounded in factual data, evidence reduces our reliance on "making things up." And when it comes to serious things, like putting my life in the hands of airline pilots, I feel confident they will transport me from place to place because of hard evidence that airplanes can fly, not mere arguments or predictions that they can fly.

In an important study of how people generate arguments, cognitive psychologist Deanna Kuhn tested whether people recognize the difference between argument and evidence.[21] In her study, Kuhn's participants first wrote about their beliefs about random topics, such as why criminals released from prison often return to crime. Kuhn then asked her participants to provide evidence for their views. Most of the responses were classified as arguments. In fact, only 16% of Kuhn's participants generated genuine evidence, with most forms of evidence being what she called *pseudoevidence* (i.e., a scenario or script depicting how things might look or how the processes described might occur).

Kuhn's results showed that people can believe things despite not understanding why or having any evidence that what they believe is true. This failure in understanding contributes to the tendency to think about argument as if it is evidence. This is a problem because the very essence of being bullible is the tendency to be influenced by arguments not grounded in genuine evidence or a concern for truth. Failing to recognize and appreciate the difference between argument and evidence makes one vulnerable to bullshit.

The good news is that the tendency to count argument as evidence can be reversed. In fact, the reversal can be as simple as replacing the tendency to ask *Why?* questions with *How?* questions. When people are asked to explain why they think something is true or why they think something works, it tends to elicit the relatively easier goal of providing opinions and mere arguments. However, when people are asked to explain how they know something is true or how something works, it tends to elicit the relatively challenging goal of providing evidence and proof. Although there appears to be a stronger disposition toward making an argument than providing evidence—because making an argument is easier—we should practice asking *how* questions. Asking questions such as "How do I know this to be true?" is a critical step toward reducing bullibility. Cognitive studies conducted by psychologists Amnon Glassner and his colleagues showed just that.[22] In Glassner's studies, participants were asked to consider frequently debated issues, such as whether the use of a mobile telephone while driving causes

[handwritten margin note: can believe w/out understanding why or how they believe]

car accidents. Half of Glassner's participants were then asked, "How do you know that the use of mobile phones while driving causes car accidents?" whereas the other half were asked, "Why do you think that the use of mobile phones while driving causes car accidents?" Those who answered "How?" were significantly more likely to produce evidence than arguments. On the other hand, those who answered "Why?" were significantly more likely to offer arguments than evidence. Glassner's subtle manipulation led to a big difference in output because the choice of argument or evidence was influenced by the goal of one's reasoning, as dictated by answering *how* rather than *why*.

Another cognitive contributor to bullibility is any factor that makes a claim easier to imagine, comprehend, or remember. The easier it is to imagine or understand something, the more likely we are to trick ourselves into believing that it is true. This fallacy in thinking is widely appreciated by advertising executives, politicians, and other "professional" persuaders because it has a potent influence on our judgments and perceptions of truth.[23] You might recall the famous Tootsie Pop television commercial that investigated the number of licks it takes to get to the center of a Tootsie Pop. The memorable classic first aired in 1968, and 20 million copies of the average-at-best candy have been produced and sold every day since.[24]

No matter how easy it is to imagine, comprehend, or remember information, it is not diagnostic of the quality of that information. Although it may be easy to imagine Elvis Presley faking his own death and that he is still roaming the grounds of Graceland, it doesn't mean it is true. A dramatic example of this self-trickery was demonstrated in a study conducted by Larry Jacoby and his colleagues. Their participants were asked to read a list of names, some of which were names of famous people and some of which were names of non-famous people.[25] While reading the names on the list, participants' attention was divided by having to simultaneously listen to random numbers read aloud by the experimenter. The next day, participants judged whether each name from a new list was of a famous or non-famous person. Some of the names were from the first list and some were entirely new. The question was, in the minds of participants, did non-famous people "become famous overnight"?

As it turns out, yes! Jacoby's participants were more likely to misidentify non-famous people as famous if they had read their name the day before. Participants confused the subjective sense of familiarity with non-famous names with famousness. Such findings suggest that simply becoming familiar with false claims can make those false claims appear true over time.

One's characteristic style of thinking also influences how bullible you are. The two general styles of thinking are intuitive and reflective thinking. To understand the distinction, try answering this question:

A bat and a ball cost $1.10 in total. The bat costs $1.00 more than the ball. How much does the ball cost?

If you are like most people, your first answer was 10 cents. Although that's the most common answer, it is wrong. If the ball cost 10 cents, then the bat would cost $1.00, and the bat would thereby cost only 90 cents more than the ball. The bat costs $1.00 more than the ball, and the only way for that to be the case is for the bat to cost $1.05 and the ball to cost 5 cents. What makes this problem difficult is that the pull of the intuitive and incorrect response is significantly stronger because it comes to mind more quickly than the correct response. In order to arrive at the correct response, you must fight against the intuitive pull and stop to reflect for a few moments—it requires reflective thinking.

The bat-and-ball question comes from the Cognitive Reflection Test (CRT), which measures intuitive and reflective forms of thinking. Intuitive thinking is a relatively effortless form of thinking that relies on instinct and reaching decisions quickly on the basis of automatic reactions. Intuitive thinkers often go with their gut feelings. Reflective thinking is the opposite: it requires considerable analytic effort, deliberation, and systematic reasoning. Reflective thinkers often question their first instincts and consider other possibilities.

[handwritten margin note: intuitive vs reflective thinking]

Experts are by no means immune to intuitive thinking—they appear to engage in just as much intuitive thinking as other people.[26] But are intuitive thinkers more bullible than reflective thinkers? Research conducted by University of Regina psychology professor Gordon Pennycook speaks to this very question. In his studies, participants completed the CRT. They also reported whether they found several of Deepak Chopra's Twitter quotes (for example, "Mechanics of manifestation, intention, detachment, centered in being allowing juxtaposition of possibilities to unfold." and "Hidden meaning transforms unparalleled abstract beauty.") to be profound or senseless bullshit. Pennycook found that intuitive thinkers are significantly more likely to perceive Chopra's senseless bullshit as profound than reflective thinkers.[27] In other words, one's susceptibility to being duped by bullshit is associated with an intuitive, less effortful, or careless thinking style. Given Pennycook's findings, it comes as little surprise that people who score high on the CRT (reflective thinkers) also tend to accurately discern fake news from real news, even for news headlines that align with their political ideologies.[28] Pennycook's perspective is that people believe fake news and other forms of bullshit not because of motivated reasoning, such as wishing false things to be true, but because they tend to engage in a "lazy" style of thinking by putting very little thought into what they are seeing on social media.

Because intuitive and reflective thinking styles are largely independent of intelligence, a high IQ does not preclude one from falling for bullshit. Even trained psychologists who predicted the results of Milgram's studies of obedience to authority, real estate agents who estimate values of homes, and physicians who make diagnoses can be as susceptible to bullshit when making judgments in their areas of expertise as novices in those fields are.[29] We don't have to go far beyond the story of Madoff's Ponzi scheme to see how intelligent people can be naive investors, neglecting risks and warning signs. There are at least two reasons for this addressed by cognitive literature: (1) even people of high intelligence fail to ask themselves basic critical-thinking questions when exposed to bullshit; and

(2) highly intelligent people are no more immune to chronic problems in thinking than are their relatively less intelligent counterparts.[30]

Many chronic problems in thinking function like cognitive illusions. And whether they emerge from a lack of motivation or a lack of the mental resources needed to critically evaluate claims, they increase bullibility.[31] Unfortunately, the list of chronic problems in thinking, serving as roots to cognitive bullibility, is long.[32] Furthermore, with most problems in thinking, part of the problem is that they usually appear to be reasonable ways of thinking. For instance, when asked, "How many animals of each kind did Moses take on the Ark?," most people report two rather than zero (the correct answer),[33] despite knowing that *Noah* was the biblical character who built the Ark.

Because of its pervasiveness and subtlety, I have a personal favorite when it comes to problems of thinking (for a more extensive list, see the appendix). It is called the *framing effect*. The framing effect describes a cognitive bias whereby our decisions are influenced by whether information is framed in a positive or negative light. The framing of options can appeal to our preferences, such as the bias to believe that a greater amount of something is usually better. Common examples of the framing effect are found in how goods are marketed. People typically prefer bottled water described as 99% pure than 1% impure, even though they are the same. Eighty-five percent lean meat is preferred over 15% fat meat, even though they are the same.[34]

How information is framed can also affect how we feel

about taking risks.[35] Imagine that you are the head physician of a large hospital where a rare disease is spreading rapidly. The disease is expected to kill 600 patients. Two drugs have been proposed to combat the disease, but you can only select one. If Drug A is adopted, 200 patients will be saved. If Drug B is adopted, there is a one-third chance that 600 patients will be saved and a two-thirds chance that none of them will be saved. Which drug would you choose?

You probably have a strong preference for Drug A. Most people are less willing to take the risk of 600 people dying with Drug B when they can be assured of saving 200 people with Drug A.

Now consider the very same scenario with Drugs C and D. If Drug C is adopted, 400 patients will die. If Drug D is adopted, there is a one-third chance that no patients will die and a two-thirds chance that 600 patients will die. Which drug would you choose?

You probably noticed that the expected outcome of Drug C is identical to Drug A and the expected outcome of Drug D is identical to Drug B. Although you probably preferred Drug A to Drug B, you may now have a strong preference for Drug D over Drug C.

When it is easier to see potential gains, people tend to behave in a risk-averse manner. When the same drugs are described in terms of their expected losses, most people are more willing to take the risk of 600 people dying with Drug D when they can be assured that 400 of those people will die with Drug C. When it is easier to see potential losses, people tend to behave in a risk-taking manner.

The framing effect is a powerful cognitive illusion. It persists even when we examine it closely and stare it in the face. I first encountered this scenario over 25 years ago, and I can honestly say I still prefer Drugs A and D to Drugs B and C. Of course, my preference is irrational.

Indeed, different versions of the notorious, lives saved/lost framing problem have been replicated in many experiments, showing that when choosing between gains, people usually prefer the riskless option, Drug A, but when choosing between losses, they usually prefer the risky option, Drug D. Once again, lives saved and lives lost frames are said to be logically equivalent, which makes the majority choice appear logically inconsistent. However, when looking more carefully at the wording of the problem, you will notice the risky options are completely specified, whereas the riskless options are not. For instance, the riskless option, Drug A, states that "200 patients will be saved," without stating, "and 400 patients will not be saved." The good news is that when experimenters have completely specified the riskless options in this way, the preferences for taking risks only when options were framed in negative ways (losses) and not taking risks only when options were framed in positive ways (gains) disappeared.[36] This important finding illustrates the very essence of bullshit detection—when provided with incomplete information (or bullshit), it is always better to search for complete information before making a judgment and/or decision.

Still, while at the supermarket, I won't select frozen yogurt described as having 20% fat. But if the very same frozen yogurt is described as 80% fat free, I'm suddenly leaning toward yes—in fact, I'll take three. Bullshit can create an equally deceptive cognitive illusion if it focuses our thinking on incomplete information or on things that are not really there.

Emotional Bullibility: How We Feel

Does our current mood affect how likely we are to believe or disbelieve other people's bullshit? Anyone who studies emotion for a living will tell you that affective experiences penetrate every aspect of our lives and heavily influence our cognitive and behavioral strategies, including how we perceive deception.

In one study, Australian social psychologist Joseph Forgas manipulated his participants' moods and assessed whether their mood affected their ability to detect deception. He had one-third of his participants watch a ten-minute excerpt from a British comedy series, another third watch an excerpt from a nature documentary, and a final third watch an excerpt from a feature film about dying of cancer. The films placed his participants in a happy, neutral, or sad mood, respectively. Following the mood induction, participants viewed video clips of people who were either honest or deceptive when denying an alleged theft during interrogation. They then made judgments about guilt or innocence and truthfulness of the people in the videos. Forgas found happy participants were more likely to make errors in detecting deceptive communications. However, sad participants showed increased skepticism and accuracy in detecting deceptive communications.[37]

Forgas expected his participants' moods to influence their

deception detection abilities for two reasons: First, a person's mood selectively influences what memories they recall. Good moods tend to bring to mind more positive, trusting evaluations of prior messages, whereas bad moods tend to bring to mind prior evaluations marked by skepticism or rejection. Consistent with an affectively induced mechanism, several empirical studies have found mood-congruent biases in the way people form many social judgments. Second, prior studies have also shown that mood can impact the way information is processed. Most often, people in a bad mood tend to process information in a more detailed and systematic manner that is conducive to detecting deception. On the other hand, those in a good mood tend to adopt a superficial processing style less conducive to detecting deception.

Forgas's research suggests that in addition to situational factors such as fatigue, divided attention, and cognitive load, the inability to detect subtle bullshit cues can result from elevated emotional states. But it should not be surprising that affective experiences can affect whether one accepts or rejects bullshit.

There are, however, other ways in which our emotions influence our level of bullibility. Consider the following scenario:

Imagine that you decided to make an investment in the stock market. Although you did your research and considered buying several stocks, you settled on an investment with shares of Stock A. After one year, you received a 0.10% return on your shares of Stock A. Not the result you wanted, but at least you didn't lose money.

Of course, you can't help but take a look at the other stocks you considered but didn't buy. You notice that you could have made 10 times as much money if you had invested in Stock B. How do you feel about that?

If you are like most people, you won't be very happy about the fact that Stock B outperformed Stock A, and you will evaluate your decision negatively. If, however, you were to find that Stock B dropped in price and that you would have lost money, it is likely that you will feel much more positively about your investment in Stock A.

People tend to evaluate the correctness of information based on their emotional reactions to that information. Do I like or dislike what the information says about me, my loved ones, or our future? In the very same way, people tend to base perceived correctness of decisions on their emotional reactions to the outcomes of those decisions. This tendency is known as the *outcome bias* because evaluations of decisions tend to be influenced more by the outcomes of those decisions than by the sensibility of the decisions.[38] Even when people are well aware of the probabilities before the decision is made (for example, Stock A has a 70% chance of profit, whereas Stock B has only a 15% chance of profit), they often cannot help themselves from perceiving the investment in Stock A to be a bad decision if Stock B turns out to be more profitable. Our emotional reactions to what occurred, and to what didn't occur, have a great impact on our views of a decision in ways that are divorced from the information that people use to make the decision. In other words, people are quick to dismiss the

sensibility of a decision once they become privy to the outcome of the decision.

Bullshit artists exploit this. They try to get us to see how
wonderful life could be if only we buy what they are selling
and how dismal it will be if we don't. Or, as economic historian
Charles Poor "Charlie" Kindleberger put it, "There is nothing so disturbing to one's well-being and judgment as to see a
friend get rich."[39] Playing on a person's emotions is a reliable
way to get them to fork over good money for the next big thing.

Motivational Bullibility: Preference for Bullshit over Truth and Facts

Another reason people are bullible is because they are sometimes motivated to disregard the truth. Our strongest social
motivations include the need to belong and feel accepted by
others, the need to be consistent in our thoughts and behavior,
and the need to feel justified in our behavior.[40] The implicit
desire to fulfill these motivations can make us especially bullible, even while awkwardly waiting, with several people, at an
elevator door whose call button has not been pressed.

As economist Robert Shiller argues, a basic mechanism
explaining the success of Ponzi schemes is humans' tendency
to model their behaviors on the behaviors of others, especially
when dealing with matters they don't fully understand.[41] In the
case of investing in Madoff's hedge fund, the fact that so many
people seemed to be making large profits on their investments,
and telling others about their good fortune, made subsequent
investments appear safe and too good to pass up. Besides, since

"everyone else was doing it," one would almost appear foolish if one failed to do the same.

Consider, for instance, the classic demonstrations of conformity provided by psychologist Solomon Asch.[42] In Asch's study, participants were shown a line (Exhibit 1) and asked which option (A, B, or C in Exhibit 2) it most resembled. The answer, as you can see, seems incredibly obvious.

"everyone else is doing it"

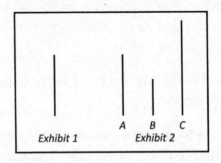

Exhibit 1   A   B   C
                  Exhibit 2

However, members of the group (in actuality five confederates, college students who were assisting the researchers) intentionally gave the wrong answer aloud, one at a time, on several trials just like this one. Now the participants faced a dilemma. The correct answer was obvious, but giving the right answer required going against a group of their peers. Conforming to the behavior of others would be easier, but required giving an obviously wrong answer.

Asch expected that his participants would ignore the answers that were blatantly incorrect and answer rationally. But that's not what happened. Seventy-six percent of his participants agreed with their peers' answers, even though they were wrong. Most participants conformed on one to three of 12 trials in which the group gave the wrong answer. However, a considerable number of participants conformed to the group's incorrect response nearly every single time.

In an important variation of Asch's study,[43] participants were led to believe that they arrived to the lab late for a critical phase of the study, and because of this, they would be required to write their answers privately on a sheet of paper. Now that participants were no longer required to publicize their responses, they rarely conformed to the others' obviously wrong answers. This variation of Asch's study showed that his participants were, in fact, seeing things clearly, but that they only felt permitted to report what they saw when they could respond privately. Asch's participants knew their counterparts were wrong, but they went along with the group because they didn't want to be excluded from the group. Asch's studies demonstrated that the motivation to be included and accepted by the crowd is a powerful one. People may hold very different private beliefs from the crowd, while at the same time publicly conform to the senselessness displayed by the crowd in order to fit in. Remaining bullible by behaving as the crowd does can fulfill the natural need to belong and is considerably easier than sticking one's neck out.

For people who work hard to base their beliefs on the best available evidence, motivated bullibility may be difficult to comprehend. They often make the mistake of thinking that all people really need is the right evidence and they will stop believing bullshit. Someone who is buying bullshit for cognitive or contextual reasons may respond appropriately to evidence clarifications, but not so for the individual who sustains their bullibility for motivational reasons. No amount of evidence

preference for bs

will keep them from buying bullshit, because it is bullshit they prefer to believe in. As soon as you realize that someone does not intend, nor prefer, to base their beliefs on evidence, you will see that their problem has nothing to do with a lack of evidence.

A litmus test for a person's motivated bullibility is to ask the person, "If it could be proven, without a shadow of a doubt, that A is not correct and that B is correct, would you believe that B is true?" If the person tells you no, then you know their endorsement of bullshit is motivationally based. In such a case, it makes no sense to continue wasting your breath. Your facts-based approach will only be met with more pushback, and you will thereby unnecessarily expose yourself to more bullshit.[44]

The sad reality is that very few people form and communicate their beliefs after a rigorous consideration of evidence and existing knowledge.[45] Although arguments for one's beliefs are often misconstrued as evidence, most attitudes and beliefs are formed on the basis of subjective, emotional reactions rather than a fair assessment of evidence. The misguided equating of argument with genuine evidence only complicates matters for people who don't really care for genuine evidence. They are motivated to confirm their beliefs by surveying data that support their conclusions. Selectively cherry-picking evidence doesn't bring anyone closer to the truth. Believing whatever one wishes to believe is true can be accomplished rather easily using many of the same types of biased, cognitive illusions that render one bullible.[46]

genuine evidence

Social psychologists refer to the mental tension created when someone simultaneously holds two conflicting thoughts as *cognitive dissonance*.[47] The act of fact-checking questionable beliefs is in contradiction with one's desire to hold those beliefs because fact-checking may prove those beliefs wrong. People are motivated to reduce cognitive dissonance when it emerges or prevent it from emerging in the first place. Rather than admitting their mistakes and letting go of bullshit-based beliefs, people tend to double down on their beliefs and rationalize contradictory evidence in order to reduce dissonance.[48] For the very same reasons, while political conservatives sort of know that Pope Francis didn't endorse Donald Trump as he campaigned for the presidency, and that Hillary Clinton wasn't directing a pedophile ring out of a Washington, DC, pizza parlor, they really want it to be true.[49] They prevent dissonance from emerging altogether by not bothering to fact-check these claims. They'd rather believe this bullshit because it fits perfectly with what they'd like to believe about these presidential candidates.

Although bullshit-based beliefs can persist in the face of scientific evidence, they shouldn't. Holding some bullshit-based beliefs will only lead to greater bullibility and suboptimal judgments and decisions.

3

WHEN AND WHY PEOPLE BULLSHIT

Learning the Conditions and Spotting the Signs

When you want to help people, you tell them the truth. When you
want to help yourself, you tell them what they want to hear.

—THOMAS SOWELL

Rebecca Bredow lived in the Detroit area with her nine-year-old son. Life was quite normal until she was sentenced to five days in jail for contempt of court. The reason? Rebecca refused to vaccinate her son a year after a county judge ordered her to do so.[1]

"It was the worst five days of my life pretty much," she told Fox 2 Detroit reporters. Yet Rebecca says that she would "do it all again."

Never in a million years did Rebecca think that she would end up in jail for standing up for her beliefs and face severe consequences for doing so. She not only lost primary custody of her son, but afterward, he was immunized anyway.

Rebecca's ex-husband took over custody and did what she refused to do. "I can't give in against my own religious belief," she argued, adding that she's not against vaccination. "This is about choice. This is about having my choices as a mother to be able to make medical choices for my child."

Rebecca isn't the only one. Surveys show that parents who refuse to vaccinate their children do so for varying reasons, but usually it comes down to religious, personal, or philosophical reasons; safety concerns; or a desire for more information from health-care providers.[2] Their primary safety concern is that vaccinations might be linked with bowel disease and autism. Autism is a developmental disorder characterized by difficulties with social interaction and communication and restrictive and repetitive behavior. It is diagnosed in 1.5% of children in developed countries.[3] If vaccinations increase the risk of developing autism, who can blame parents who wish to protect their children by not having them vaccinated? It is perfectly natural to demand the truth about the potential relationship between autism and vaccines before exposing our children to them.

The problem for anti-vaxxers like Rebecca is that the "facts" about vaccines placing children at greater risk for autism are based on an elaborate, fraudulent research report.[4] The original study suggesting a link between vaccines and autism was reported by someone who didn't care to know the truth—a discredited ex-gastroenterologist named Andrew Wakefield.

In Wakefield's original study, he examined 12 autistic children. He collected case histories, blood tests, colonoscopies, and spinal fluid from the children, and his findings revealed that eight of the children had received the MMR (measles, mumps, and rubella) vaccine shortly before experiencing developmental delays. Wakefield published his findings in the highly respected medical journal *The Lancet*. Shortly following the paper's publication, Wakefield held a press conference where he openly criticized the "triple-jab" MMR vaccine. Wakefield claimed that the triple-jab vaccine could affect children's immune systems, speculating that the measles virus in the vaccine caused proteins to leak from the intestines and impair neurons in the brain. Although Wakefield's publication never actually claimed that the MMR vaccine caused autism specifically, he did make this claim consistently afterward.

Sunday Times investigative journalist Brian Deer wasn't buying any of it.[5] By 2004, Deer discovered several problems with Wakefield's study and accused him of serious ethical violations, leading *The Lancet* to retract the original article. Most importantly, Wakefield's paper featured case studies (not more conclusive clinical trials) of the 12 children. It doesn't take a statistician to know that 12 observations aren't nearly enough to be definitive regarding a relatively weak causal relationship between vaccines and autism.

By 2011, Deer had enough data to prove that his accusations against Wakefield were correct. As it turned out, 5 of the 12 children in Wakefield's study had case histories reflecting developmental issues prior to getting the vaccine, and three of the children didn't even have autism at all. Most damning was the fact that before his 1998 article in *The Lancet*, Wakefield had been funded by Legal Aid Board, a law firm planning to bring a lawsuit against vaccine manufacturers—an apparent conflict of interest. Had he been like other scientists, Wakefield would have disclosed any conflicts of interest, but he didn't identify any in his report.[6]

While many researchers were initially skeptical of Wakefield's reported findings, panicked parents in both Great Britain and the United States pushed vaccination rates down sharply. It wasn't long before rates of measles, mumps, and rubella on both sides of the Atlantic began to rise.

The most important thing to know is that the link between vaccines and autism has been completely, widely, and repeatedly debunked. The research data are clear—vaccines do not cause autism. Dozens of top journals, including the *New England Journal of Medicine*, *Journal of Pediatric Infectious Diseases Society*, and *Journal of Autism and Developmental Disorders*, have all published research reports on a possible causal link between vaccines and autism and they have found none. A study involving over 95,000 children was published in the *Journal of the American Medical Association* in April of 2015.[7] The authors concluded that their findings "indicate no harmful association between MMR vaccine receipt and [autism spectrum disorder] even among children already at higher risk." Another effort by the United Kingdom's Medical Research Council concluded there was no evidence linking the vaccine to autism. In the largest study, published in *Annals of Internal Medicine*, which involved over 657,000 Danish children, the researchers concluded, "The study strongly supports that

MMR vaccination does not increase the risk for autism, does not trigger autism in susceptible children, and is not associated with clustering of autism cases after vaccination."[8]

Had Wakefield been concerned with the truth and genuine evidence, he would have accepted the medical establishment's conclusion that he was wrong and continued on with a promising career. But Wakefield refused to back down. In 2010, Wakefield was struck from the medical register and forbidden from practicing medicine after being found guilty of unethical behavior, misconduct, and dishonesty for authoring a fraudulent research paper.[9]

Yet, amazingly, many anti-vaxxers do not care that Wakefield's infamous case study has long been discredited and retracted. Nor do they care that Wakefield was removed from the UK medical register. Unfortunately, once anti-vaxxers become convinced that vaccines cause autism and share their beliefs publicly, it appears nearly impossible to dissuade them. Meanwhile, because parents are refusing to vaccinate their children, the rates of measles and mumps continue to rise. For these reasons, I believe Wakefield's bullshit deserves three flies on the Bullshit Flies Index.

Like it or not, we live in a world that pays more attention to bullshit than facts, evidence, and science. We live in a world that gives more credence to motivated bullshitters than to scientists and truth seekers.

The influence of cardiothoracic surgeon Dr. Mehmet Oz is another case in point. On *The Dr. Oz Show*, Dr. Oz spends an hour each weekday discussing health and wellness concerns. No subject is off-limits—from sex to diet to exercise, Dr. Oz addresses viewers' questions and chats with health experts. On March 28, 2013, Dr. Oz began his show like this:

[The large screen behind Dr. Oz displays "TOXIC TEETH" in large letters and is visible during much of the broadcast.]

Our show today concerns every one of you watching who's ever had a cavity filled, because if your filling is made with silver, it probably also contains the highly toxic element mercury. How toxic? This thermometer contains mercury. If I were to drop it, we would have to evacuate this entire studio immediately. So why are dentists still putting fillings containing mercury in your mouth? If they're already there, could your fillings be poisoning you and making you sick? They're called amalgam fillings, and more than a hundred million Americans to date have had them in their mouths. They're made of silver and other metals, but it's mercury that binds these fillings together and keeps them sturdy. Dentists have been using mercury in dental filings for more than 150 years. But are they safe? It's a question that first sparked a firestorm 30 years ago when major news reports brought to light the potential toxicity of mercury fillings. The concern is that these fillings may cause serious health problems from memory loss to mood swings, anxiety, even autoimmune disorders. The American Dental Association insists your fillings are safe, but now there's mounting new evidence showing mercury is released when you eat and drink and even when you brush your teeth. According to one report, half of dentists surveyed no longer use them. And, if they're inside your mouth, what should you do?

The show continues "asking" if our silver fillings are making us sick, suggesting that amalgams are sufficiently risky and that all people who have them should immediately have them removed. This message conflicts with contemporary medical research. Not only are amalgam fillings safe, inexpensive, and durable, the liquid mercury stored in thermometers differs from the mercury in amalgam. Bound to other ingredients, the mercury in amalgam poses zero risk of toxicity. Furthermore, the fact that mercury is released from fillings has been known for decades. When dentists drill out old amalgam fillings, they and their patients are exposed to mercury dust, yet they have no higher rates of any disease or death. Finally, there is no scientific evidence that amalgam fillings cause serious health problems. What should we do? Absolutely nothing. Given that amalgam bullshit can strike fear and panic in people with silver fillings in their teeth, it warrants at least two flies on the Bullshit Flies Index.

Amalgam does not Harm!

If you have something to sell and it is even remotely health-related, being featured on *The Dr. Oz Show* is a dream-come-true endorsement. Dr. Oz appears perfectly willing to use his name and credentials to push alternative medicines and quack treatments for personal financial gain. Because Dr. Oz is very personable, charismatic, and influential, an endorsement by him is one of the best ad campaigns a company can run.

Because Dr. Oz's viewers take him seriously and want

to believe they can improve their health and well-being by watching him, truth should be the principal concern on *The Dr. Oz Show*—but that isn't something viewers can count on. Research reported by Christina Korownyk, professor of family medicine at the University of Alberta, found that fewer than half of the recommendations on *The Dr. Oz Show* are based on reliable evidence.[10] What is more, when confronted about his claims that largely untested remedies are "miracle cures" by a Senate subcommittee in 2014, Dr. Oz responded, "My job, I feel, on the show is to be a cheerleader for the audience."[11] Dr. Oz certainly does cheer for his viewers to keep an open mind, but clearly, the motivations of his viewership are given precedence over providing accurate information. Keeping an open mind is a good thing, but it makes little sense to keep an open mind if it means that our brains fall out and we completely ignore evidence from real health science. Unfortunately, bullshit can be dangerous to one's health.

It is for this reason that I decided to devote the rest of my research career to the empirical study of bullshit—it pains me to recognize the devastating effects bullshit can have on society.

empirical study of BS!

ATMOSPHERIC CONDITIONS OF BULLSHIT

Recognizing the consequences of disregarding the truth may motivate us to search out and reject bullshit, but we need to understand what facilitates bullshit in order to to effectively detect and call it out. The primary goal of my research is to better understand the conditions under which bullshit is most likely to thrive. If we are more aware of the conditions under which we are most likely to be exposed to bullshit, as well as who is most likely to bullshit us, we can better position ourselves to dodge and dispel bullshit's many unwanted effects.

TRUE

↳ better equipped to detect BS

Obligation to Provide an Opinion

Philosopher Harry Frankfurt surmised, "Bullshit is unavoidable whenever circumstances require someone to talk without knowing what he is talking about. Thus the production of bullshit is stimulated whenever a person's *obligations or opportunities* to speak about some topic are more excessive than his knowledge of the facts that are relevant to that topic."[12]

My Bullshit Studies Lab at Wake Forest University decided to test Frankfurt's assertions with a very simple experiment. Our participants read a scenario describing the personality of either Jim or Tom. Half of the participants learned about Jim's personality and nothing about Tom's, whereas the other half learned about Tom's personality and nothing about Jim. Subsequently, participants learned that Jim was running for a seat on the city council and had a strong lead in the polls, but that one month before the election, Jim pulled out of the race. Participants were then asked to explain why they thought Jim pulled out. Critically, half of our participants were told they were *obligated* to complete a thought-listing task, whereas the other half of our participants were explicitly told that they were under *no obligation* to share their thoughts. After writing their thoughts about why Jim pulled out of the race, participants then rated each thought with respect to their *level of concern for evidence when writing the thought* (this served as our measure of bullshitting).

Of particular interest was the total percentage of their own thoughts that our participants regarded as bullshit. Participants who had some knowledge of Jim's character estimated 33% of their own statements were bullshit, while participants who knew nothing about Jim's character produced a bullshit percentage that was only slightly greater, at 36%. Whether participants were knowledgeable or unknowledgeable had little effect on how much they bullshitted. However, unobligated participants' bullshit percentage was only 24%, while obligated participants bullshitted almost twice as much, at 44%. Obligation, rather than lack of knowledge, increases the amount of bullshit. That is, people who have some knowledge about a topic or no knowledge about a topic appear equally willing to bullshit when they feel obligated to provide their opinions.[13]

The results of our experiment showed that Frankfurt appeared to be correct. People are willing to communicate about things they know nothing about when they feel some obligation or opportunity to do so. People will sometimes be expected, if not obligated, to talk about things they know nothing about—and what often comes out is bullshit.

Ease of Passing Bullshit

Frankfurt theorized that no matter how "studiously and conscientiously the bullshitter proceeds, it remains true that he is also trying to get away with something." If Frankfurt is correct, bullshitting should be more likely to emerge when bullshitters expect people to accept or tolerate it. If listeners don't appear to hold knowledge about the topic or informed opinions, "getting away" with bullshit should be easy. In other words, a bullshitter should feel more confident of receiving a social pass for bullshitting when talking about things that most other people also know very little about.

other ppl also know little (ab)

My lab also tested these ideas within the Jim and Tom experiment. We included additional conditions. Participants were led to believe that their explanations for Jim's decision to pull out of the race would later be evaluated for their accuracy by either people who *knew Jim very well* or by people who *did not know Jim*. Frankfurt was right, once again. Confirming that people are more likely to bullshit when they expect to get away with it, the bullshit percentage was significantly greater, at 41%, when participants were led to believe their thoughts would be evaluated by unknowledgeable coders (when it would be easy to pass bullshit). However, when they were led to believe their thoughts would be evaluated by knowledgeable coders (when it would be difficult to pass bullshit), bullshitting was reduced to 29%.

Consistent with Frankfurt's theories, people appear more willing to bullshit when no one can judge whether they know what they are taking about. In my case, I would not try to bullshit my auto mechanic about my car—the only thing I know about cars is that you must put gas in them. But I might bullshit my daughter when she asks how the brakes in my Volvo station wagon work. Anything that signals to a bullshitter that

Ppl BS when no one can judge → fear of judgement

it will be easy to pass bullshit provides a license to play fast and loose with the truth—and what often comes out is bullshit.

Producing bullshit is simple (see conceptual flowchart below). When people do not feel obligated to provide an opinion or sense that it would be difficult to get away with bullshitting, they tend to refrain from bullshitting. However, when people feel an obligation to provide an opinion (even if it is something they know little to nothing about) or sense that they can get away with it, their motivation to bullshit will increase (stage 1). Because bullshitting does not require providing facts and seeking out the truth, people find it extremely easy to bring to mind bullshit (stage 2). Once bullshit is mentally available, the content can be shared at will (stage 3).

confused by this !

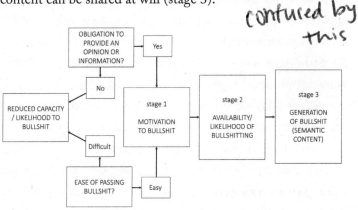

Any factor that increases either the obligation to provide an opinion or the chance of getting away with bullshit will increase the likelihood of bullshit.

THE FACTORS

Both situational and interpersonal factors influence whether one feels obligated to provide an opinion and how easy it is to get away with bullshit. *Situational factors* are factors in one's context or social environment that increase or decrease the likelihood of bullshit production. *Person factors* are factors specific to individuals that increase or decrease the likelihood of bullshit production.

Social Expectations to Know Everything

Implicit social pressures to have an opinion can create an obligation to provide one (even if that opinion is bullshit). We expect an auto mechanic to tell us why our car is leaking oil, a financial advisor to tell us how we can save money on insurance packages, and a doctor to tell us how to treat a persistent sinus infection. The pressure we place on experts to provide answers is justified because they have extensive training in their domains of expertise, but we also often place that expectation on ourselves and others in our lives.

In the twenty-first century, with a 24-hour news cycle and the Internet in our pockets, we are constantly inundated with information. We expect ourselves and others to have opinions about everything—from politics and the economy to the environment and the latest Pixar movie. Of course, it's impossible to have an informed opinion about everything, but this doesn't stop us from having that expectation.

authority vs advising

What happens when experts don't have answers to our questions? Revealing that they don't know the answers could put their very identites at risk. And this is when social pressures can compromise their concern for truth. If an auto mechanic doesn't at least sound like he knows what he's talking about, I and other customers will be more likely to take our business elsewhere. The same will happen with the financial advisor's clients and the doctor's patients if they cannot confidently provide an answer. This is why it is very rare to hear an expert, doctor, or anyone with a PhD say, "I was wrong" or "I don't know." → *financial bias*

social expectatic

Experts merely sounding like they know what they're talking about, in place of actually knowing, create a great cost to society. Consider a study conducted by Gerd Gigerenzer and his colleagues at the Max Planck Institute for Human Development. Gigerenzer and his colleagues presented 160 gynecologists with the following scenario:[14]

Assume you conduct breast cancer screening using mammography in a certain region. You know the following information about women in this region:

1. The probability that a woman has breast cancer is 1% (prevalence).
2. If a woman has breast cancer, the probability that she tests positive is 90% (sensitivity).
3. If a woman does not have breast cancer, the probability that she nevertheless tests positive is 9% (false-positive rate).

A woman tests positive. She wants to know from you whether that means that she has breast cancer for sure, or what the chances are. What is the best answer?

A. The probability that she has breast cancer is about 81%.
B. Out of 10 women with a positive mammogram, about 9 have breast cancer.
C. Out of 10 women with a positive mammogram, about 1 has breast cancer.
D. The probability that she has breast cancer is about 1%.

With this information, the very best that a doctor can give the patient is a conditional probability—the probability the patient has cancer given a positive test result. There are two ways to determine a conditional probability. Both methods require knowing the prevalence of the disease in the region (perhaps specified by sex and age), the sensitivity of the test (the chance that the test detects cancer when cancer is present—the true positive rate), and the specificity of the test (the chance that the test result is negative when there is no cancer—the true negative rate).

The first method requires a bit of math, and most doctors learn how to calculate conditional probabilities in medical school. Although not as precise, the second method is simpler and usually results in an accurate estimate. This method requires doctors to translate the prevalence, sensitivity, and specificity into natural frequencies:

1. Ten out of every 1,000 women have breast cancer.
2. Of these 10 women with breast cancer, 9 will test positive.
3. Of the 990 women without cancer, 89 will test positive.

Looking at the natural frequencies, it is easy to see that mammographies have false positives about 10 times more often than true positives and that the probability that the patient has breast cancer after a positive test is about 10%.

Gigerenzer's study, however, demonstrated that the gynecologists in his study apparently neglected to employ either method. A majority of the gynecologists (60%) estimated the chances that a woman has breast cancer after receiving a positive mammogram to be 81% or greater. They would have told 8x greater the woman that the chance of her having cancer was eight times greater than it actually was. The gynecologists either ignored the fact that mammograms produce a high frequency of false-positive test results or they could not perform the basic calculation required. The saving grace was that when gynecologists were trained to translate prevalence, sensitivity, and specificity into natural frequencies, 87% of them understood that one in ten was the best answer for the patient.

Doctors and patients make better treatment decisions when they know that the chances of having cancer is 10% rather than 81%. Such knowledge should also help to reduce over-testing, over-medicating, and over-treating. Not only do patients deserve to know what a positive or negative test result actually means, it is critical that doctors know what test results actually mean.

Doctors can easily obtain tests' sensitivity and specificity rates from lab technicians, the tests' labels, or the Internet. As Gigerenzer and his colleagues concluded, "Gynecologists could derive the answer from the health statistics provided, or they could simply recall what they should have known anyhow." Yet the effects of false positive test results, in the form of emotional stress, unnecessary biopsies, and mastectomies, are nothing new. From the late 1970s to today, several empirical reports have documented that physicians, college students, and staff at Harvard Medical School have difficulty estimating the conditional probability of a disease given positive or negative test results.[15]

medical industry misleading data

The medical industry is notorious for misleading portrayals of medical data. For many years, women were informed (and many still are today) that early detection of ovarian cancer through screening can reduce the risk of dying from ovarian cancer by 20%. Although many people believe this means that for every 100 women who participate in screening, 20 lives will be saved, it is absolutely not the case. Providing screening information in this way is known as a *relative risk reduction frame*, whereby the risk of a screened group is referenced in light of an unscreened group. It sounds precise, but the estimate is ambiguous. The cold reality is that of every 1,000 women who are screened for ovarian cancer, 4 would be expected to die from ovarian cancer within 10 years, but of every 1,000 women who are not screened, 5 would be expected to die from ovarian cancer within 10 years. Of course, the difference between 5 and 4 is the 20%. Yet, when the very same risk rate is expressed in an *absolute risk reduction frame* (from 5 to 4 in 1,000), it is more obvious that the benefit of screening is 1 in 1,000 or 0.1% (one tenth of 1%). Cancer organizations, health departments, and some doctors inform people of their relative risk reductions, which makes the benefit of screening appear larger than if it were framed in absolute terms.

Miscalculations, misrepresentations, and extra careful ovarian cancer screening may not sound like terrible problems until you consider a study published in the *Journal of the American Medical Association* (*JAMA*) in 2011. The study included over 78,000 women aged 55 to 74 (all with an average risk of ovarian cancer) who either underwent annual screening (screening group) or usual care (non-screening group).[16] Three women in 1,000, in both the screening and the non-screening groups, died of ovarian cancer within ten years. A total of about 85 in 1,000 women in each group died of other causes. However, the study revealed ovarian cancer screening can cause substantial harm. Ninety-six in every 1,000 women screened received false-positive test results. Thirty-two women who received false-positive results had their ovaries unnecessarily removed based on inaccurate test results.

With no survival benefits and considerable potential harm, it is no surprise that no medical organizations currently recommend ovarian cancer screening. But this hasn't changed the medical practices of many health-care professionals. Seven years after the seminal *JAMA* report, Odette Wegwarth and Gerd Gigerenzer asked 401 US outpatient gynecologists whether they followed the universal recommendations of their medical organizations in daily practice and reported to their patients estimates of ovarian cancer screening's effectiveness based on current best evidence.[17] On average, 62% reported estimates of and beliefs about ovarian cancer screening's effectiveness that diverged from available evidence. Furthermore, more than 57% reported regularly recommending the screening! However, after the gynecologists were presented with a fact box summarizing current best evidence, 51% of those who reported providing inaccurate estimates of the screening's benefits significantly revised their initial estimates of, and beliefs concerning, the effectiveness of ovarian cancer screening. This means that a substantial number of gynecologists continued to recommend unnecessary ovarian cancer screenings.

unnecessary screening

A doctor's miscalculations and mistaken beliefs can increase patients' anxiety and generate unnecessary tests, consultations, and surgeries. Teaching doctors to calculate accurate probability estimates will improve the diagnostic process and, ultimately, the quality of medical care. But this won't occur unless doctors are committed to evidence-based reasoning or patients collectively begin to detect when their doctors are bullshitting and call them out.

What doctors should do:

Doctors often talk with their patients about the implications of positive test results in vague ways and opt to test ($), test ($), and retest ($) until they are subjectively satisfied of a diagnosis. Doctors do have specialized knowledge, but they are often under considerable pressure to speak about things they do not know. Because of these expectations, doctors rarely tell their patients that they simply do not know the answer to a question—and what often comes out is bullshit.

It's crazy to me that BS can directly relate to a life or death situation

Accountability

Accountability is the condition of having to answer, explain, or justify one's actions or beliefs to an audience. Through accountability we can expect to be rewarded by others if our actions are justified and held responsible and punished if our actions cannot be justified. Decision makers who believe they will be held accountable for their decisions tend to employ evidence-based reasoning. It comes as little surprise that accountability typically improves decision quality as it tends to discourage the reliance on bullshit-based reasoning.[18]

In line with the idea that people will bullshit when they expect to get away with it, introducing elements of social accountability should reduce bullshit. My Bullshit Studies Lab tested this idea in another study.

This time, all of our participants were asked to report their attitudes toward three social issues, including affirmative action quotas, a nuclear weapons freeze, and capital punishment, and to then list reasons for their attitudes. Just before listing their thoughts, participants were randomly assigned to either a *no-accountability condition*, simply asked to list their thoughts about the issues, or an *accountability condition*, again asked to list their thoughts about the issues but this time informed that they would be required to explain and justify their opinions to a sociology professor (who was described as an expert on the social issues in question). Participants in the accountability condition were also led to believe that the discussion would be audiotaped to "facilitate analysis of the communication process."

If you can place yourself in the shoes of our participants, you probably know what happened. Sure enough, participants assigned to the no-accountability condition engaged in significantly greater bullshitting behavior than participants assigned to the accountability condition.

Introducing accountability is one of the easiest ways to reduce bullshit. Accountability signals to potential bullshitters that someone is listening carefully. In our study, we signaled accountability by telling our participants that someone with actual knowledge, competence, and skill would be assessing their statements and could conceivably call them on any bullshit. However, there are other social cues of accountability that we can use to discourage bullshit (for example, no-bullshit instructions pointing to the critical importance of evidence). If people choose to ignore accountability cues or fail to recognize them, however, they will expect to get away with pushing their incompetence off as something worthy of consideration—and what often comes out is bullshit.

Bullshit Contagion

In his bestselling book *Thinking, Fast and Slow*, Nobel laureate Daniel Kahneman wrote that "people can maintain an unshakable faith in any proposition, however absurd, when they are sustained by a community of like-minded believers."[19] Relatedly, Frankfurt stated that participants in a bull session "try out various thoughts and attitudes in order to see how it feels to hear themselves saying such things and in order to discover how others respond, without it being assumed that they are committed to what they say: It is understood by everyone in a bull session that the statements people make do not necessarily reveal what they really believe or how they really feel."[20]

We tested these ideas within our study with the alleged sociology professor. We divided the accountability condition participants into three different groups: one-third of the participants were told nothing about the sociology professor's attitudes; another third of the participants were led to believe that the professor happened to be like-minded, sharing the same general positions as the participant; the final third of the participants were led to believe that the professor was unlike-minded, not sharing the same general positions as the participant.

What we found was that bullshitting was reduced, compared to the no-accountability condition, when participants had no knowledge of the sociology professor's attitude or believed that the professor held different attitudes. However, when participants were led to believe the professor held the same attitudes, they bullshitted just as much as they would have under the no-accountability condition. In other words, if people expect to be held accountable for the validity of the thoughts and opinions they express, we can safely expect to reduce bullshit. However, even when people do expect to be held accountable, accountability will have little effect on how much they bullshit if they expect us to agree with them—and what often comes out is bullshit.

*If expectation = agreement →
- BS will occur

People Most Likely to Bullshit

Although bullshit is affected by situational factors, bullshit is also infleunced by the individual people within the social situation. Having a clear understanding of the type of people who have a high propensity to bullshit should make you better at successfully detecting and repelling bullshit.

One's general propensity to bullshit is strongly tied to one's motives. These motives are very similar to the motives for lying. When people lie, they usually do so to protect themselves from embarrassment, make a positive impression, avoid a negative judgment, gain an advantage, or avoid punishment.[21] Although everyone, at one time or another, has these motives, people with a high propensity to bullshit hold these motives relatively often.

High-propensity bullshitters are remarkably easy to spot. They are the type of people often found evangelizing and proselytizing about their beliefs to anyone willing to listen. They do this because convincing otherwise rational people to agree with their opinions reduces any psychological discomfort they may feel for believing their own bullshit. Because relying on evidence to make decisions does not appeal to them, high-propensity bullshitters tend to show signs of irritation when asked to provide reasons for their beliefs. The *Star Wars* character of Darth Vader is the quintessential high-propensity bullshitter. He uses his telepathic powers and oddly mesmerizing voice to obsessively rap on about the destiny of the Dark Side and ruling the Empire. When anyone resists him in the slightest, he completely loses it. Importantly, however, Darth

Vader doesn't know what he is talking about. He constantly tries to persuade everyone, including his son, Luke Skywalker, to join the Dark Side, but he is too wrapped up in the rigid doctrines of the Jedi Order to recognize that he is being used by the scheming, powerful, and evil-to-the-core Emperor to destroy the Jedi Order.

A disregard for evidence and established knowledge, paired with motives to protect oneself from embarrassment, make a positive impression, avoid negative judgment, gain an advantage, push an agenda, feel good about the decisions they've already made, or avoid punishment can lead to bullshitting. However, there are at least four individual factors that impact a person's motivation to bullshit: the need for evidence; one's level of domain-specific knowledge; a desire for attention, fame, or wealth; and a need to belong.

Need for Evidence

During his presidential inauguration on January 20, 2017, President Donald Trump noted, "Every four years, we gather on these steps to carry out the orderly and peaceful transfer of power, and we are grateful to President Obama and First Lady Michelle Obama for their gracious aid throughout this transition. They have been magnificent. Thank you."[22] Yet this didn't stop White House press secretary Kayleigh McEnany from stating on November 20, 2020, "Something that I would note is that we talked a lot about transfer of power and the election, and it's worth remembering that this president [Trump] was never given an orderly transition of power."[23]

This is a hallmark of the high-propensity bullshitter—a chronic disregard for genuine evidence.

An individual with a high need for evidence is one who possesses a healthy degree of skepticism and finds it important to hold only those attitudes that are supported by evidence.[24] High-need-for-evidence individuals do not believe in something just because there are pragmatic benefits in believing it, and they don't find it annoying when people ask them to provide reasons for their opinions. Instead, high-need-for-evidence individuals determine whether something is good or bad only after weighing the evidence. They tend to refrain from contributing their thoughts to a discussion until they have all the facts. People with a high propensity to bullshit possess none of these evidence-based goals.

How many people do you know with a high need for evidence? I doubt you know very many. Consistent thinking and behaving with a high need for evidence require a great deal of work—and few people are willing to do such work.

Not only are high-propensity bullshitters indifferent to truth and evidence, they tend not to react kindly when presented with evidence. Receiving consistently irrational responses to cold, hard evidence indicates that you are probably dealing with a high-propensity bullshitter. A sure sign of a low-need-for-evidence individual—and likely a high-propensity bullshitter—is a person who appears willing to fabricate evidence or data. They often refer to data that only they have access to—and what often comes out is bullshit.

Knowledge

Research conducted by cognitive psychologists Sarah Brem and Lance Rips demonstrates that when people possess adequate knowledge about a topic they usually provide arguments based on genuine evidence and refrain from providing baseless arguments.[25] That is, when people are knowledgeable, they do not need to bullshit—they are more aware of evidence and tend to use it. On the other hand, when people are unfamiliar with a topic, they bullshit when they feel obligated to share their opinions, and expect their bullshit to be accepted.

While knowledgeable people are less likely to bullshit in their domain of expertise, what about people who just *think* they're knowledgeable? If unknowledgeable people feel knowledgeable about a topic, they are especially likely to bullshit. And people are surprisingly bad at assessing their own competence and knowledge. It is true that people who say they have knowledge are less likely to *report* that they bullshit in their respective domains of "expertise"—but don't take their word for it.[26] In fact, people are likely to bullshit when they *feel* more knowledgeable about something than their audience. That is, a feeling of knowing, not actual knowledge, can be enough to produce bullshit.[27]

Bullshit-based judgment and decision-making can occur when people have no clue as to what they're talking about. The story of McArthur Wheeler is a striking demonstration. In 1995, Wheeler strolled into two banks in Pittsburgh and robbed them in broad daylight, with no attempt to conceal his identity. Wheeler was arrested later that same night, and videotapes from bank surveillance cameras were broadcast on the 11 o'clock news. When the police later showed Wheeler the surveillance tapes, he stared in confusion. "But I wore the juice," he mumbled. Apparently, Wheeler was under the mistaken impression that rubbing one's face with lemon juice rendered it invisible to video cameras.[28]

Social psychologists Justin Kruger and David Dunning demonstrated that people tend to hold overly favorable views of their own abilities in social and intellectual domains.[29] People overestimate their own knowledge, in part, because people who are unskilled in a domain lack the ability to distinguish competence from incompetence. In other words, incompetent individuals are prone to erroneous conclusions and unfortunate choices because they usually do not know they are incompetent. In one study, Kruger and Dunning had Cornell University undergraduates complete a 20-item multiple-choice test of English grammar. Instead of giving the students performance feedback, they asked them to rate their overall ability to recognize correct grammar and how their performance compared with that of their peers. In this way, Kruger and Dunning could see if those who did poorly would recognize their poor performance.

Four to six weeks later, participants received a packet of five completed, but not scored, tests by other students. The packet of completed tests reflected the range of performances that their peers had achieved. Participants then graded each test. Participants were then shown their own test and asked to once again rate their own ability and test performance relative to their peers. Kruger and Dunning were especially interested in what students who performed in the bottom and top quartiles thought about their abilities and performance. Consistent with the now-famous *Dunning-Kruger effect*, students at the bottom quartile grossly overestimated their test performance and ability. Although their actual test scores put them in the 10th percentile, they initially estimated themselves to be in the 66th percentile. After they reviewed their peers' tests, they readjusted their perceived grammar knowledge to be at the 63rd percentile. Students at the top quartile underestimated their test performance and ability. Although their actual test scores put them at the 88th percentile, they initially estimated themselves to be in the 71st percentile. But after they reviewed their peers' tests, top quartile participants readjusted their perceived grammar knowledge up to the 77th percentile.

The mental skills one needs to be competent in a domain are the very same skills one needs to recognize competence. This is why we require heavy training and a series of tests for airline pilots and surgeons. Evidence is prized and taken very seriously in these domains. If your own domain doesn't value evidence, it's likely you will find bullshit.

Desire for Attention, Fame, or Wealth

Because she has over 167 million Instagram and 33 million Twitter followers, Kylie Jenner is paid as much as $1.2 million for making sponsored posts. A sponsored post is a new brand of advertising known as *influencer marketing*, whereby brands or products are promoted by influential and well-known people, like celebrities. Most of the time, Instagramers will see a "Paid Partnership with [Sponsor Name]" disclosure at the top of the post. But marketers don't seem to worry about the disclosure or any negative reactions by potential consumers. Marketers know their investment is a wise one. They understand that millions of people will believe a new soap or skincare cream is better than the old one if Jenner says so. It's all unsubstantiated—unless, of course, Jenner has consulted Consumer Reports or conducted trials to support the claims she's been asked to make by her sponsors. Marketers are well aware that people who are famous for being famous have great social influence. They also know that millions of people will recognize and purchase the products they promote through social media without expending effort to research the differences that they're paying for—which are often minimal at best. The last time I checked, all soaps and skincare creams do basically the same jobs.

If you are willing to sell out to the masses of people who don't care for scientific evidence or are unable to differentiate pseudoscience from real science, you too can use bullshit to gain fame or wealth. All you have to do is find the right niche.

Take for instance the abuse of *harnessing neuroplasticity*. Neuroplasticity refers to the brain's ability to change continuously throughout an individual's life. Neural networks in the brain can form and reorganize synaptic connections. In response to injury, the brain can exhibit significant neuroplasticity and compensate for brain damage in one region by having another region take on some of the injured region's functions. Over the past three decades, research on neuroplasticity has received increasing attention because it can be used to treat brain damage, vision impairments, ADHD, chronic pain, and phantom limbs. But in the cloud of dust that is neuroplasticity research, several commercial "brain-training programs" have exaggerated the "boundless possibilities" of neuroplasticity and made a lot of money as a result.

One such example is the Arrowsmith Program, which claims to help students with a wide range of learning disabilities. Offered in schools throughout the world, the Arrowsmith Program uses "cognitive exercises" that are claimed to have been drawn from the neuroscience research of Arrowsmith's founder, Barbara Arrowsmith-Young, author of *The Woman Who Changed Her Brain*.

In her autobiographical account, Arrowsmith-Young describes how she overcame her own severe learning disabilities and details 30 case studies of children with learning disabilities who she claims overcame similar problems by using her method. However, the Arrowsmith Program has been criticized by several scientists for basing its claims on anecdotal evidence and pseudoscience. In fact, to date there are no peer-reviewed randomized control studies published that evaluate whether it is more effective than other "brain training" programs.[30]

People like Arrowsmith-Young are good writers, but bypass well-established, peer-reviewed scientific processes in favor of pseudoscience and anecdotal evidence to promote their treatments.[31] Accolades such as "worldwide bestseller" and "widely praised," without the backing of a community that cares about evidence and truth, may signal "full of bullshit"

and "snake oil salesperson." But it should come as little surprise that people will ignore truth if doing so is sure to gain
them notoriety or make them money—and what often comes
out is bullshit.

Need to Belong

The human need to belong is a fundamental and powerful motivation for high- and low-propensity bullshitters alike. People
desire frequent, positive interactions with others. People form
social attachments quite readily under almost any conditions
and resist the dissolution of existing bonds. When people lack
interpersonal attachments and a sense of belonging, they often experience ill effects on their thoughts, emotions, physical
health, psychological adjustment, and well-being.[32]

People will do all sorts of strange things to belong. I recall
a conversation I was having with some friends about a new
Batman movie. Now, I knew for certain that my friend Joe had
yet to see the movie. Yet Joe didn't skip a beat—he skillfully
fronted and contributed to the ongoing conversation as if he
had watched the movie. No one asked Joe if he had watched
the movie and everyone appeared to assume he had. I knew
damn well Joe hadn't watched the movie and that he didn't
have a clue what he was talking about. That didn't matter at all
to Joe—it was more important to be included in the conversation, and as you might imagine, out came bullshit.

Just like Joe, everyone knows that bullshit can have social
benefits. For instance, we can be rewarded for bullshitting
if it helps to identify people on our "team." If a person in

the stadium stands yells, "LeBron was fouled!" or "He did have the biggest gathering at his inauguration!" you can be certain which team they support. And if you are looking to sit alongside highly committed members of that team, after that one bullshit comment, you know with whom to sit. Because team and tribalism are important to our sense of belonging, bullshit is a convenient way to signal which team you are on.

In my earlier training as a counseling psychologist, I spent many hours leading group psychotherapy sessions. I've learned that our daily social lives can be much like group therapy sessions. At some point or another, people will look to you and it will be your turn to say something. If you waste too many opportunities to speak or if you rarely have anything purposeful to say, you lose your opportunity to connect with the group. You become a nonfactor and you don't belong. You are much better off bullshitting than saying nothing.

Kipling Williams's research on *social ostracism* is a prime example of just how important it is to feel included and have a sense of belonging.[33] In one of Williams's experiments, participants were led to believe that two other alleged participants (confederates) would work with them during an experiment. The confederates and the participant were asked to sit in a circle and engage in small talk. A small foam ball was sitting on the floor. One of the confederates would pick up the ball and begin tossing it around the group. But then, the confederates would begin talking exclusively to each other, speak abruptly to the participant, stop making eye contact with the participant, and cease throwing the ball to her.

quick to change!

Within a few moments, the participant would begin to show nonverbal expressions of sadness and rejection.[34]

You might be thinking, "Well, I wouldn't let it bother me." Don't bet on it. In another set of studies, Williams reasoned that in all previous experiments involving ostracism, there had never been any costs to inclusion or benefits for ostracism.[35] What would happen if being included meant losing money and being ostracized meant earning money? Would individuals still be distressed when ostracized? To answer this question, Williams "loaded the dice" in favor of ostracism. Participants played Cyberball, a computerized simulation of the ball-tossing game. But this time, participants lost money for each ball toss they received. Surprisingly, even when being ostracized meant earning more money, participants found it painful not to receive positive attention from complete strangers.

so interesting

No matter the situation, being ignored and excluded is extremely painful for social animals. We are sensitive to the slightest hint of social exclusion. To avoid this, we could choose to refrain from conversations about things we know nothing about. But with this approach, we run the risk of excluding ourselves from the group by not contributing our share. On the other hand, by bullshitting, we have the potential benefits of ingratiating ourselves with the group and increasing our sense of belonging to it. To maintain a sense of connection with others and to avoid feeling excluded, we sometimes talk about things we know nothing about—and what comes out is bullshit.

→ *so connection = source of bs sometimes*

4

BULLSHIT ARTISTS

Douglas, Donald, and Deepak

As the vilest writer hath his readers, so the greatest liar hath his believers: and it often happens, that if a lie be believed only for an hour, it hath done its work, and there is no further occasion for it. Falsehood flies, and truth comes limping after it.

—JONATHAN SWIFT

Parents and caretakers of a child with autism know that autism can sometimes really suck. Autism is a developmental disorder characterized by difficulties with social interactions and communication, affective processing, and exhibiting restricted and repetitive behavior. Some children with autism exhibit only mild symptoms of the disorder, but others show great difficulty with speech, with some being entirely nonverbal. Up to 50% of children diagnosed with autism never develop spoken language beyond a few words or utterances. Parents commonly complain that everyday conversations can be difficult, reducing their ability to regulate their children's behavior.[1]

Compassionate social scientists have studied nonverbal

autism for decades. Enter Dr. Douglas Biklen, who was a dean at Syracuse University. He specialized in the cultural foundations of education, disability studies, and teaching and leadership programs. Biklen is famous for introducing *facilitated communication* to the United States in 1989.

Facilitated communication is a technique whereby a trained facilitator helps "stabilize" a nonverbal autistic person's hand above a keyboard so that "they" are able to "freely move" their arm and hand to type a message. Convinced of the efficacy of facilitated communication, Biklen staunchly promoted it for over 30 years, becoming a leader of the Institute on Communication and Inclusion at Syracuse University—the world's foremost champion of the pseudoscientific practice of facilitated communication. Through his research, Biklen provided compelling and emotional accounts of nonverbal autistic children using facilitated communication to communicate their emotions, such as "My mother thinks I'm stupid because I can't use my voice properly."[2]

At first, Biklen's technique was warmly received and acclaimed as a major breakthrough in the treatment of nonverbal autism. That is, of course, until skeptical researchers began looking more closely at the inner workings of the technique.

The typical experimental procedure used to test facilitated communication goes like this: An autistic child sits at the end of a long table with a keyboard and a trained facilitator. The visual fields of the facilitator and the autistic child are separated by an opaque wall that stretches the length of the table, allowing experimenters to independently manipulate what the facilitator and child see. At the other end of the table,

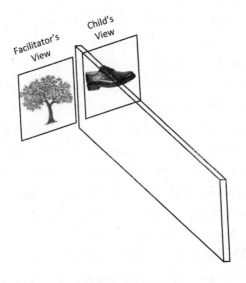

experimenters place clearly visible cards with objects depicted on them, such as a tree or a shoe. Another method involves both the facilitator and child wearing headphones that play a recording of "tree" for the facilitator and "shoe" for the child. The facilitator and autistic child work together to type what the child sees at the end of the table (or what the child hears over her headphones).

From validation procedures like these, there appeared to be a very big problem. Trial after trial revealed that what children "typed" on the keyboard, with the help of the facilitator, was never what the child saw (shoe) but always what the facilitator saw (tree). Hundreds of failed trials were recorded without a single hit. In fact, the only time the nonverbal autistic child typed the correct answer was when the picture card shown to the facilitator matched what was shown to the nonverbal autistic child. Facilitated communication failed.[3]

Each study revealed that facilitated communication simply did not work. Remarkably, however, dozens of controlled studies weren't enough to convince Biklen, and the thousands of parents and caretakers who heralded him as a hero, that it didn't work. Biklen turned tens of thousands of people into believers in facilitated communication without presenting a shred of scientific evidence. With excitement, parents believed their nonverbal autistic children miraculously learned how to spell (without looking to position their hand on the keyboard—something a trained typist cannot do) and express thoughts with the help of a facilitator.

As an advocate of facilitated communication, Biklen claimed that the method could unlock expressive literacy in nonverbal autistic individuals. Yet under controlled scientific conditions in dozens of studies, the method did not work. When Biklen was confronted with the results, he maintained a confident posture and began spouting pseudoscientific flim-flam. Of the simplest validation studies, he said, "I think that test has severe problems. One, you're putting people in what might be described as a confrontational situation. That is, they're being asked to prove themselves. As I pointed out, confidence appears to be a critical element in the method. If people are anxious they may in fact freeze up in their ability to respond, they lose confidence, they may feel inadequate."[4] The reality was that if there were any biases in the studies, they were biased toward proving that facilitated communication was real: The picture cards selected were things that nonverbal autistic individuals experienced in their everyday lessons, autistic individuals were paired with facilitators they'd had the most "success" with in the past, and the studies were conducted in their usual school setting. If facilitated communication worked, there was no reason it wouldn't work in controlled studies.

Still, Biklen pushed on, claiming that many nonverbal autistic individuals have difficulty finding the right words for objects yet are capable of writing beautiful prose and poetry. But this assertion only sidesteps the fact that what was always typed matched the pictures viewed by the facilitators in the validation studies—a most improbable finding if facilitated communication was real.

Again, Biklen surged on. "It's very easy to fail in one's attempt to demonstrate something, it's usually more difficult to be successful. So, it almost doesn't matter how many instances of failed studies we have. What we need with any one individual are instances where the person succeeded." Biklen does not appear to understand how scientific inference actually works. The dozens of studies showing that facilitated communication fails do matter. The cold reality, however, is that Biklen never wanted scientific evidence. All he needed to do was invite readily willing people to join him in ignoring the overwhelming disconfirming evidence showing that facilitated communication did not work.

I'm of the opinion that Biklen's facilitated communication bullshit deserves at least three flies on the Bullshit Flies Index, given that the method puts the facilitators' words in the mouths of nonverbal autistic individuals without their consent and provides false hope to parents and caretakers.

No matter the number of swarming bullshit flies, we cannot expect promoters of pseudoscience and bullshit to be weeded out by default. In fact, all of the science that proved facilitated communication to be a hoax has had little effect on Biklen and his method. Despite receiving heavy criticism from the Commission for Scientific Medicine and Mental Health and the special education research community, Biklen became the dean of the School of Education at Syracuse University in August 2005.[5] He has never faced professional consequences for his insistent advocacy of pseudoscience and continues to work with nonverbal autistic individuals and their caretakers.

TACTICS OF THE BULLSHIT ARTIST

To promote their own bullshit, bullshit artists use the same influence tactics that everyone else uses, except the bullshit artist uses them a lot and has considerably more practice.[6] Knowing the six tactics commonly employed by bullshit artists can make you a much more effective bullshit detector.

Completely Disregard All Evidence That Disproves the Claim

In the classic film *12 Angry Men*, one can appreciate the great value that should be placed on genuine evidence that disproves a claim. Evidence that disproves a claim can sometimes (though not always) demonstrate that the opposite of the claim must be true. As demonstrated by Juror 8, played by Henry Fonda in the 1957 original and Jack Lemmon in the equally good 1997 remake, disconfirming evidence proved most powerful. The prosecution argued that the defendant, an 18-year-old impoverished youth, stabbed his own father to death with a knife. During their deliberations, the jurors disregarded details in the murder case that would disprove their initial conclusion: guilt beyond reasonable doubt. The jurors ignored significant details such as the fact that the key eyewitness was not wearing her eyeglasses when the stabbing occurred and the knife used to kill the victim was not at all unusual (the prosecution implied the knife's uniqueness added to the presumption of guilt). They also failed to recognize that a noisy L train would have made it impossible to hear the defendant threaten, "I'm going to kill you!" All of these details would have disconfirmed their prior assumptions, but were overlooked until Juror 8 persistently drove them home—demonstrating that evidence disproving a claim is as important as evidence that supports a claim.

The last thing bullshit artists want anyone to do is focus on evidence that disproves their claims. In the uncanny case of Dr. Biklen, he wants us to disregard all of the relevant evidence disconfirming that facilitated communication works. To compensate, skillful bullshit artists not only find creative ways to dismiss or ignore disconfirming evidence, they capitalize on people's motivations to believe their claims. If people are not already motivated to believe their claims, bullshitters can derail natural skepticism by distracting people from disconfirming evidence and dazzling everyone with anecdotal evidence.

Despite the fact that facilitated communication has been discredited, schools around the world continue to spend millions of dollars to hire and train facilitators.[7] Some parents of

↳ use empirical evidence!

nonverbal autistic children pay to have their child's facilitator accompany them to college. These parents and their children's teachers and therapists choose to ignore the facts. They believe facilitated communication is a breakthrough technique that redefines nonverbal autism. The messages their autistic children "type" are all the validation many parents, teachers, and therapists will ever need.[8]

That sane people believe facilitated communication works, despite all evidence to the contrary, is a testament to just how difficult it can be to see bullshit when one wants to believe in it.

Focus Attention on Unreliable, Anecdotal Evidence That Supports the Claim

Bullshit artists typically share their favorite anecdotal evidence in the form of stories.

> I think I may be psychic. In fact, just yesterday I was thinking about Grandma Anne, and seconds later she called me on the telephone.

> I threw a coin in the fountain and made a wish for Maxie and he was drafted by the Houston Oilers. I forgot to make a wish for Mark—and well, he went nowhere fast. Wishing fountains clearly work.

> I have no doubt that Ouija boards are real. My brother used one just last week to talk to our departed mother. And he's a trustworthy man not prone to making things up.

A good story is a particularly effective method of influence. Not only does a story distract people from focusing on relevant data, it is often more memorable. The more anecdotes *ethos* a bullshitter can pile up, the more convincing their bullshit becomes. Anecdotal evidence can convince people that alternative medical treatments are effective despite abundant evidence that they don't work.[9] → CAM! & supplements

As most writers, successful persuaders, and psychologists know, stories and anecdotes (true or false) have much more impact than evidence and statistics.[10] International organizations and charities understand this well. Rather than confusing us with statistics and facts about thousands of people in need, they tend to select a single impoverished child and tell us about their life, providing specific details sure to tug at the heartstrings. People are much more willing to assist specific, identified victims of unfortunate events than they are unidentified, general, or "statistical" victims.[11]

Our most confident beliefs—about the way things really are and how the world really works—should be based on genuine evidence. But bullshit artists communicate as if this rule does not apply to them. As science historian and professional skeptic Michael Shermer puts it:

> Stories about how your Aunt Mary's cancer was cured by watching Marx Brothers movies or taking a liver extract from castrated chickens are meaningless. The cancer might have gone into remission on its own, which some cancers do; or it might have been misdiagnosed. . . . What we need are controlled experiments,

not anecdotes. We need 100 subjects with cancer, all properly diagnosed and matched. Then we need 25 of the subjects to watch Marx Brothers movies, 25 to watch Alfred Hitchcock movies, 25 to watch the news, and 25 to watch nothing. Then we need to deduct the average rate of remission for this type of cancer and then analyze the data for statistically significant differences between the groups. If there are statistically significant differences, we better get confirmation from other scientists who have conducted their own experiments separate from ours before we hold a press conference to announce the cure for cancer.[12]

Relying on anecdotal evidence is convenient because it requires doing the least amount of work to substantiate a claim. However, drawing inferences exclusively from anecdotal evidence leads to several shortcomings in the bullshit artist's judgments.[13] Bullshit artists tend to accept at face value anything that supports their beliefs (counting their "hits"), while ignoring anything that contradicts them (discounting their "misses"). They like to make bold assumptions based on a few observations, distracting everyone from the fact that extraordinary claims require extraordinary evidence. And perhaps most disappointing to statistics professors, bullshit artists are prone to conflating observed relationships between things (correlation), like rooster crowing and sunrises, with the idea that one thing causes the other (causation).

Pseudo-Profundity

He has a natural charisma and presentation skills, he wears Mandarin-collar suits and Clark Kent/Superman glasses with rhinestones embedded in the frames, and he speaks with a strong Indian accent. His name is Deepak Chopra, and he is a prominent figure in the New Age movement whose books and videos have made him one of the best-known and wealthiest figures in alternative medicine. Deepak was trained in internal medicine and endocrinology, but claims to be an authority on "perfect health" and transcendental meditation. He gained popularity in 1993 after being interviewed about his self-help books on *The Oprah Winfrey Show*. No one can touch the depths of concepts like Deepak Chopra. Consider this Tweet:[14]

Deepak Chopra ✔
@DeepakChopra

The purpose of existence is awareness of existence . It spontaneously evolves as creativity & maximum diversity of expression. Me & mine are fictions. Only reality is pure consciousness . Everything else is sensations images feelings and thoughts . All stories are fabrications

profound ?

Does this mean anything to you? Although it sounds incredibly profound, I honestly haven't a clue what it means.

Since he first became a celebrity, Deepak has promoted *pseudo-profundity*. Pseudo-profound language is intentionally obscured through exaggerations, ambiguous references, insider jargon, buzzwords, and the authoritative pretense that the speaker knows about things that no one else can possibly comprehend.

Deepak believes that a person can attain perfect health and become free from disease, pain, and aging. He speaks of the "quantum mechanical body" and how it is composed not of matter but of energy and information. Deepak believes that one's state of mind can prevent chronic disease because "human aging is fluid and changeable; it can speed up, slow down, stop for a time, and even reverse itself."[15]

A 2015 paper by psychologist Gordon Pennycook and his colleagues examined the reception and detection of pseudo-profound bullshit. They had survey respondents rate the profundity of various quotes. Some of the quotes were artificial and some were taken directly from Deepak's Twitter feed because it contains plentiful examples of pseudo-profundity. Unsurprisingly, Pennycook and his colleagues found little difference in the perceived profundity of Deepak's Tweets and artificial Deepak quotes generated by an algorithm.[16]

When propped up with pseudo-profundity, even the most senseless bullshit (for example, "Everyday reality is a dreamscape projected by consciousness") can be confused with the profound.[17] But Deepak's claims aren't pseudo-profound because I can't make heads or tails of them. They are pseudo-profound because even if the opposite of his claims were true (or false), it would make no difference. The philosopher G. A. Cohen offered a convenient test to determine when an obscure-sounding statement is bullshit.[18] Called the *unclarifiable unclarity* test, it requires an answer to this question: Would the claim have a different effect if it were reversed? Consider the claim "Hidden meaning transforms unparalleled abstract beauty." If the opposite claim—*"Revealed* meaning transforms unparalleled abstract beauty" (or "Hidden meaning transforms *commonly found concrete ugliness*")—would have a different effect on reality, then the claim is not pseudo-profound bullshit. However, if one can discern no differences between the effects of a claim and the effects of its opposites, then the claim is pseudo-profound bullshit. Pseudo-profound bullshit contains vacuous and confusing buzzwords that obscure meaning and invite people to fill in the gaps with whatever they think the nonsense means—meanwhile, Deepak comes away sounding brilliant.

Pseudo-profound analogies are common in business jargon: "If you cut off a spider's head, it dies" in reference to the top-down management structure of traditional organizations, or "If you cut off a starfish's leg, it grows a new one" in reference to nimble companies that shift and grow in response to business demands.[19] Great. Spider. Starfish. They make the point; let's move on. Using analogies sparingly can compellingly make a point or clarify abstract concepts, but if someone insists on using an entire lexicon of senselessly obscure jargon to describe the simplest of things, it's a pretty good sign you are dealing with a bullshit artist.[20]

Using contradictory slogans and clichés—war is peace, freedom is slavery, and ignorance is strength—is fair game for the pseudo-profound bullshit artist.[21] Not only does such Orwellian bullshit sound profound and postmodern, but ambiguous language permits the bullshitter to behave as if she really didn't mean what we thought she said when confronted with disconfirming evidence because the claim has several possible interpretations.

Another surefire way to determine if someone is using pseudo-profundity is to ask them to clarify what they mean: "So you say, 'Defund the police.' What do you mean by that? What would that look like? How would it work? Tell me the logistics. How would we know it's working?" There will be a stark difference in how academics and serious criminal-justice reform activists respond to these questions and how those who blindly advocate the phrase on Twitter respond. Clarification is a major antidote to bullshit because bullshitters find it difficult to clarify pseudo-profound bullshit by saying something that actually makes sense or reflects truth and evidence.

important

When you ask a bullshit artist for clarity, listen carefully to their response. When a claim has been challenged or disproven, bullshit artists often *move the semantic goalposts.*[22] For instance, Deepak is well known for his unconventional "quantum healing hypothesis" that people can reach their personal subjective well-being and life-satisfaction goals through visualization, meditation, journaling, traveling, practicing yoga, and becoming more "aware of the ego."[23] According to Deepak, all we have to do is use the principles of quantum mechanics, as he has, and we'll arrive at the panacea for any ailment, including aging—we just have to think and "will" our molecules to do it. Furthermore, he uses enough technical terminology to convince nonscientists that he understands physics.[24] Yet when ethologist and evolutionary biologist Richard Dawkins asked Deepak to clarify how quantum physics applies to his

just 'good enough' to convince ppl of his BS

theory of consciousness, Deepak moved the semantic goal-posts. He suggested that he only uses the term *quantum physics* as a metaphor and that his theory actually has little to do with quantum theory.[25]

There are two major problems with pseudo-profundity. The first is that it masks the real meaning of just about everything. Despite the fact that it is pretentious and annoying, bullshit artists use it because people often accept pseudo-profundity as a substitute for thinking hard and clearly about "the expert's" message, goals, and directions. The *Sokal Hoax Article* is a case in point.[26] A professor of mathematics at University College London and a professor of physics at New York University, Alan Sokal found himself increasingly dissatisfied with postmodern cultural scholarship. He decided to test the field's intellectual rigor by submitting for publication "Transgressing the Boundaries: Towards a Transformative Hermeneutics of Quantum Gravity" to *Social Text*, a top postmodern cultural studies journal whose editors included luminaries such as Fredric Jameson and Andrew Ross. Unbeknownst to the editors, Sokal's manuscript was a hoax. It appeared to be a synthesis of relevant literature, but was instead full of pretentious-sounding, pseudoscientific nonsense. If Sokal's study had any hypothesis at all, it was that he could get an article, liberally salted with utter nonsense, accepted for publication in a leading cultural studies journal. All Sokal really needed to do was flatter the editors' ideological preconceptions and ensure that the paper sounded good.[27] The paper was accepted. The editors of *Social Text* were unable to discern real theory from Sokal's pseudo-profound bullshit because it made as much sense as other pseudo-profound papers they were publishing in their journal.

But there is a second major problem with pseudo-profundity. Because pseudo-profundity often sounds like evidence, it tends to disguise its true nature and, thereby, increase its perceived feasibility. In his first appearance on *The Oprah Winfrey Show*, Deepak claimed that Oprah could use the "power of her mind" to move objects. He challenged her to hold a string with a small metal weight tied to the end and, without moving her arm or hand, "will" the weight to move with her mind. To Oprah's amazement, within a few moments the weight began to gently swing back and forth. Deepak explained:

> You see, your expectancy determines outcome. And as long as you're not attached to the outcome, the outcome will be guaranteed. Whenever we fulfill, whatever that desire is, certain things happen. And this is living proof that every cell in your body is eavesdropping on your internal dialog. And by changing your internal dialog you can influence the chemistry—the fundamental chemistry—of every cell.

Deepak's demonstration was short of miraculous. Never mind the facts that the weight at the bottom of the string was never perfectly still, Oprah was breathing right over the string, and her arm and wrist continued to move ever so slightly. Yet, Deepak's explanation for the effect was completely off the mark. The effect is the result of the very natural *ideomotor effect,* whereby mere thought or mental suggestion brings about correspondingly subtle muscular reactions, often outside one's awareness.[28] The body can react automatically and reflexively to ideas without consciously deciding to take action—as when we reflexively remove our hand after touching something very hot before feeling the burning sensation. The ideomotor response has also been implicated in the use of facilitated communication and Ouija boards.

If you would like to experience the ideomotor effect yourself, close your eyes and imagine a tart lemon. Think about the yellow pulp and the lemony aroma. Then imagine placing a piece of lemon in your mouth. Taste the lemon's tart flavor. Is your mouth beginning to water? If so, you have experienced the ideomotor link between mind and body.

You can try Deepak's trick at home. Get any small object with some weight, like a ring or pendant, that can be attached to a string about 15 inches in length. Hold the string from the top and let the object dangle freely. Position your arm and hand away from the body. Now close your eyes and try to keep very still. Imagine that the pendulum begins to slowly move, gently swinging back and forth, from left to right. Picture it vividly in your mind. Making sure you don't deliberately move or interfere with the hand holding the string, focus as hard as you can on the image of a swinging pendulum. Visualize the rhythmic sweep of the swing becoming longer.[29] After two to three minutes, open your eyes and look at the pendulum. Most likely, you will find it is swinging back and forth, just as you imagined.

It is very easy to produce an ideomotor response. Imagined

movement can be translated into real movement. It is very seductive to believe that we can somehow will inanimate objects to move freely. That is why I don't believe Deepak or Oprah was faking it. However, a disregard for truth and consistent endorsement of pseudo-profound nonsense is dangerous. Not only does it promote jumping to conclusions and carte blanche rejection of science and reason, it encourages us to believe whatever we wish to believe.

not faking it, but disregarding truth!

By claiming to have mystical knowledge of advanced science, health and wellness, and the supernatural, Deepak has developed a large following.[30] He can say almost anything without fear of being challenged. Mixing and matching the study of consciousness and quantum mechanics is fine, as long as it sounds very heady and "science-y." It also doesn't hurt his chances to pander to people's hopes and fears, to speak with authority about things very few people understand, and to misappropriate the language of various fields of study. Capitalizing on the guru image like nobody's business, Deepak gains notoriety for his contributions to our understanding of the "connection between our consciousness and the cosmos."[31]

Although I can't honestly say that I can make sense of Deepak's bullshit, I do feel more confident interpreting more subtle forms of pseudo-profundity often found in the corporate world.

Enron's performance in 2000 was a success by any measure, as we continued to outdistance the competition and solidify our leadership in each of our major businesses. We have robust networks of strategic assets that we own or have contractual access to, which give us greater flexibility and speed to reliably deliver widespread logistical solutions. We have unparalleled liquidity and market-making abilities that result in price and service advantages. We have metamorphosed from an asset-based pipeline and power generating company to a marketing and logistics company whose biggest assets are its well-established business approach and its innovative people.

This is part of Enron Chairman Kenneth L. Lay and President/CEO Jeffrey K. Skilling's final letter to shareholders in 2000.[32] It is an example of *corporate gibberish* that defies comprehension. Such content is considered suitable for sales pitches, e-mails, and corporate websites because most people in the corporate world actually communicate this way. This text is full of ambiguous and obscure language and makes claims that are completely unsubstantiated by evidence. Using a simple computer algorithm, such corporate gibberish can be generated by one of the many online bullshit generators—and it can hardly be differentiated from the real thing.[33]

While working for Deloitte Consulting, Brian Fugere and his colleagues held a brief contest to identify bullshit words used in corporate America.[34] In less than two weeks, the team received nearly 10,000 entries from people within their corporate network. Among the thousands of entries received were made-up words (for example, *envisioneer*), real words used out of context (for example, *let's talk off-line, out-of-context*), real words abused and overused (for example, *global*), and real words combined in nonsensical ways (for example, *knowledge capital*, *thoughtware*). Among the most frequently submitted words were *leverage, value add, bandwidth, touch base, incentivize, synergy,* and *win-win*.[35]

Perhaps you sometimes use these words. If you do, it doesn't make you a bullshit artist. What distinguishes a bullshit artist is the fact that they use corporate gibberish a lot—more frequently than most and in all sorts of contexts.[36] For example, the word *leverage* may be used in place of the more straightforward word *use* (for example, "Our company can leverage its knowledge capital to incentivize new buyers")—not only at the office but at the dinner table and park.[37]

A major problem with corporate gibberish is that its use can influence thinking and decision-making in unwanted ways. People who chronically rely on corporate gibberish are the same people who pay incompetent consultants to sell them the latest personality "predictive index" that promises more than it delivers.[38] They are the same people who pay other people to perform jobs they don't actually need someone to do (for example, performance managers, leisure coordinators, leadership coaches/consultants).[39]

Exaggerate Levels of Credibility

Articulate and seemingly well-informed by science and her own anecdotal experiences, the aforementioned Barbara Arrowsmith-Young sounds like she is the world's foremost authority on learning disabilities. She is the leader of the worldwide Arrowsmith Program, designed to help children and adults with learning disabilities "build stronger brains," "create new realities," and "transform their futures."[40] As she has overcome her own learning disabilities, as detailed in her book *The Woman Who Changed Her Brain*, Arrowsmith-Young claims that people with severe learning disabilities can overcome their difficulties. All they need to do is practice 19 cognitive exercises, which supposedly correspond to 19 areas of learning dysfunction. She claims that her exercises, provided exclusively by her program that costs up to $24,000 annually, encourage *neuroplasticity*—the idea that the adult brain is capable of changing physiologically and functionally.[41]

There is one problem with Arrowsmith-Young's miraculous claims about her program—they are not supported by existing scientific knowledge. In fact, no controlled studies have ever linked the Arrowsmith Program's exercises to improvements in the areas of learning dysfunction she identifies.

Instead of referring to evidence supporting her program, Arrowsmith-Young speaks almost exclusively about her own experience and the fact that she has an undergraduate degree in child studies and a master's degree in school psychology. Never mind that she is not a bona fide neuropsychologist, nor a scientist at all. Arrowsmith-Young can come off sounding like the world's foremost authority on learning disabilities because she speaks about things most people don't understand and exaggerates the persona of an expert by making a huge deal about reading a textbook by Alexander Romanovich Luria (a Russian neuropsychologist, often credited as the father of modern neuropsychological assessment). She also makes you aware her program is inspired by the research of psychologist

Mark Rosenzweig, whose work on neuroplasticity in animals indicated that the brain remains capable of change through one's life. But it's all smoke and mirrors propped up to distract her audience from the fact that she has no replicable evidence for her claims that her cognitive exercises harness neuroplasticity.

What bullshit artists like Arrowsmith-Young try to do is confuse us by bolstering their own credibility by name-dropping other "experts." Credibility refers to a person's ability and motivation to provide accurate and truthful information. A speaker is deemed credible if they demonstrate expertise and trustworthiness. Credibility has been a long-standing topic of study in persuasion and attitude change research, with the general finding that high-credibility speakers are more persuasive than low-credibility speakers.[42] Bullshit artists bolster their credentials by overhyping their skills on their resumes or counting watching two-hour online videos as valid certifications in something like CPR (cardiopulmonary resuscitation).

Bullshitters also use their own legitimate credentials as rite-of-passage licenses to bullshit about anything and expect people to buy it (and unfortunately, many do). Dr. Andrea Pennington, author of *The Real Self Love Handbook* and *The Pennington Plan*, is one such example. Pennington followed the latest fad in fast-tracking a career. The track includes five simple steps: (1) get an advanced educational degree from anywhere; (2) read a few books (possibly in quackery similar to what you will try to produce); (3) write a book or two of your own; (4) set up a super fancy website to sell the book(s); and (5) give a clichéd self-help TED Talk to market the book(s)—all to create an illusion of credibility to score guest speaker gigs for thousands of dollars.

Pennington received her MD from Washington University in St. Louis, but a PubMed search of her research contributions returns absolutely nothing. Can someone who has contributed nothing to existing medical knowledge actually have anything new to say that we do not already know about health? Anyone who claims that they specialize in longevity and age management medicine, discredited traditional alternative medicine, and discredited acupuncture and has more guest appearances on *The Oprah Winfrey Show* and *The Dr. Oz Show* than they do contributions to medical research is unlikely to be a pioneer in advancing medical science.[43] Pennington has a better chance of becoming the next Deepak Chopra than she has of actually telling you something you can't already find in the latest issues of *Cosmopolitan* and *Woman's Day*.

One question you should ask a bullshit artist is, "Where did you get that idea from?" Such questions signal to them that perhaps their audience suspects they don't know what they are talking about. But they know the question is coming and they double down by giving us reasons to believe they do know what they are talking about. The best bullshit artists have a canned and reasonable-sounding answer bolstered by the illusion of credibility (for example, "There was a study done at Harvard Medical School . . ."). They do this because credibility usually signals competence. However, in the case of a bullshit artist, appeals to credibility are often nothing more than illusions. Once again, Deepak Chopra doesn't fail to provide an example. On *The Oprah Winfrey Show* in 1993, Deepak claimed that you should never eat a meal with people you don't like. "Because your state of awareness will influence how your food is metabolized. . . . So it's not just the food you eat but what your awareness, what your consciousness, and your state of emotions is at the time you're eating it [that] will metabolize the food into an appropriate or inappropriate metabolic pathway."[44]

Deepak remembered that the audience would be more satisfied with his miraculous claim if he could provide a seemingly credible source for it. "There was a study done in Ohio State University where they were feeding rabbits diets that were extremely high in cholesterol. And they found, to their amazement, there was one group of rabbits that never caught the high cholesterol levels. After a while they found out the technician who was feeding these rabbits instead of just throwing the food at them, he would stroke them and pet them and cuddle them and kiss them and then feed them the same poisonous food. But now as a result of that experience of happiness, they made chemicals inside their brains and their bodies that turned the cholesterol into a completely different metabolic pathway, making the crucial difference between life and death from what kills more people in our civilization than anything else."

Interestingly, the "study" Deepak refers to is the stuff of urban legend. There are no scientific studies that make such claims. In fact, the practice of therapeutic touch has long been discredited by several simple demonstrations, including one conducted as a fourth-grade science project by nine-year-old Emily Rosa.[45] When you hear someone say, "There was a study done . . . ," it is often code for "I really don't know the details, and I really don't care, because I prefer to imagine that the conclusions of the research fit with the arguments I'm trying to make."

Unsubstantiated Character Building and Assassination

In addition to exaggerating their own credentials, bullshit artists opt to use their no-evidence-based approach to build up people who support them and discredit and disparage those who do not. They do this to create the façade that only they and those who agree with them know what they are talking about.

When President Donald Trump liked him and appointed Steve Bannon senior counselor to the president and White House chief strategist, Trump said, "I've known Steve Bannon a long time. If I thought he was a racist or alt-right or any of the things, the terms we could use, I wouldn't even think about hiring him."[46] Campaign manager Kellyanne Conway, who often spoke for President Trump, said, "Steve Bannon is a Georgetown Harvard MBA grad, a former naval officer, a former Goldman Sachs vice president and really the general, the field general in our successful campaign effort—a brilliant tactician and serves president-elect Donald Trump very well."[47] But when Trump no longer liked him and fired Bannon seven months later, he said, "When he was fired, he not only lost his job, he lost his mind. . . . Now that he is on his own, Steve is learning that winning isn't as easy as I make it look. . . . Steve had everything to do with the loss of a Senate seat in Alabama held for more than thirty years by Republicans. Steve doesn't represent my base—he's only in it for himself."[48] When he liked him in April of 2018, President Trump appointed John Bolton as national security advisor and said, "Bolton has been fantastic," and, a year later, declared "John Bolton is doing a very good job." But five months later when he no longer liked Bolton, President Trump began accusing Bolton of impeding his administration, attacking Bolton's reputation on Twitter as a "military hawk," and claiming his forthcoming book was "nasty and untrue."[49] And, when he still liked Omarosa Manigault Newman and appointed her as director of communications for the Office of Public Liaison, President Trump said, "Omarosa, who's actually a very nice person . . . She's actually a very, very fine person and a pastor." But when he no longer liked her after she published a book about her time in the Trump administration, he resorted to calling her "disgusting and foul mouthed," accusing her of going "for some cheap money" by publishing a book, and tweeted, "I am currently suing various people for violating their confidentiality agreements. . . . I gave her [Omarosa] every break, despite the fact that she was despised by everyone. . . . Numerous others also!"[50]

President Trump's character-building and -assassination tactics are simple to employ because they are not based on genuine evidence. When Trump liked particular people, he promoted their character and said positive things about them with the very best of words.[51] But when President Trump no longer liked these same people and fired them because they opposed

not genuine evidence

his policies or methods, he had not-so-nice things to say about them.

A related method employed by bullshit artists is to indirectly attack their critic's "positions" using the *straw man technique*. The straw man technique involves mischaracterizing an opponent's argument or position in a distorted or oversimplified way, and then knocking down that mischaracterization.[52] When a political bullshit artist starts a sentence with "Some say . . . ," what they're doing is almost assuredly setting up a rhetorical retort. The device is usually code for "the other political party." In describing what others advocate, political bullshit artists often omit important nuances or substitute an extreme stance that bears little resemblance to their opponent's actual position. The bullshit artist then follows with, "Well, I strongly disagree . . . ," conveniently knocking down a straw man of their own making. For example, when President George W. Bush said that when it came to battling terrorists, "I need members of Congress who understand that you can't negotiate with these folks," he was straw manning Senator John Kerry and implying that Democrats backed talks with Al Qaeda. Similarly, when President Barack Obama took on Washington and Wall Street, two of his favorite straw men, he said, "I know some folks in Washington and on Wall Street are saying we should just focus on their problems. . . . It would be nice if I could just pick and choose what problems to face, when to face them. So I could say, 'Well, no, I don't want to deal with the war in Afghanistan right now; I'd prefer not having to deal with climate change right now. And if you could just hold on, even though you don't have health care, just please wait, because I've got other things to do.'"[53]

I find it comforting to know that straw man bullshit doesn't always work for bullshit artists. Social psychologist George Bizer and his colleagues have shown that straw man arguments can be effective when people are not able or willing to think deeply about a set of arguments. However, when people are able and willing to think deeply, the straw man technique may be unsuccessful or even backfire.[54]

Appeal to Interpersonal Relationships

Within five minutes of meeting Lance Murphy, you would think you'd found a natural-born communicator.[55] He is charismatic, pleasant, upbeat, profound when he talks, and down-to-earth. You wouldn't be surprised to learn that Murphy is a former point guard who led his small college basketball team to a national championship. No longer scoring three-pointers, Murphy spends much of his time talking with doctors as the Boliftoclax US national sales director for oncology and biosimilars. As a pharmaceutical sales representative, his business is to educate physicians and other medical professionals on new developments in the rapidly advancing pharmaceutical industry. He connects doctors with the knowledge, drugs, and treatments necessary to provide cutting-edge care to their patients. With over 20 years of experience in the pharmaceutical industry, including stints with large companies (like Merck and Eli Lilly), Murphy's broad background in account management serves him well.

I asked Murphy about his work. "Point blank—I think of my work as creating and managing relationships with health-care professionals. That's it. Not everyone can do the work I do. What I say or don't say to doctors will inevitably impact people's lives," he said.

Trained as a public relations specialist, Murphy endorses the idea that beliefs, not necessarily truths, are what matter to his success. As Murphy explains, "I'm not an oncologist. I don't know everything there is to know about tumors and treating cancer. So if I work my way through talking about it, you might call it bullshit. But I call it high-class interpersonal communication skills."

Murphy must be extremely careful in what he says to doctors. He walks the very fine line between effective sales techniques and potential legal ramifications. "I can't be perceived as promoting something 'off-label.' I can't say, well, this drug may not have FDA approval for treating breast cancer, but it works for lungs. I can't tell them, 'You should go and check out the research on that.' I must be savvy in my vernacular, while keeping it surface so I don't go too deep and they think I'm really just fluffing through it. I never went to medical school, but I can talk with any doctor, using their language, about anything."

But why would a doctor use Murphy's products given the dozens of other alternatives? Why would a doctor prescribe Murphy's biosimilar and not a generic? Murphy knows which products are successful and which are not for other doctors who have already signed on with Boliftoclax. And he knows that consensus among doctors is very useful information. Ethical guidelines and laws prohibit pharmaceutical sales representative from broadcasting what their colleagues and competitors might be using and finding useful for their patients. In his business, there are boundaries he is not permitted to cross. The game is really all about how close you can get to those boundaries without stepping into unethical quicksand. "I can't say directly to Dr. Jones, 'Oh, Dr. Smith uses this drug with his patients.' But I might use a subtle name-drop regarding Dr. Smith with something completely unrelated, like 'Say, Dr. Jones, when will you be on deck for getting that comfy corner office? You know, I was just meeting with Dr. Smith yesterday, and you know what? He's got that comfy corner office.' Now, the doctor I'm speaking with knows he's not about to go rogue on selecting any new treatment drugs because now he knows Dr. Smith, who very rarely talks with anyone and is a world-renowned surgeon, actually let me into his office. And if anyone is trying get to what Dr. Smith prescribes to his patients, it will be Dr. Jones."

Murphy's drug line is in oncology and cardiovascular health. His sales success boils down to getting doctors to endorse and prescribe his drugs to their patients and not someone else's drugs. Because Murphy is restricted by commercial sales ethics and prohibited from intentionally persuading health-care professionals, he is forced to use more creative strategies.

"What I find most useful is to focus on the relationship. If the interpersonal relationship is good—if there is trust and a freeness to talk about anything—yes, there might be more bullshit involved. And doctors know fully well that I didn't go to medical school and they are inclined to think that I have no idea what I'm talking about. So, I can't get away with saying, 'There are data on this in *JAMA* [*Journal of the American Medical Association*],' when I don't know if there really is, with someone who doesn't at least believe that I know what I'm talking about and who doesn't trust me on an interpersonal level." Of course, most people wouldn't claim they are bullshit artists, but Murphy does a lot of bullshitting.

"More often than not, doctors find it intriguing, admirable, and even a compliment to them and their field to have this salesperson in their office who at least sounds like he knows what he's talking about, and doesn't sound like someone who is just trying to baffle them with bullshit. That's the key—you can't sound like you're bullshitting. It's like being able to speak a language in a foreign country. If you go to Vietnam as an American and you've taken the time to learn Vietnamese, you would receive more respect. And now you have doors open that would never be open otherwise. And now you have your foot in the door of them liking you. Am I right?

"In my line of work, compliance regulation violations can be very severe. You might receive fines or be blacklisted by Medicare for violating the sales communication standards. So, I focus on the patient at the end of my line whose life is going to be affected by what I share with doctors. I believe in our biosimilars. So, I dress the part. I try to have the right demeanor, not pushy or hurried. I try to sound like I have the right depth of expertise, and never, ever sounding like I think I know more than the doctor. No one knows more than the physicians in my work. But they love it when I meet them halfway. I say, 'I've never put my hands on a patient. I've never so much as put on a lab coat. . . .' When they ask if I've read *JAMA*, I say, 'Yes, of course, and the *New England Journal of Medicine*.' You see, because a doctor I want to speak with might go through 50 patients in a day, and I may never get another chance to meet with them, I focus on what will make me stand out. What will make me worth ten minutes? Because I'm sitting on a drug treatment that could save thousands of lives. Another salesperson might be pushing an even better product, but if he/she isn't special in some way, I've already won the game."

What matters, in other words, is the human connection that may have nothing to do with oncology and medication, but is key to landing a sale. Here bullshit is useful. "The doors of selling a commodity don't really open unless I connect on a human level, and yes, bullshit can do wonders for this. I show interest in the more human side of sales. I comment on family pictures on a wall. 'Hey, is that Pebble Beach?' Cities, states, schools in common. Sports, kids, the best golf courses in the area, whatever. I want to leave their office with a strong association between my brand, Boliftoclax, and everything oncology. But I can't even open that door if they don't like me. It's much harder to say no to someone you like than someone you don't."

Much of what practicing physicians know about treatment drugs is what sales representatives tell them. Although Murphy's pitch must be sharp, he doesn't need to know everything. He only needs to know how his products are better than others on the market. Murphy admits to practicing sound bites for these opportunities. When doctors inquire about research data, he has the perfect response memorized. The one thing Murphy explains that he never does is promise more than his products can deliver. But no matter how fantastic his company's products are, his company won't be in business for very long if he isn't able to effectively develop relationships with doctors on an interpersonal level—and for this, bullshitting skills can come in handy.

Murphy is not the first, nor last, person to capitalize on established friendship and mutual liking. People are frequently influenced by bullshit because it comes from someone they like and trust.[56] Detecting and disposing of bullshit is much more difficult with friendly and likeable bullshitters because bullshit detection involves evaluation—and it is difficult to accurately evaluate a friend. Receiving bullshit from a friend produces a natural conflict of interest, but it is bullshit all the same. And just because we like our friends, it doesn't mean that they won't bullshit us.

5

BULLSHIT DETECTION WHEELHOUSE

TED Talks and Fifteen Minutes of Bullshit

The most essential gift for a good writer is a built-in, shockproof, shit detector. This is the writer's radar and all great writers have had it.—ERNEST HEMINGWAY

Viewed by millions on YouTube every day, TED Talks are influential and creative talks by professionals. TED Talks are billed as "ideas worth spreading," which is an admirable goal. People enjoy watching them because they are often inspirational and are marketed as the best education you can get for free. Each talk comes with a brief speaker bio that establishes their expertise. Because viewers tend to trust experts, they often accept TED Talk content as fact. But the truth is, TED Talks often proliferate substantial bullshit.[1]

One video that drew my attention was Cynthia Thurlow's TEDx Talk, titled *Intermittent Fasting: Transformational Technique*. Thurlow's talk was first posted online in May of 2019. Viewed over 7 million times, her video scored nearly 2 million views in its first month. For a TED speaker, this is a dream come true—I know this for certain, as my own TEDx Talk on bullshit scored only 25,000 views in the same time frame.

Thurlow sounds and looks like an expert. She is attractive, slim, and in great shape. Her tagline reads:

Trained nurse practitioner and functional nutritionist who is passionate about female hormonal health. She believes that the inherent power of food and nutrition can be your greatest asset to your health and wellness journey. She works 1:1 with female clients and is the creator of Wholistic Blueprint a 6-week signature program for female hormonal health, she's also the co-host of Everyday Wellness podcast and a recurring segment contributor on her local ABC affiliate in Washington, DC.[2]

Thurlow begins her talk with two questions: "What if I told you that breakfast being the most important meal of the day was wrong? What if I told you it is more important when you eat than what you eat?" Thurlow argues that meal timing and how frequently people eat are crucial to losing weight, sleeping better, and aging more slowly. She also claims that the focus on calories consumed and burned through exercise and daily activity is outdated and no longer adequate—this dogma, Thurlow adds, "makes me want to cry."

Thurlow warns people that they shouldn't waste their money on supplements, potions, powders, snake oils, and quick fixes that are not effective long-term solutions to weight gain. She contends, "I've got a better idea. There are lots of strategies that I use with my female patients, but none more powerful than intermittent fasting. Intermittent fasting can help fuel fat loss as well as many other benefits. . . . [I]t also can improve interpersonal relationships and self-esteem . . . and for many women it is the magic bullet that permits them to gain back their former selves."

Thurlow pushes intermittent fasting as a "free, flexible, and simple method," defining it as the absence of food during a prescribed time period. To fuel fat loss, she prescribes a "16–8" schedule, whereby we fast for 16 hours and only eat during an eight-hour window. She claims that "we know that it improves mental clarity because insulin levels are low . . . we know that it spikes human growth hormone, which helps us with lean muscle mass . . . we know that it lowers insulin levels, blood pressure, improves our cholesterol profile, and we know that it can reduce your risk of developing cancer and Alzheimer's disease."

In Thurlow's talk you will also hear her use the word *auto-phagy*, which she claims is akin to spring cleaning for cells and only occurs when one is fasting. Autophagy is supposed to be the primary mechanism that makes intermittent fasting work. In concluding, Thurlow urges all health-care professionals to discuss intermittent fasting with their patients.

First, Thurlow's claims must be clarified. She claims that meal timing is important to our sleep quality and the rate at which our body ages. She is making a causal claim that intermittent fasting will not only help us lose weight, but that it will result in all sorts of physical and psychological benefits. Are there any good reasons to believe Thurlow's claims?

Second, Thurlow argues that the diet math of calories consumed and calories burned is outdated. I understand that earlier scientific conclusions might be wrong and overturned, but I'm quite certain that any diet that has ever worked for anyone has a very important and simple rule: consuming more calories than one burns leads to weight gain and consuming fewer calories than one burns leads to weight loss. What I still want to know is: How did Thurlow come to her astounding discovery that calories are no longer useful for understanding how people gain or lose weight?

What is desperately needed are scientific experiments designed to test if intermittent fasting produces the results Thurlow claims it does. It might take a long time to test if intermittent fasting affects things like cancer, Alzheimer's disease, interpersonal relationships, and self-esteem, but it should be relatively straightforward and less time-consuming to test if it has an effect on weight loss over and above other common diet plans.

Krista Varady, a professor of kinesiology and nutrition from the University of Illinois at Chicago, offers some clarity. Varady has run dozens of clinical trials on weight loss and fasting in hundreds of people. Her data show that people do lose weight through intermittent fasting methods.[3] However, her data also show that the cause of the weight loss with intermittent fasting is not because it puts the body in a special fat-burning mode (as Thurlow suggests). Rather, her data suggest that people on intermittent fasting diets lose weight because they eat less overall—they are consuming fewer calories.

Third, as Thurlow lays them out, the *causal effects* of intermittent fasting sound incredible: improvements in self-esteem and interpersonal relationships; greater mental clarity; more muscle; better insulin, blood pressure, and cholesterol levels; and lower risks of cancer and Alzheimer's disease—and all of this just from eating from noon to eight. Yet throughout her talk, Thurlow fails to reference any genuine evidence to back these claims. After searching databases that house reports of all the published medical and psychological science, like PubMed and PsycINFO, I was unable to find any evidence that suggests intermittent fasting *causes* the body to burn fat faster or do all of the great things Thurlow claims it does. It simply isn't there.

Fourth, Thurlow never actually explained in her talk what autophagy is, which she tags as the primary mechanism that makes intermittent fasting work. Interestingly, autophagy is part of the process by which cells recycle themselves to make new cells. This process preserves the health of cells and tissues by replacing outdated and damaged cellular components with fresh ones. When people starve themselves, autophagy provides an internal source of nutrients for energy generation. Some evidence suggests that autophagy can prevent degenerative diseases, but there is no evidence that autophagy prevents cancer in people.[4] What you hear in Thurlow's talk is that intermittent fasting "ramps up" autophagy, leading us to believe that we can get rid of more fat cells, live longer, and prevent cancer. Once again, however, Thurlow was wrong. Claims that intermittent fasting increase autophagy are only supported by studies conducted with mice and rats. That is, there have never been any human studies suggesting that calorie restriction or

no way to measure autophagy

fasting directly help people live longer. Furthermore, any studies suggesting a link between autophagy and cancer prevention are preliminary. In fact, science doesn't have a clear way to measure changes in autophagy in people.[5]

If I could have asked Thurlow some questions, I would have asked her: This all sounds very exciting, but *how do you know* that intermittent fasting has all the benefits you claim it does? What sort of evidence supports your conclusions? Have the proposed benefits of intermittent fasting been tested in randomized, controlled clinical trials? Show me the data!

Available literature on intermittent fasting shows there is absolutely nothing transformational about it. Intermittent fasting may help you to lose weight, not because it burns fat faster but because it will help you consume fewer calories. People who are physically healthy and feel good about themselves are likely to have better self-esteem and more positive relationships with others, but there is nothing extraordinary about intermittent fasting that facilitates such outcomes.

There probably isn't much risk in trying intermittent fasting—it might help you shed a few pounds. However, it would be very risky to expect intermittent fasting to lead to better mental clarity; more muscle; better insulin, blood pressure, and cholesterol levels; higher self-esteem; and improved interpersonal relationships or to expect intermittent fasting to be a panacea for cancer and Alzheimer's disease. That is why I believe Thurlow's bullshit warrants at least two flies on the Bullshit Flies Index.

In my final analysis, not only do I consider Thurlow's talk bullshit, I don't consider it an expert opinion. People who are not interested in the truth and readily available evidence in their own domain of expertise can hardly be considered experts—they are bullshitters. I feel I have a right to call bullshit on Thurlow because the two hours I spent fact-checking her claims was probably more time than she spent seeking the truth about intermittent fasting.

We shouldn't be surprised by such nonsense. After all, bullshit, quackery, pseudoscience, crackpot science, and outright fraud are ubiquitous and often considered acceptable in our postmodern, misinformed, fake news world—and it even sells. People will continue to consume false information from bullshit artists like Thurlow unless they begin asking critical questions.

Many people believe that the only thing one needs to detect bullshit is good old *common sense.* I understand the temptation. But if common sense was so useful, it wouldn't prescribe so many contradictions, as found in our most commomsensical knowledge (for example, haste makes waste vs. time waits for no man; you're never too old to learn vs. you can't teach an old dog new tricks; look before you leap vs. he who hesitates is lost). If common sense is the only tool you use to defend against bullshit, you will find it difficult to avoid bullshit's unwanted effects. If you want to become a better bullshit detector and a more critical consumer of information, you must first understand *common sense is not enough*. If common sense were a reliable reasoning method, we wouldn't need science or critical thinking.

If you find learning unappealing, are reluctant to critique authorities and experts, strongly dislike finding out that you are wrong sometimes, are indifferent to supporting your beliefs and behavior with fact and reason, dislike critically evaluating your own beliefs and actions, have no desire to intelligently explain to others your reasoning, or are uninterested in focusing on details, bullshit detection isn't for you. Bullshit detection requires *critical thinking*.

Critical thinking is a learned process of deliberation, fact-finding, and self-reflection used to comprehend and appropriately evaluate information in order to decide what to believe or what to do. It involves a broad range of skills and attitudes designed to purposefully self-regulate judgments and decisions with reasoned and fair-minded consideration of the evidence. When good critical thinkers suspect they have been exposed to bullshit or discover that their own beliefs and actions may be based on bullshit, they ask themselves five important types of questions:

- *Collect Data*: Have I obtained and reviewed the right types, amounts, and levels of information to comprehend and evaluate the claim?
- *Recognize Potential Bias*: Have I treated the claim or its implications like ideas, refraining from assuming it to be true or false on the basis of my emotional reactions before evaluating the evidence?
- *Minimize Bias*: Have I accurately identified the positions, arguments, and conclusions of the claim and the degree to which any assumptions are sensible, false, or

unfair? Have I considered and fairly weighed evidence that opposes, and evidence that supports, the claim?

- *Assess the Validity of Conclusions*: Have I reviewed and drawn logical, valid, and justifiable conclusions provided by the relevant evidence of multiple, independent viewpoints or sources?

multiple sources

- *Elaborate and Apply*: Can I reasonably draw my own well-informed, well-reasoned, and compelling conclusions from the evidence to form arguments convincing to other critical thinkers?

Asking critical-thinking questions is the gateway to evidence-based reasoning and optimal decision-making. People who think critically make sound judgments on issues and problems and are more likely to generate potential solutions. They become aware of things that really matter. They make better decisions about their purchases and business transactions. Critical thinkers are more likely to correctly interpret requirements, terms, and conditions before agreeing to the "fine print." They are also conscious of the consequences of their decisions for themselves and others. Essentially, critical thinkers are the antithesis of bullshit artists.

If you *desire to know the truth and make better decisions*, you must become a critical thinker. The good news is that you don't need to learn dozens of techniques to dispose of bullshit. Critical thinking can be thought of as a *process* rather than as facts to remember. Operate from the reality that people are often wrong—even scientists—and you will naturally and consistently be asking questions. Remember, better decision-making always requires better information. In pursuing our goal, I urge you to develop two important habits: an *attitude of skepticism* and a *practice of questioning*.

BULLSHIT DETECTION WHEELHOUSE

A wheelhouse is the part of a boat that serves as a shelter for the captain. Just like a wheelhouse shelters the captain and contains the wheel of the boat, an effective *bullshit detection wheelhouse* will protect you from bullshit and help guide your questioning, thinking, and decision-making.

The two general tools in the bullshit detection wheelhouse are an *attitude of skepticism* and a *practice of questioning*. Skepticism in the context of bullshit detection means bringing a healthy element of polite doubt when evaluating evidence for or against a claim. If you bring skeptical thinking to the process, it doesn't mean that you are close-minded and unwilling to accept new ideas. It means believing in that which can be verified by genuine and compelling evidence and requiring extraordinary evidence for extraordinary claims. I am perfectly willing to accept the possibility that aliens exist—but show me the spaceship, let me inspect it, allow me to get some expert opinions, let me ask some questions, let me see the bodies, and let me see the dissections.

The oldest continuously operating scientific society in the

world, the Royal Society, adopted as its motto over 350 years ago the Latin phrase *nullius in verba*, meaning "take nobody's word for it." This shall be our motto as well. Long appreciated by scientists and philosophers, a distinguishing feature of science is that its claims are expected to be verifiable. It is in the process of verifying what may or may not be bullshit that bullshit is successfully detected.

Given the pervasiveness of bullshit, an attitude of skepticism and practice of questioning work best if you keep in mind four assumptions:

1. You will encounter bullshit claims frequently—especially when an individual is motivated to influence you.
2. Individuals rarely recognize and fully appreciate the complexity of the phenomena or systems they're bullshitting about.
3. Individuals do not always take the time and effort necessary to evidence-proof their claim(s).
4. You need to ask questions to verify if claims are based on evidence or bullshit—treat ideas as ideas and not as facts.

4 assumptions - skepticism necessary!

WHEELHOUSE QUESTIONS

Bullshit detection requires being sensitive to bullshit cues. When you suspect you are being bullshitted, it's essential that you ask critical questions and keep your eyes and ears open for bullshit cues. Whether an individual's claim is true or false, if they haven't bothered to verify their claims they're bullshitting you.

Although critical questioning will take some practice, consistently asking critical questions is the key to effectively detecting and disposing of the unwanted bullshit in your life. You don't need to ask all of the following questions every time you suspect someone's bullshitting you. Just asking a question or two will allow you to assess the claim and will prompt additional, diagnostic follow-up questions.

Questions to Ask Yourself

Clarify the Claim:

(handwritten: ① Understand the claim!)

- What precisely is the claim?
- Does the claim rest on underlying assumptions or apply only to a certain group of people or in certain situations?[6]
- Are there any unfair apples-to-oranges comparisons being made?
- Is the claim extraordinary? If so, is there extraordinary evidence in support of it?
- Does the claim sound too good or too bad to be true?
- Of all the ways the individual could have possibly stated the claim, why did they state it this way?

Assess the Individual Communicator:

Read the individual!

- How credible is the individual making the claim? What is their expertise in the area?
- Do they appear concerned with evidence supporting their claim and willing to engage in a critical conversation without unfairly dismissing evidence that might oppose their claim?
- How does the individual know this?
- What is the individual's motivation for sharing this claim with me? Are there any reasons for them to bullshit?
- Are they employing rhetorical signs of bullshit: "Some people say . . . ," "I read somewhere . . . ," and/ or shifting the semantic goalposts when asked for clarification; inaccurately representing competing claims, explanations, and arguments; using tautological reasoning (repeating an idea or statement using different words that essentially say the same thing); or using pseudo-profundity?
- How does the individual react when asked questions? (Properly diagnose defensive responses by the individual. The individual could sound defensive or irritated for a number of reasons—they may sense that their bullshit was detected, they may feel discomfort realizing they were bullshitting, or they may be frustrated because you don't appear to comprehend their claim.)

Evaluate the Claim and Its Evidence: *Evidence!*

- What exactly are the plausible reasons for the claim? Do any reasons contradict common knowledge, such as mathematical or scientific laws, semantic or empirical knowledge?
- How strong or compelling is the relevant evidence?
- What problems does the claim have? What doesn't the claim explain? How might the claim be wrong?
- What significant information might have been omitted? Are the statistics or how they're displayed deceptive in any way? Are any mere arguments or anecdotal evidence being treated as genuine evidence?
- Is it possible to conduct a simple thought experiment to test the claim?
- Given the available evidence and established knowledge, what are the most reasonable conclusions?

Assess the Self: *Self - introspection!*

- Are my conclusions about the claim based on genuine evidence?
- Have I sought any information beyond what I was given? Would someone say that I've thought this through like a fact-checker?
- Is there anything about the individual that would cause me to look beyond the substance of their claim

and its evidence (for example, attractiveness, liking, disliking, etc.)?

objectivity →

- Am I being objective in my assessment of the evidence? Have I tried another perspective? Have I honestly considered the possibility that the opposite of the claim is true or am I jumping to conclusions?
- If I accept or reject the claim as true, what other beliefs of mine might need to change? Do these implications affect my evaluation of the claim's validity or its evidence?

Questions to Ask the Individual Communicator

You are in an excellent position to detect bullshit if you have the opportunity to gain additional information from the individual. If there is a key to detecting bullshit in conversation with others, it is adhering to this general structure of questioning: **What? How? (not Why?) And Have you considered . . . ?** Asking, "What exactly are you saying?" or "What do you mean by that?" prompts people who are bullshitting to clarify their claims and provides them with an opportunity to clean up parts that don't make sense. Try not to ask *why* questions. When bullshitters are asked why they believe what they believe, they tend to provide theoretical or philosophical arguments and leave out evidence. It is always better to ask *how* they came to their conclusions. Answering how they've come to believe what they believe encourages bullshitters to muster evidence in support of their claims.[7] Asking bullshitters if they've considered alternatives to their claims will help to

Don't ask 'Why?'

uncover the sophistication and complexity underlying their reasoning (or lack thereof).

Follow-up questions are especially diagnostic if you have *control data* for comparison. That is, if you can first establish a behavioral baseline for the individual, you will be better positioned to detect bullshitting cues. How does the individual usually communicate? How does the individual usually respond to questions? Is the individual's behavior different now than it usually is? If you know how the individual tends to communicate things that could not possibly be bullshit, and you know how they tend to answer purely factual questions, you are well positioned to identify their verbal and nonverbal bullshit behaviors.

When you ask clarifying questions, don't be surprised if what you receive in response is even more bullshit. Resist the temptation to make it personal—you will likely meet resistance and not get anywhere. People base most of their beliefs on moral and motivational reasons rather than epistemological or empirical grounds.[8] Don't expect questioning bullshit to result in the pinnacle of rationality and logic. The goal is to reveal understandable errors in reasoning. Doing so is a more efficient method of getting to the truth than making accusations.

Consider softening questions: "I'm very interested, and I just want to understand your idea clearly. . . ."

Clarify the Claim:

- What do you mean by ___?
- What can ___ look like?

- Is there another way to state ___?
- When and where is ___ most likely to occur?
- Could you give me an example or illustration?
- Are there specific conditions under which ___ is true and conditions under which ___ is not true?

Evaluate the Evidence:

- How do we know ___ to be true?
- Why should we believe that ___ is so?
- What sort of evidence supports the conclusion about ___?
- What is the best single piece of evidence for ___?
- How could we check that to find out if that is true?
- Has anyone tested ___ with an experiment?
- What were the results of any experiments?
- Can you tell me a bit about the methods used in those experiments?
- How were the data collected?
- Were the right metrics for drawing valid conclusions used?

Play Devil's Advocate with Disconfirmatory Questions:

- How might ___ be wrong? (Don't ask, "How might you be wrong?" Keep the discussion about the claim.)
- Under what conditions could ___ be false?
- What would it take for ___ to always be true?
- What would it take for ___ to be rejected?

- What sort of evidence might someone provide—even hypothetical evidence—that would show a need to revise the claim?
- Have you, or has anyone else, considered alternative possibilities, like ___ or ___?
- Suppose ___ was tested and failed. Why might it fail?
- What kind of evidence would it take for you to conclude your claim was wrong?
- Is confidence in ___ justified by available evidence?
- Does available evidence lead us to ___?
- Have you considered or ruled out any viable alternative hypotheses?

Dealing with Numbers and Statistics

On the rare occasions that bullshitters use numbers and statistics, they tend to exploit them in ways that do not reflect evidence-based reasoning. Remember that even when numbers and statistics are factual, they can be interpreted in many different ways.

There are four basic *questions* that you can ask yourself to determine if someone is trying to bullshit you with numbers and statistics:

- Are the numbers *plausible*?
- Are the *descriptive statistics*, like frequencies, averages, percentages, or charts, consistent with the claim?

- How were the numbers *collected* and what other numbers have been collected but not reported here?
- What are the *probabilities* of the numbers reported, and do they accurately depict reality and what is implied by the claim?

plausability check

Just because something sounds plausible doesn't mean it is true—don't accept claims as facts without first running a *plausibility check*. The plausibility of a claim can be checked by using logic and working out the numbers. If someone tells you they can do 300 full-extension pull-ups at the gym in under five minutes, you might be impressed until you realize that it's not plausible—300 pull-ups in under 300 seconds would require one pull-up every second and no time at all for rest. You don't need to go to a gym to realize this is impossible.

Sometimes claims and statistics can sound perfectly plausible and pass the plausibility check, but are irrelevant to the point. For instance, one might argue that the Pittsburgh Pirates are historically a better baseball team than the New York Yankees because the Pirates' World Series win percentage is 71.5% whereas the Yankees' is only 67.5%. The data might look like it supports the claim, but it doesn't.[9] In fact, the Yankees have played in 40 World Series and won 27 of them, while the Pirates have only played in 7 World Series and won 5 of them. After looking at relevant evidence, one should conclude that the claim is false: the Pirates are not historically better than the Yankees.

Bullshitters like to obscure facts with relevant but less diagnostic data. For instance, a friend of mine claimed that before

COVID-19 hit the United States, more Americans were employed than at any other time in history. My friend supported their claim by pointing to the fact that the total number of Americans employed immediately prior to the pandemic was higher than at any other point in history. However, the total number of employed Americans does not take into account the fact that the population of the United States was at an all-time high. The percentage of workers employed (employment rate) is a much more diagnostic marker of employment. The greatest employment rate in US history occurred in April of 2000 at almost 65%, whereas it was only 61% just before COVID-19 hit the United States.

Descriptive statistics describe basic features of the data in a study. Using frequencies, averages, and percentages, descriptive statistics provide a summary of the sample. Bullshitters often tell you only part of the relevant data—showing you those statistics that support their claim and ignoring data that don't. Descriptive statistics do not prove anything on their own. The best way to determine if descriptive statistics accurately depict reality and support a claim is to examine the raw data. Look at the distribution of the data. Sometimes you will find that something as straightforward as an average doesn't describe the data at all. One might claim that the average weight of people in the United States is 185. However, you won't find the greatest frequency of Americans to be at 185 pounds. You will find much greater frequencies at 170 pounds and 200 pounds because the distribution is bimodal—the average woman weighs 170 pounds and the average man weighs 200 pounds. But you wouldn't know this unless you looked more carefully at the distribution of weights.

BSers: correlation

Bullshitters frequently use correlation—a statistic that measures the strength and direction of the relationship between two things—to support claims that one thing *causes* another. However, correlation does not imply causation. For instance, sunscreen sales and ice cream cone sales are highly and positively correlated because they tend to increase and decrease at relatively similar rates. But of course, their correlation doesn't mean that variation in sunscreen sales causes ice cream cone sales to fluctuate.

A particularly frequent and annoying form of bullshit involves the many ways of manipulating how data are displayed to make it appear that the data support a claim. For example, suppose that when asked how much they like chocolate ice cream on a scale of 1 to 7, men reported an average of 5.37 whereas women reported an average of 5.47. The difference between men and women is only .10. Is this a large or small difference? A chart that displays a range of only 5.00 to 6.00 makes the difference look enormous, yet the more appropriate figure using the full range (1.00 to 7.00) clarifies that women and men enjoy chocolate ice cream about the same amount. The only way you will see the relevance of that difference is to find the scale of the measurement actually used to collect the data, and not the one that the communicator wants you to see.

Determining how the data were *collected* is critical to assessing a claim that provides numbers and statistics as evidence. Who or what was sampled? Who or what did the sampling? Remember, the questions a scientist asks and how they ask them inevitably shape the answers.[10] Scientists employ strict rules for how they sample data and what measurement tools they use.

Use Visuals. You will almost never find a bullshitter referencing the probabilities or likelihoods of outcomes inherent in the phenomena they describe. To evaluate a claim with numbers, you need to know what the likelihoods of the numbers presented or implied by the claim are. The best tool for roughly estimating likelihoods is to draw a picture of the claim's *sample space* (that is, a picture or diagram that shows all the possibilities the claim covers and what it doesn't cover; sometimes referred to as problem space).

Consider an easy claim without numbers:

Jack is looking at Anne but Anne is looking at George. Jack is married but George is not. My claim: A married person is not looking at an unmarried person.

If you are like most people you probably think that my claim is correct. But it's wrong. Don't be disappointed if you don't see it right away. Many Ivy League students don't see it either, and when David Robson, author of *The Intelligence Trap*, published

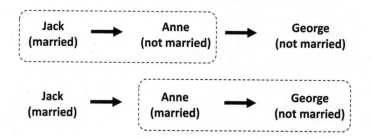

this test, he received an unprecedented number of letters claiming that the answer was a mistake.[11] However, if you had drawn the *sample space*, you would clearly see my claim is false.

Regardless of whether Anne is married or not, a married person would be looking at an unmarried person. The trick is to think through all possible scenarios—this is the sample space—only then is it easy to see.

Now consider a claim with numbers. Imagine you are on a game show and you are presented with three doors. Behind one of the doors is a car and behind the other two are goats. The game-show host asks you to pick a door. You pick Door 1. The host knows where the car is. To make things more interesting, the host always reveals a goat behind one of the doors you did not pick. In this case, the host reveals a goat is behind Door 2. The host asks you to make a final decision: stick with your original Door 1 or switch to Door 3. I claim that sticking or switching doesn't matter because you have a 50/50 chance of winning the car.

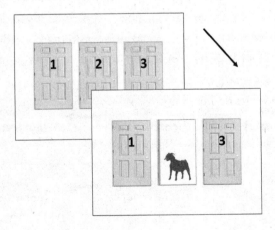

What will you do?

If you are ever presented with a three-doors dilemma, please switch! No matter how many trials you are presented with, you should always switch.[12] My claim that it doesn't matter if you stick or switch is complete bullshit—it deserves at least two flies on the Bullshit Flies Index—believing that the final choice doesn't matter would greatly reduce your chances of winning the car. By drawing out the sample space (see below), you can easily recognize that my claim that it doesn't matter is bullshit.[13]

All possible outcomes of sticking or switching after initially picking Door 1 in each case

Behind Door			Host Reveals Goat Behind Door(s)	Result of **Sticking** with Door 1	Result of **Switching** to Remaining Door
1	2	3			
Goat	Goat	**Car**	2	Win Goat	**Win Car**
Goat	**Car**	Goat	3	Win Goat	**Win Car**
Car	Goat	Goat	2 or 3	**Win Car**	Win Goat

At the beginning of the game, you had a 33% chance of picking the car and a 67% chance of picking a goat. After you've made your first choice and the host opens another door to reveal a goat, you have more information about the remaining door but no new information about your original choice. There is still a 33% chance there is a car behind your original door, but there is now a 67% chance there's a car behind the remaining closed door. While there's a risk that you originally chose the correct door, you double the probability of winning if you switch to the remaining door. In other words, the switch strategy is the winning strategy because it wins if you chose the wrong door on your first try—which, whether you know it or not, will have occurred 67% of the time. If you are like most people, you still don't think the decision to stick or switch matters—but it most certainly does matter—to claim otherwise is bullshit. Imagine there are 100 doors, 99 goats, and 1 car. You select Door 32. The host opens 98 doors, except Door 32 and Door 78, revealing goats behind each one. Are you still going to stick with Door 32, assuming it is equally likely to contain the car as Door 78? In this case, the chances Door 32 has the car is only 1% but the chance that Door 78 has the car is 99%.

Fermi Estimation. Nobel laureate Enrico Fermi created the world's first nuclear reactor and is regarded as an architect of the atomic bomb. Excelling in both theoretical and experimental physics, Fermi was known for making quick and relatively accurate estimates of quantities that seemed difficult or near impossible to determine precisely (without a computer). For instance, what do you suppose the circumference of the Earth is? If you folded a large piece of 0.1mm-thick paper 100 times, how thick would it be?[14] Fermi estimated the distances are thousands and trillions of miles long, respectively.

Fermi's approach to such questions was to use a series of logical assumptions, rough estimates, and a bit of common sense to piece together a ballpark value. *Fermi estimation* is a fantastic tool to employ on the rare occasion that a bullshitter tries to pretend that he/she is actually interested in genuine evidence to baffle you with big numbers or wild estimates of things that don't seem right.

In December of 2016, *Fox & Friends* ran a story claiming that $70 million had been lost that year to food stamp fraud in the United States and that such high fraud rates were a good reason to eliminate the program (now known as SNAP, Supplemental Nutrition Assistance Program).[15] Losing $70 million to fraud sounds like a lot of wasted money. But given the size of the food stamp program, is $70 million actually a lot of money?

A standard of comparison or reference point would help you form an evidence-based opinion about whether losing $70 million to fraud is a big deal. This is where Fermi estimation comes in very handy. First, you may not know exactly how expensive the food stamp program is, but you could calculate it rather quickly. Let's say you guesstimate that about 15% of Americans are on food stamps. Second, you are probably aware that there are about 325 million people in the United States. Hence, you figure there are around 48,750,000 people on food stamps. Now you really only need one more piece of information to make a decent Fermi estimation—what is the average annual benefit paid to US food stamp program recipients? You might figure that it would be reasonable for recipients to receive $125 per month in supplemental food aid ($1,500 per year). Multiply that by the number of Americans who receive the benefit (48,750,000) and you get $73.1 *billion*. Using your Fermi estimate, you find that the United States loses less than 1% of the money it invests in the SNAP.

15% of Americans are on food stamps

325 million people in the USA

325 million people × .15 = approximately 48,750,000
   people on food stamps

The average benefit paid to recipients annually is
   $1,500

48,750,000 people × $1,500/person = $73,125,000,000

$70,000,000 / $73,125,000,000 = approximately 0.001
   = one-tenth of 1%

At this point, you've got enough information to see what's wrong with the argument made on *Fox & Friends*. As it turns out, the Fermi estimation was impressively accurate, despite the fact that *Fox & Friends* severely underestimated SNAP's 2016 losses to fraud.[16] A loss of $70 million may sound like a lot of money, but in light of the total amount spent on the program, the notion that $70 million in losses is significant is bullshit. Put another way, say you have a 100 dollars in your wallet. If you lost the equivalent percentage that SNAP lost a year to fraud, it would amount to ten cents.

After receiving criticism from the US Department of Agriculture (USDA), *Fox & Friends* corrected their report about food stamp fraud, stating that their calculations from the USDA information from 2009 to 2011 showed $853 million in fraud, or 1.3% in those three years. Nationally, food stamp trafficking was on the decline.[17] Apparently, the Fermi estimator at *Fox & Friends* could use a few recalibrations.

Linguistic Red Flags of Bullshit

Linguistic research shows that when people are not interested in truth and evidence, they tend to produce more words overall and rely on sense-related words (for example, *seeing*, *touching*, *hearing*).[18] They tend to take the focus off themselves by using a smaller proportion of self-oriented pronouns (for example, *me*, *myself*, *I*) and by placing the focus on others by using a greater proportion of other-oriented pronouns (for example, *you*) and third-person identifiers (for example, *he*, *she*, *it*, *they*, *him*, *hers*, *them*, *their*, *his*, *its*, or *theirs*).

When people are not concerned with truth, they tend to avoid using causal words (for example, *because*, *therefore*) and increase their use of negation words (for example, *not*, *none*) and negative emotion words (for example, *hate*, *worthless*). Bullshit tends to be expressed in simpler terms with more motion verbs (for example, *walk*, *move*) and fewer exclusion words (for example, *but*, *without*).

You can also take a look at how others react to bullshit. People tend to unknowingly change their behavior during deceptive conversations, even when they don't know they are being deceived. They tend to ask more questions with shorter sentences when they're being bullshitted and match the bullshitter's linguistic style.

Below is a list of red-flag words and phrases that should set off your bullshit detector whenever you hear them. Although none of these words and phrases are—in isolation—indicative of bullshit, a combination of several of them together is.

- "My guess is . . ."
- "My gut tells me . . ."
- "Look, I just know . . ."
- "Many people don't know this, but . . ."
- "You're probably not going to believe this, but . . ."
- "Isn't it amazing . . ."
- "Trust me . . ."
- "All I know is . . ."
- "Hey, don't look at me . . ."
- "I know it when I see it."
- "What if I told you . . . ?" [the hands-down favorite of TED Talk bullshitters]
- "That looks great on you." [providing no reasons]
- "His proposal will cripple the economy . . ." [providing no reasons]
- "This place sucks." [providing no reasons]
- "All . . ."; "Every time . . ."; "Everywhere . . ."; "Everyone/Everybody does it . . ." [sweeping generalizations or hasty conclusions without providing evidence-based reasons]
- "They are saying . . ." or "They are out here saying . . ." [Who are they? Where are they? And how many are there?]
- "That's how they get you." [Who are they? And how exactly do they get you?]

Bullshit Masquerading as Science

If you've ever watched the evening news or opened a magazine, you've witnessed just how common the word *science* has
become. Stories leading with "A new study shows" air just before that day's astrological horoscope.

> "A new study shows eating bacon will make you live
>   longer."
> "A new study suggests hugging your dog may be bad
>   for your dog."
> "A new study shows that drinking a glass of red wine is
>   just as good as spending an hour at the gym."

market

Bullshit masquerading as science sells stories and consumer
goods. Take for example the multibillion-dollar essential oils
industry. Millions of people believe that aromatherapy using
lavender, chamomile, rose, hyssop, sandalwood, or eucalyptus
oils can relieve stress, boost energy, aid digestion, calm nerves,
and improve skin conditions. But scientific research on the
effectiveness of essential oils for health purposes has been, at
best, jam-packed with methodological errors. In a systemic
review of 201 published studies on essential oils as alternative
medicines, only 10 were found to be of acceptable methodological quality, and even these 10 were still weak by scientific
standards. As far as the ability of aromatherapy to alleviate
hypertension, depression, anxiety, pain, and dementia, the authors of the review found the evidence unconvincing.[19]

Medical scientists from the University of Exeter Medical

School published an article in 2014 titled "The synthesis and functional evaluation of a mitochondria-targeted hydrogen sulfide donor, (10-oxo-10-(4-(3-thioxo-3H-1,2-dithiol-5-yl)-phenoxy)decyl)triphenylphosphonium bromide (AP39)" in *Medical Chemistry Communication*.[20] Soon after, someone at the University of Exeter goofed and published a press release titled "Rotten egg gas holds key to healthcare therapies."[21] This was all that *Time* and dozens of other news outlets needed to run articles such as "Scientists say smelling farts might prevent cancer" and "Sniffing your partners' farts could help ward off disease."[22]

The authors of the original article made no claims whatsoever that smelling flatulence had any medical benefits. The actual article showcased a compound—AP39—that in laboratory experiments delivers very small amounts of hydrogen sulfide to mitochondria, an organelle that is the powerhouse of cells. None of the medical research says you should inhale farts.

It is a sad case to see good science go to waste. Public misunderstandings about science often follow a familiar route: Scientist conducts an experiment and makes preliminary claims (for example, "eating and digesting celery burns more calories than it adds") → Reporters take the idea and grossly overgeneralize the findings, adding cute titles to their articles to get attention (for example, "Celery, the New Wonder Food") → Public consumes incorrect or misleading interpretations of science → Scientist attempts to correct the misinterpretations for the next two decades → Public rarely gets the full story and recalls the incorrect or misleading interpretations → Public feels that scientists change their stories

How science can get twisted

and call "bullshit" on science altogether, dismissing and distrusting any subsequent scientific claims that challenge their ideologies or interests.

It can be difficult to distinguish between science and bullshit that masquerades as science. And, unfortunately, scientists pointing to their many successes has had little influence on public perceptions of science. Scientists and advocates of science would do better to proselytize about why we should trust the scientific method as a way to know knowable things. And we would do better to respond to scientific reports as they are, not as a sensationalized recasting of knowledge to sell newspapers and magazines.

The scientific method (i.e., asking a question, doing background research, constructing a hypothesis, testing the hypothesis with an experiment, analyzing data, drawing conclusions, and communicating the results) doesn't prove anything on its own. The scientific method can only tell us what, if any, evidence there is for or against an idea. Whether we should conclude one thing or another requires interpretation of that evidence. Once again, approximating truth with evidence-based interpretations requires asking critical questions.

Questions to Ask About Scientific Evidence

When a person asserts that a claim is supported by *science*, *experiments*, or a *new study*, you should ask:

- *What* does the study actually say?
- *Where* is the scientific paper published?

← important!

- *Who* authored the scientific paper? What is their expertise? Were there any conflicts of interest?
- Is the report or claim really a result of science? [Not only are all scientific studies not created equal, but there are several reasons to believe that many "scientific" claims are not as legitimate as we would hope them to be.]
- What is the validity of the research conclusions? How rigorous were the tests of the hypothesis(es)?
- Is this the first report of its kind, or are there other reports relevant to the validity of the research conclusions? How many are there? What are their conclusions?

Why We Can Trust Science

An often overlooked step in the scientific process is how scientists communicate their results. Once a scientist completes their experiment and analyzes the data, they write up their hypotheses, methods, and conclusions in a paper and submit it to a journal. The editors of that journal then find peer reviewers who are experts in the field to assess the paper and try to find fault with the methods and conclusions. Peer reviewers are expected to recuse themselves if they have a relationship with the authors of the paper or other conflicts of interest and are charged with asking tough questions, providing honest criticism, and requesting further evidence (experiments) to substantiate strong claims. The peer review process allows the scientific community to weigh in and ensures faulty claims are less likely to be published in the literature. Once published, the entire community can weigh in by publishing rebuttals, conducting their own experiments, or criticizing the authors and the peer reviewers on social and mainstream media.

Of course, the communal process of science can go wrong. Not only are scientists human, with their own motivations, but the scientific process is not foolproof. However, over time, science is self-correcting. Looking carefully at historical cases, whether they be important discoveries that were first denied by the community or cases whereby science went awry, over time there is consensus among the scientific community or there is not. No one enjoys criticizing the work of scientists more than other scientists. This is one reason why the most sensational scientific claims, and even unexceptional ones, are not accepted by the scientific community until there's a substantial body of research replications supporting them.

As with many things, in science, patience is a virtue. It takes time to make new observations, test new ideas, form new interpretations, and reconcile competing claims. In the face of new evidence, scientists do change their minds—they revise their theories and make new recommendations—but these are strengths of science, not weaknesses.

peer reviewed!

6

EXPERT BULLSHIT DETECTORS

Used Cars, Diamonds, and Real Estate

You can fool some of the people all of the time, and you can fool all of the people some of the time, but you cannot fool all of the people all of the time. —ABRAHAM LINCOLN

If Abraham Lincoln was correct, then there should be people who are rarely duped by bullshit. Who are these people? Can they help us understand the moments when critical thinking fails and how to overcome them?

These are the questions I've asked in my qualitative research on bullshit and bullshitting. It involves identifying expert bullshit detectors and understanding their styles of thinking.

From my research, I am convinced that there are many specialized, expert bullshit detectors in our midst. Through years of experience, they've "seen everything." They've been witness to every bit of bullshit pulled in their respective professions and industries. They have highly specialized knowledge that makes it very difficult for people who don't know what they're talking about to get away with bullshit. We have much to learn from them. And so, I went out into the field to discover what they do differently from the average person.

CURTIS BAKER AND USED-CAR DEALERS

As an automobile hobbyist and enthusiast, most days Curtis Baker can be found working on an old car. I joined Baker while he refinished a 1995 Porsche 911 Carrera Cabriolet in his 60,000-square-foot warehouse. After discovering the car on CarGurus.com, he flew to Dallas, Texas, and drove it all the way home to Charlotte, North Carolina. I've never known anyone like Baker, who can work with tools, weld, talk, and eat spaghetti and meatballs, all at the same time. Baker is the perfect person to ask why car buyers are so often duped by used-car dealer bullshit.

"I don't think people are duped so much by direct bullshit from sellers. People are duped more by the facts sellers don't share with them. And only someone who doesn't really want to sell is going to tell you something that would make you avoid the car. The seller of that sweet 2006 Mercedes-Benz SL500 with 50,000 miles isn't going to tell you that soon enough you'll need to replace the hydraulic suspension that will cost you anywhere between $3,500 and $5,000. Dealers bullshit by omission." Baker believes that information omission is orchestrated by both sellers and buyers. The seller is not readily forthcoming, but the buyer participates by not asking the right questions. He believes that if buyers can demonstrate to the seller that they know what they're talking about by the questions they ask, there is considerably less room for the seller to bullshit.

What are the questions that Baker asks himself and sellers when he's interested in buying a car?

Baker explains, "I ask myself, if I was to buy this car, how could I drive it for free for the next two to three years?" Baker never buys a car he knows he can't sell at a profit later. He points to a 2010 Toyota FJ Cruiser he bought last year for $16,000. "I will drive it for a couple of years, put miles on it, and still sell it for $20,000 without doing anything to it. Why? Because I've done my homework on the Toyota FJ Cruiser. Not only are they not the gas guzzlers you think they are, but after 2014, Toyota stopped making these cars. So every day there are fewer and fewer on the roads. And when I'm ready to sell it, there will be even fewer. And people absolutely love these SUVs, so the demand will remain steady, but the supply will continue to diminish."

Baker is convinced that every car has a price that would enable you to drive it for free. "You really just need to do your homework so that no seller can bullshit you into buying something you don't really want. Almost every car model has an online forum you can check out for free. Say you're still interested in that 2001 BMW X5. Get on the online forum and see what people who have the model are complaining about. You'll find out real quick which models have crap parts and when common problems are likely to emerge. Doing your homework will also place you in a better position to develop a strong BATNA. And when the dealer says to you, 'You don't have to be such an asshole,' that's when you know you're getting a great deal."

A BATNA is the best alternative to a negotiated agreement, and whoever has a stronger BATNA wins in negotiation.[1] If you've done your homework and know everything there is to know about the make and model and invested some time to find multiple alternatives, then you're likely to have a strong BATNA. Essentially, having a BATNA means having a viable plan B.

Don't let dealers bullshit you into believing there is only one car for you. As the buyer, you have multiple dealers and cars to choose from. And with readily available alternatives from CarGurus, Autotrader, and eBay in the game, you have hundreds if not thousands of cars to choose from. Baker believes that one of the easiest ways to develop a good BATNA is to connect with multiple car sellers and "fall in love with" at least two cars—or as many as you can. Falling in love with that special one-and-only is fine when it comes to people, but not when it comes to cars and properties. Baker explains, "Falling in love with only one car or one house or one job is almost guaranteed to make you a sucker. Why? Because if you're so head-over-heels with a single option, you have no choice but to submit to details of the deal made by the single seller—you have to accept whatever terms they're offering."

If you give the illusion that you've been swept away by another car at another dealer, then you are building some leverage for your BATNA. You will feel much more comfortable pushing back on the original, higher-priced deal when you have this leverage. At a minimum, your homework will teach you something about the market for the car you want and cultivate your confidence when you try to sound like you know what you are talking about. Although there are more sophisticated BATNA schemes, Baker claims there is no chance of driving a car for free without one.

When he has an eye on a car, Baker digs to discover its true value. That is, what are the total costs given the inevitable maintenance, risks, interest to be paid, insurance costs, and depreciation of the model? And what price would he likely get for the car when he's ready to sell it? So many car buyers focus on the payments for four, six, or even seven years of financing. They focus too much on monthly payments and not enough on the true value and costs of the car. But as Baker explains, the right focus is to ask, "What are the objective facts concerning this car? What does the Carfax report say? If you see a collision on the Carfax report, you don't want that car, because unless you're planning on driving the car for the next ten years, you're going to have trouble selling it with that red flag. Let's say there was never any damage to the car, it has only 10,000 miles, and is only five years old, but has had seven different owners. The Carfax will tell you that, but you really don't want it because it could be a hot rock and you don't want to take a chance at holding it."

Baker's most useful recommendation for learning about a car is to ask the seller or dealer to take the car to a nearby, certified auto dealer to have a *pre-purchase inspection* done at your cost. Usually this runs about $350, but it's worth it. The dealer will look at everything closely and tell you about any problems. If the car has no problems, great. If the car has some problems, even better. You can use those officially reported problems as leverage with the seller. A pre-purchase inspection might sound excessive if you're buying from a trusted dealer, but you don't want to pass up this level of investigating and questioning when purchasing a used car. As Baker claims, "I've seen BMW X5s with only 35,000 miles and the transmissions fall right out of them. Because I will tell you, that oil that you see in a small puddle under the car, the dealer will just tell you that they just changed the oil and spilled a bit. Bullshit. Get the pre-purchase inspection and thank me later."

Before buying a car, Baker also likes to get a feel for whether the seller will consider an absurdly embarrassing offer. He argues that one never knows what kinds of pressures sellers or banks are under. "You might only have a 5% chance of success with the absurdly embarrassing offer, but you'll get a hit 5 out of every 100 absurdly embarrassing offers, and that's equity you just earned. I'm always amazed at how many people don't do this. And if you've done your homework and can actually sound like you know what you're talking about, you might just remind the dealer why the car might be otherwise difficult to sell. If you bring up the fact that you'll need to spend at least $1,000 on four new tires when just one of the tires blows on that four-wheel-drive Cadillac Escalade, you can get the price reduced by $1,000 just like that."

Finally, Baker adds, "I ask myself: Is this an emotional buy I'm considering? Would this be an impulse decision? The one thing I avoid at all costs is to make an emotional or impulse buy. Base your decision on facts and reason and not emotion. The only time I've ever lost money on a car was when I bought a car on emotion. I always loved the 1994 Pontiac Trans Am. It had white wheels, and I just had to have it. But I had a hell of a time getting rid of it when it came time to sell. Dealers know fully well that people buy cars for emotional reasons. That's why they want you to test-drive it. See what it feels like to ride in it with the top down. Feel its horsepower. Smell the leather. Imagine yourself driving off with it today. They really just want you to fall in love with the car so that they have some leverage in your decision. They are more than ready to give you a load of bullshit because, despite the fact that they may refer to themselves as a Customer Sales Consultant, A-Team Representative, Sultan of Sale, Sir Close-a-Lot, Sir Come Sale Away, or Mr. Miracle Worker, they are car dealers and their livelihoods depend on selling as many cars as they can. Don't forget that."

"DIAMOND" TIM TERRY AND THE DIAMOND BUSINESS

When I was a poor graduate student in 2005, I fell madly in love. Sure enough I found myself on the market for another expensive item surrounded by a whirlwind of bullshit. Fortunately, I happened to meet another expert bullshit detector who helped me out. The item was a diamond engagement ring, and that expert was Tim Terry.

Terry's opening advice to me was spot-on: "If you are looking for a diamond engagement ring, do not take your fiancée-to-be along with you." If only I had listened to Terry.

Terry believes that retail jewelers only need to pander and bullshit one of two people. Any reasonable jewelry dealer will choose to focus on the person wearing the piece—"What does she like? What does she want?"—and not on the one purchasing it. Jewelers love to see two lovebirds shopping together. As Terry warns, "If you take your fiancée-to-be along with you, you will be wrong to assume that you are on the market for a $2,000 ring. Because once she has an up-close look at what's available and starts comparing this with that, you're now looking at purchasing a $4,000 ring because it's that other ring you know she really wants."

I caught up with my old friend and master jewelry maker in Bloomington, Indiana. Owning jewelry shops in Endicott, New York, and now in Bloomington, Terry has been in the retail jewelry business for over 40 years. He left graduate school in the 1970s to pursue his passion full-time. His specialty is creating sophisticated designs, frequently inspired by nature. Anything you could possibly want in a custom piece of jewelry, Terry can produce it. But for all of his artistic skills, what I admire most about Terry is his breadth and depth of knowledge about the jewelry industry and his no-bullshit willingness to speak candidly about it.

"Even the earliest surveys conducted by De Beers Diamond Syndicate, Gerold M. Lauck, and the N. W. Ayer advertising agency found that men were the key to the market. After all, it is men who buy the large majority of all engagement rings. So, even if your fiancée-to-be isn't along with you, any jeweler worth their weight is going to know you're looking for that special ring, and they are not going to let you leave their shop without suggesting, and you thinking, that the one and only special ring can be purchased exclusively from their shop. That's why the jewelry business promotes the idea that diamonds are the gift of love. The bigger, the finer, the more exclusive the diamond, the greater the expression of love. Although they may not admit it, diamond sales suggest that young women dance to the same tune. For almost a century now, women have been encouraged to perceive diamonds as a vital part of romantic courtship and of their status and self-worth. But of course, you know that is bullshit."

The real cost of any piece of jewelry is in its details. But a surprising fact is that people spend good money for this detail, which they and others will never even notice. Terry's favorite part of the process is the addition of the fine, intricate details on the band and bezel of a ring, though not many people see the work on the band because much of it is hidden when worn.

In the United States, over 80% of women receive diamond rings (that lose over 50% of their value once they leave the shop) when they're proposed to. Why diamonds? Because the international diamond exploration, mining, retailing, trading, and manufacturing corporation De Beers Diamond Syndicate, along with a brilliant marketing campaign led by Gerold M. Lauck and the N. W. Ayer advertising agency, said so. Ever since the early 1940s, the De Beers Diamond Syndicate has fabricated the illusion of diamond scarcity, justifying the cost of diamonds by carefully restricting their supply (they've tried to purchase all the diamond mines). In reality, however, diamonds are not the rare commodity most consumers assume them to be.

With the advent of lab-grown diamonds, which are virtually

indistinguishable from their naturally sourced counterparts and often aesthetically flawless, diamonds are even less scarce. The Federal Trade Commission (FTC) requires lab-grown diamond manufacturers to use a qualifier that clearly distinguishes lab-grown diamonds as "man-made and not of natural origin." Yet the FTC's requirement is only a stand-in for implied bullshit because the reality is that lab-grown and natural diamonds are virtually the same chemically and visually. In fact, their differences are not visible to the naked eye. These diamonds only differ in their origin. If you happen to be on the market for a diamond with superior color and cut, chances are you're looking for one made in a lab. It's much easier to make than find a perfect diamond. But all of these realities don't stop jewelers from pricing natural diamonds at a 30% markup compared to lab-grown diamonds. A .75-carat natural diamond will cost you between $2,000 and $3,000, whereas a 1-carat lab-grown diamond will only cost you about $1,600.

Terry pulls out an old, tattered article by Edward Epstein published in a 1982 issue of the *Atlantic Monthly*. In the article, Epstein explains why you can't sell a used diamond for anything but a fraction of what you paid for it.[2]

Retail jewelers . . . prefer not to buy back diamonds from customers, because the offer they would make would most likely be considered ridiculously low. The "keystone," or markup, on a diamond and its setting may range from 100 to 200 percent . . . if it bought diamonds back from customers, it would have to buy them back at wholesale prices.... [R]etail jewelers almost invariably recommend to their clients firms that specialize in buying diamonds "retail."

When the four *C*s of diamonds—cut, color, clarity, and carat weight—are not enough to entice potential buyers, retail jewelers prefer to push the bullshit notion that a diamond is an investment. But no one in the diamond business believes this. In fact, the opposite is true. As Epstein explained:

> Because of the steep markup on diamonds, individuals who buy retail and in effect sell wholesale often suffer enormous losses. For example, Brod estimates that a half-carat diamond ring, which might cost $2,000 at a retail jewelry store, could be sold for only $600 at Empire.

Terry believes that consumers should be more attentive to the fact that jewelers are already dealing with an item that has an awful lot of uncertainty that comes with it. With all of the complexities of the 4 *C*s, jewelers cannot make apples-to-apples comparisons between diamonds and often just make up prices.[3]

Terry explains, "To put it delicately, gemstones like diamonds are bullshit. Even that $1,600 lab-diamond is bullshit. That lab-diamond probably shouldn't cost more than $100. The cost to harness a natural diamond requires moving tons of kimberlite from underground kimberlite pipes or offshore marine mining. That's partly why natural diamonds cost what they do. But the notions that natural diamonds are scarce, a good investment, and not just a status symbol, are not only complete bullshit, they are simply wrong. Besides, if diamonds were so rare, why is it that everyone's got one?"

Terry's belief is that if you want something special, unique, and truly rare, find someone who can make a custom piece worthy of presentation. And buy it as a symbol of love, commitment, and unity, not status. If you try to do all of that with a diamond, you're just bullshitting yourself. I'm inclined to believe Terry, especially if his claim that lab-diamonds come with an amazing 1,500% markup is correct.

"People also like to completely bullshit themselves into believing that the diamond they are wearing is brand-new. But the stark reality is that you have absolutely no idea where your diamond actually came from. Unscrupulous jewelers are notorious for switching stones—where that particular diamond came from is really a moot point. Maybe the jeweler got the diamond from a pawn shop—which is exactly where I would *CRAZY* tell a friend to get a diamond. You'll get a pawn shop diamond for one-quarter the price of wholesale and it may be better than any 'brand-new' diamond you will find otherwise."

Like Baker's dealings with used-car dealers, Terry believes that the best consumer is the informed customer. To get a fair deal, he suggests being more inquisitive. "Customers rarely ask the right questions, let alone enough questions about jewelry." Their failure to ask the right questions and focus on the key factors that reveal the true value of a piece of jewelry are central to why they are duped by jewelry bullshit time after time. Terry explains: "Customers rarely make price comparisons.

informed customer!

212 · THE LIFE-CHANGING SCIENCE OF DETECTING BULLSHIT

Asking questions about price is treated like a sacred place you don't go. But if you want to find a good deal, ask questions. Why are they charging this much for this piece? How does this piece compare to another? Is there any way to look up a price comparison? Are there any clues that the imperfections of the gemstone have been disguised by a temporary oil? There are no dumb questions—just bite the bullet and ask."

CHRISTINA PRYCE IN THE WORLD OF REAL ESTATE

With over 25 years of experience in the Lake Norman area just north of Charlotte, North Carolina, and as a 16-time winner of the Five Star Real Estate Agent Award, Christina Pryce is as knowledgeable and trustworthy as real estate agents come.[4] She also happens to be an expert bullshit detector. I know this firsthand, as both a buyer and seller. Her no-bullshit approach to real estate has literally saved me thousands of dollars.

One of the things that attracted me to Pryce is that she only holds five to six listings at any one time and doesn't overwhelm herself with dozens of clients who are looking to buy a home. It comes as no surprise that 100% of her business is obtained by word-of-mouth referrals—she doesn't advertise and has no web presence. This approach affords her time to study the market and fine-tune her craft. As she notes, "I'm not a real estate appraiser, but I've taken an appraisal course three times. Things change over time in the real estate business." She knows zoning laws and how to find appropriate houses for comparisons, as she explains, to "help" appraisers do their jobs. "People in this area often want to live on Lake Norman. When buyers ask if they could put a boat dock where there currently isn't one, the vast majority of agents will say, 'Sure thing, you can put a dock there.' But most of the time they really don't know what they are talking about. Lake Norman is a man-made lake built by Duke Energy to service their nuclear power plant—any docks must first be approved by Duke Energy, and their rules change all the time. It is heartbreaking to someone who buys a home on the lake only to discover they will never be approved for their very own dock. I avoid this altogether by doing my homework rather than bullshitting my clients."

Her "spider-sense" is founded on the recognition that bullshit is much more influential than most people realize. Pryce believes that appraising homes can be as subjective as valuing art. I find this somewhat disturbing. In an interesting study, cognitive psychologist Jonathan Fugelsang and his colleagues presented people with over 140 artist- or computer-generated abstract paintings and asked them to rate the profundity of each piece. Some of the paintings were tagged with art curator language known as International Art English (IAE).[5] IAE is a style of communication commonly employed by artists and curators to discuss artwork.[6] Rather than employing clear and concise language, IAE uses morphing verbs and turns adjectives into nouns (for example, *potential* to *potentiality*), pairs like terms (for example, *internal psychology* and *external reality*), and favors hard-to-picture spatial metaphors (for example, *culmination of many small acts achieves mythic proportions*).

In Fugelsang's studies, abstract paintings included IAE titles such as "The Pathological Interior" or "Undefined Singularity of Pain," mundane titles such as "Canvas No. 8" or "Color Mixing," or no title at all. The title had a remarkable effect. Those paintings tagged with IAE titles were rated as more profound than paintings tagged with a mundane title or no title at all.

Title! matters

The very same attempts to influence perception through language can also be found in real estate. Savvy real estate agents never use words that might convey negative things about a home they are listing. *Cozy*, *dollhouse*, or *cottage* might sound cute and whimsical, but usually these words are code for "very small." *Custom* or *unique* might characterize the pride held in a home, but potential buyers tend to think "weird corners," "tacky colors," and "wild additions" when they see these words. *Modern*, *vintage*, and *rustic* can mean that a property makes you feel like you are stepping back in time, but buyers hear "ridiculously outdated." "TLC" or "lovingly maintained" may sound to sellers like the home has so much "potential," but to buyers it signals that a property needs serious work. The worst is "buyers to verify permits," which is code for "unpermitted additions or conversions." Instead, your realtor will use code words like "beautiful," "turnkey," "spacious," "backyard paradise," "open floor plan," "redeemed to perfection," and "suite." Every realtor knows that when it comes to writing real estate ads, a surefire approach is to "sell the sizzle, not the steak"—and what often emerges is bullshit.

What most sellers don't understand is that all of the coded language is really for other *real estate agents* who represent the buyers and understand their expectations. In the business of real estate, coded language must be accurately applied. As Pryce explains, "I don't pull any punches in how I describe a listing I have for sale. If another agent shows up with interested buyers to see my listings and they don't see what they've come to expect from my description, that only damages my reputation—and reputation among real estate agents in the area is absolutely essential to a surviving and thriving real estate business." → Curse of Cassandra

When I was selling my home in the middle of the summer of 2014, two weeks after listing the home on the market our air-conditioning unit died. It turned out to be a $2,500 repair. Little did I know, Pryce had already registered my home with a seller home warranty. The repair cost me $50 to register and $100 for a service fee, saving me $2,350. Pryce explains, "I do this automatically with any sellers I'm working with because no matter how new or old a home is, things can unexpectedly go wrong. People who have a 30-year-old home want to bloviate about how their home is like new and worth at least $20,000 more than it actually is. It isn't. It's 30 years old, and worth $20,000 less than you think it is—and no one's 30-year-old home is like new—something will break before it's sold."

One of the most annoying tactics that Pryce encounters is when buyers bloviate about their ability to buy a home. "When looking at a house, a potential buyer says, 'Oh, this house is smaller than the one I'm in now. I could pay cash for this.' And more often than not, it turns out he can't, because a week later he's telling me, 'Well, interest rates are so low, I think I'll get a mortgage.' Just as it is with sellers, it is best to assume that, for whatever reason, buyers will somehow try to bullshit me."

She also dislikes when other real estate agents bloviate about their own credentials. "Reputation is everything in the real estate business. Any home valued at $400,000 or less is going to have multiple offers. Now the home seller decides which buyer they will work with, but agents can inevitably influence this decision. Agents working for the home seller do not want to work with someone who is inexperienced because the more experienced agent will be expected to do 'everything'—and nobody wants that. So, what you have is agents who are new to the area, don't really know what they are talking about, and exaggerate their experience and success. I just had another agent tell me he was doing so well in real estate that he was on pace to clear $20 million this year—and it was September. I thought to myself, 'Well, you must expect to have a killer last quarter then, because I already looked you up on the multiple listing service that shows you only cleared $5 million.' It is much better to be transparent with people you are dealing with."

She also demands that her clients be clear-eyed and realistic when it comes to the process. "My very first question is 'How are you going to buy this home?' Because the reality is many people are not ready to buy a home—they think they are, but they really are not—and I'm not interested in just taking you, or anyone else, on a grand tour of Lake Norman. Once the ability to buy a home is established, then we can start working together. And next, I want to know what my clients really want. Do they want a home for the next five to ten years? Are they looking to make a profit? What is this potential home buy really all about?"

Even if her clients have decided that they will buy a home, deciding which one can be overwhelming. To help, Pryce suggests her clients do something research scientists are all too familiar with. She asks that they open an Excel spreadsheet. In the first column of the spreadsheet, they have to list the various features of a home they want to buy, including price, location, kitchen, bathrooms, size of master bedroom, flooring, ceilings, landscaping, neighborhood, school district, distance to work, even an X-factor they might not be able to fully describe. Let's say they have 25 features that are important to them. They then decide which of the features are most and least important to them and list the features in descending order of importance. They assign each feature a weight, ranging from .00 to 1.00, to represent how much influence each feature should have in their final decision—they put that in the second column—and make sure the sum of the weights is equal to 1.00. They then add a column for each home on their short list. They rate each home on each of the features they've already identified they want to include in the decision using a one-to-five scale. They then multiply each rating by the feature's respective weight. Finally, they sum each of the products. The home with the greatest weighted-sum score is declared the winner.[7] Many judgment and decision-making experts refer to this method of decision-making as the *weighted additive model*, and it happens to be a very effective way of making decisions when multiple alternatives and features are available. It is comforting to know that some real estate agents are not relying solely on the bottom line to nudge their clients in one direction or another. Yet as a social psychologist on the lookout for bullshit, I'll continue to rely on the Excel spreadsheet.

An important discovery I've made through my qualitative research on bullshit and bullshitting is the fact that having 10–40 years of experience in bullshit does not make one a bona fide expert any more than 13 years of public schooling made me an expert student. What distinguishes a high-performing expert from the highly experienced professional is that the expert understands two things.

First, experts understand the complexity of the *sample space.* In mathematics and the study of human problem-solving, as noted earlier, a problem's sample space is all of the possible values of a broad range of variables.[8] For instance, determining the probability of obtaining a 7 on a roll of a pair of 6-sided dice requires knowing the six different rolls that could result in a 7: 1–6, 2–5, 3–4, 4–3, 5–2, and 6–1. Looking at all of the other possible outcomes of a roll of a pair of dice enables one to clearly see that a roll of 7 is the most likely outcome. The idea of a sample space can also be applied to providing consumers a product or a service. For example, an experienced auto mechanic might have enough of an understanding of what goes on in an automotive engine to get my car back up and running. An expert auto mechanic knows how to get my car back up and running but also knows the physics and mechanics of an automotive engine and how to modify it for greater efficiency. If your car is leaking oil, you want an expert, and not just an experienced auto mechanic, to diagnose the leak. That is because there are literally dozens of technical reasons a car might be leaking oil. The expert auto mechanic is better able to find and fix the source of the leak because she more fully understands all of the possible sources of the problem—she understands the sample space.[9]

Second is that all experts describe operating in their domain much like an investigator or scientist would. Experts know how to think critically about their domains of expertise. intro-spective They understand the questions that must be asked to gain important information critical to problem-solving and optimal decision-making that nonexperts may never think to ask. With intellectual humility, they are careful not to make too many assumptions, they dig deeper to clarify unsubstantiated claims and reduce uncertainties, and they refrain from forming conclusions about things until they have compelling evidence.

Over my years of research, I have asked hundreds of people I consider to be expert bullshit detectors to explain why so many people are duped by bullshit in their professions and industries. What failures in critical thinking and questioning do they see? Each and every expert bullshit detector has reported to me the very same things:

1. When people have good information they typically make good decisions. Better information doesn't always lead to better decision-making, but better

decision-making almost always requires better information.

2. Failed bullshit detection is usually about things people don't do and the questions they don't ask.

The good news is that we can learn from their approach.
Below, I've listed some common habits that will help you weed
out bullshit and make smarter decisions.

THE COLUMBO MINDSET OF EXPERT BULLSHIT DETECTORS

My ideal bullshit detector is Lieutenant Frank Columbo,
played by Peter Falk in the 1970s television series *Columbo*.
He was a homicide detective and famous for solving complicated "whodunit" murder mysteries by asking suspects "just
one more question." The last question would always be the one
that cracked the case. If you analyze empirical research on
critical-thinking skills, you will find many commonalities between the ideal critical thinker and Columbo.

What exactly does it take to put the Columbo mindset to
work? Unfortunately, there are no evidence-based answers to
these questions just yet. However, we would be remiss to ignore
well-established research on critical thinking as a guide to competent bullshit detection. Research characterizes this mindset
along four basic dimensions: inquisitive truth seeking, open-
mindedness, analytic-systematic analysis, and confident and
judicious reasoning.[10]

By asking probing, critical questions (like those listed in Chapter 5), *inquisitive truth seekers* refrain from intellectual dishonesty by bravely and actively seeking the most accurate and valid knowledge. Rather than being indifferent, inquisitive truth seekers desire to be well-informed and seek to learn new things even when the immediate usefulness of the knowledge is not entirely clear. For instance, consider this data-based claim expressed according to relative risk: "The annual injury risk per Michigan driver, resulting from a blowout with standard tires is about average, but with the improved, more costly tires the risk is half that for standard tires." Inquisitive truth seekers don't simply take this information at face value. Rather, they are willing to do the research to find the absolute risk rates, such as the probability of a serious injury due to a standard tire blowout (for example, .0000060) and compare it to the probability of a serious injury due to an improved tire blowout (for example, .0000030).[11]

By tolerating opposing views, *open-minded* people are sensitive to the possibility that their own biases shape their conclusions. It is well established that a person's attention is usually drawn to what is novel and appears relevant to them.[12] However, this fundamental tendency is countered when open-minded people resist the influence of irrelevant information on their thinking. For instance, if asked if there are more or less than 20 active volcanoes worldwide, both close- and open-minded individuals know that the number is greater than 20. Yet open-minded people tend to be more aware of how their perceptions may be biased by the information provided (20) and more likely to adjust their final estimates upward and closer to the correct answer (1,500) than close-minded people.[13]

Remaining alert to problems and anticipating the consequences, *analytic-systematic* people attempt to foresee the short- and long-term outcomes of events, decisions, and actions. Disdaining disorganization and chaos, they employ an organized and thorough approach to identifying and resolving problems. At their best, systematic people are orderly, focused, and persistent in their approach to solving, learning, and asking the right questions. Not only are analytic-systematic thinkers the type of people who use spreadsheets to organize information before making decisions, they happen to be the very same people who don't find pseudo-profound bullshit to be very profound.[14]

People who display *confident and judicious reasoning* trust in the process of critical thinking, convinced that better reasoning tends to follow from access to better information. Confident and judicious thinkers know that multiple plausible solutions to problems exist. They possess the intellectual maturity to understand that most issues are not black and white and that decisions will sometimes be made with uncertainty.

What does the Columbo critical-thinking mindset look like in practice? We can list the basic habits of critical thinking as the following:

- Having a passionate drive for clarity, precision, accuracy, relevance, consistency, logic, completeness, and fairness.

- Having sensitivity to the ways in which critical thinking can be skewed by wishful thinking.
- Being intellectually honest, acknowledging what they don't know and recognizing their limitations.
- Not pretending to know more than they do and ignoring their limitations.
- Listening to opposing points of view with an open mind and welcoming criticisms of their beliefs and assumptions.
- Basing beliefs on facts and evidence rather than on personal preference or self-interest.
- Being aware of the biases and preconceptions that shape the way the world is perceived.
- Thinking independently and not fearing disagreement with a group.
- Getting to the heart of an issue or problem without being distracted by details.
- Having the intellectual courage to face and assess ideas fairly even when they challenge basic beliefs.
- Loving truth and being curious about a wide range of issues.
- Persevering when encountering intellectual obstacles or difficulties.

Philosopher Peter Facione and the American Philosophical Association identified five critical-thinking skills in the landmark 1990 *Delphi Report*: *interpretation, analysis, evaluation, inference,* and *self-regulation*.[15] Each of these skills is essentially a different way of asking questions.

You are best able to detect bullshit when you are able to accurately *interpret* the claim. If you can answer the following questions, you can better understand the meaning and significance of a claim:

- What does the claim mean? How is it meant to be understood?
- Is there anything unclear, ambiguous, or not understood about the claim?
- How can the claim be best characterized and classified?

An expert bullshit detector *analyzes* the arguments that could be made in support of and against a claim. Engaging in analysis involves asking these questions of the claim:

- On what basis is the claim being made?
- How does the individual know the claim is true?
- What assumptions must be made to accept the claim and its conclusions as true?

When critical thinkers assess the logical strength of a claim, they engage in *evaluation.* They determine if the arguments and evidence for the claim justify the conclusions. Evaluative questions include:

- How compelling is the evidence supporting the claim?

- How well does the claim follow from a reasonable interpretation of the evidence?
- Do the results of relevant investigations speak to the truth of the claim?

Expert bullshit detectors engage in *inference,* which occurs when the relevant information needed to draw reasonable conclusions is secured and connected to the implications of the claim's truth. Inference is promoted when you can gain answers to questions like: *infer*

- What does the evidence imply?
- If the claim is true, what are the implications moving forward?
- If major assumptions supporting the claim are abandoned, how does the claim's truth stand?

Self-regulation involves assessing one's own motivations and biases and asking whether these influence one's interpretations, analyses, inferences, and evaluations of a claim. *Self regulation* Self-regulation works best when engaging in metacognitive thought (thinking about one's thoughts) by answering questions such as:

- How good was my method in evaluating the claim?
- Are my conclusions based on evidence and data, or are they based on anecdotal evidence or what I read in the news?

- Is there anything I might be missing (or wanting to miss), and are my conclusions about the claim motivated by something other than the truth in any way?

STANDARDS OF COMPARISON, REFERENCE POINTS, AND BENCHMARKS

Expert bullshit detectors tend to see things differently than the rest of us and know things we don't. Specifically, expert bullshit detectors recognize the usefulness of different standards of comparison, reference points, and benchmarks from the ones that everyone else uses. For instance, if you are asked to think about the concept of *political leaders* in general and then asked how to rate Bill Clinton, George W. Bush, and Barack Obama, you might rate them negatively. However, if you are asked to think about specific political leaders, like Adolf Hitler, Benito Mussolini, and Saddam Hussein and then rate Clinton, Bush, and Obama, you might rate them more positively. All judgments depend on standards of comparison and reference points.

Before purchasing a car, rather than focusing on specs and financing, Baker focuses on what will increase the likelihood he can sell it for a profit. When judging the value of a piece of jewelry, rather than focusing on the size of a diamond, Terry considers what went into making the piece and the finer details consumers rarely pay attention to. When dealing with clients buying homes, rather than having her clients objectively assess their subjective preferences, Pryce encourages them to create weighted additive models. Experts do not focus on what everyone else is looking at. They tend to employ effortful, critical thinking within their areas of expertise, something that does not come naturally.

Suppose a man named Dr. D makes a claim that he can miraculously locate undiscovered underground water. He claims that, rather than using expensive scientific tools, he can find water by surveying the field with two L-shaped rods about the size of metal coat hangers. Would you pay Dr. D for this service? Some people would. In fact, there is a lot of money to be earned through this method, better known as *dowsing*. But is there something to Dr. D's claim, or is it just bullshit?

An expert bullshit detector is keen to understand the claim and the basic reasoning underlying it. Dr. D's claim is that he can find undiscovered underground water with a tree branch, and he offers three arguments to prove his claim:[16] Like other professional dowsers, Dr. D tells you that objects made of natural materials, like metal rods, can be "attuned" to physical forces that emanate from other objects. He tells you that he can harness the psychic powers of the conscious self to "connect" with the item being sought. Dr. D also tells you that the subconscious "knows" the answers to all questions and some other nonsensical gibberish. Of course, none of these arguments makes any sense. An expert bullshit detector would treat Dr. D's arguments as strike one.

Second, an expert bullshit detector would be keen to notice that when dowsers like Dr. D employ their methods, they usually appear to be influenced by an extrasensory power infringing on their attempts to be perfectly still. But dowsers are not faking it. An expert bullshit detector does not appeal to the supernatural when a more natural explanation will suffice. In fact, just like Deepak Chopra's plumb bob string trick, dowsing behavior can be explained by the ideomotor effect. If you take any highly sensitive object, like a weighted string or thin, handheld metal rods greased with silicone lubricant, they will move all over the place in response to your slightest of movements, though you may remain convinced that you've stayed perfectly still all along.

Third, if we want to know if dowsing is useful for detecting water, it is critical to evaluate the method in light of an appropriate reference point. We first need to find out the likelihood of finding water by chance alone. That is, how likely are we to discover water if we were to drill random holes in a field at a depth of anywhere between 10 and 300 feet? Considering the nature of the land in which the dowser operates (i.e., the sample space) reveals the appropriate standard of comparison for evaluating a dowser's ability to detect water.

Despite widespread misconceptions that ground water is available through narrow, underground rivers, ground water more closely resembles large lakes and can be found almost everywhere beneath the land surface in the United States (albeit at varying depths). In fact, the abundance of drinkable ground water provides water to about one-half the US population.[17] Dowsers, by random chance, have a high probability of finding water in favorable terrain. That means that if ground water is present, it is hard to miss. To demonstrate that dowsing actually works, dowsing must lead to better than the already high chances of finding ground water.

After identifying an appropriate standard of comparison, an expert bullshit detector would conduct a test. One such test could involve concealing a bottle of water inside 1 of 20 numbered and otherwise empty containers. Dr. D and other dowsers (who often claim to be 100% accurate outside of controlled trials) would then be asked to use their dowsing rods to detect which container holds the bottle of water. A similar test was conducted with 500 self-proclaimed dowsers in Munich, Germany.[18] The experimenters rigged up the bottom floor of a large barn with a water pipe that could be moved along the width of the barn. Dowsers were positioned on the second floor and asked to locate the position of the pipe. After thousands of trials, the only thing demonstrated by the Munich study was the decisive failure of the dowsers. In fact, many of the dowsers performed significantly worse than chance.

With a bit of critical thinking and a careful test, it is easy for most any bullshit detector to see the truth. Paying Dr. D or any expert dowser to "find" ground water would be a lot like paying someone to tell us which water hazards on a golf course have golf balls hidden in them. Almost all golf course water hazards contain golf balls—hundreds, if not thousands of them—so it wouldn't be a remarkable thing to discover what cannot be seen directly from the surface.

Careful investigation has demonstrated that dowsing simply does not work. But you would be mistaken to think dowsing is the stuff of pseudoscience enthusiasts and has no impact on society. Indeed, belief in dowsing-like bullshit can have a much more insidious effect.

Since 2007, the annual number of terrorist incidents world-wide has averaged over 10,000, and injuries and deaths resulting from terrorist incidents have averaged more than 15,000 and 20,000, respectively. Most terrorist attacks have occurred outside the United States in places such as Syria, Iraq, Nigeria, Afghanistan, Pakistan, India, China, and Russia. The unsettling reality is that terrorist attacks can and do occur anywhere in the world. As a result, multiple efforts have been made to better detect this threat.[19]

One such effort was Advanced Detection Equipment (ADE) 651. The ADE 651 was a handheld device designed to detect explosives by the British company Advanced Tactical Security and Communications (ATSC). It had a plastic handgrip with a swiveling antenna mounted on a hinge and it required no battery, as it was powered by static electricity. All that was required was for an operator to walk a few paces to "charge" the device, holding it at a right angle to their body. The antenna swiveled in the user's hand and "tuned into the frequency" by pointing in the direction of an explosive.

The ADE appeared to be groundbreaking technology and an answer to detecting hidden terrorist explosives. With so much excitement about its potential, Iraq, Afghanistan, and 20 other countries in the Middle East and Asia entered into contracts to supply security forces with the detectors for a price of up to $60,000 each.[20] ATSC profited £50 million from sales of more than 7,000 units, and the Iraqi government alone is believed to have spent £52 million on the devices.[21] The ADE

651 was quickly adopted as a bomb-sniffing device because it offered a fast solution to a difficult problem.

There was only one problem with the ADE 651—it didn't do what ATSC's founder, Jim McCormick, claimed it could do. In fact, the ADE 651 was a piece of junk produced in the 1990s by American car dealer, commercial diver, and treasure hunter Wade Quattlebaum. Quattlebaum originally promoted the device as the Quadro Tracker to find lost golf balls. With mountains of golf balls produced as "proof," he reasoned that his device could also be marketed as a detector of other important things, like hidden stashes of marijuana, explosives, and weapons.

The Quadro Tracker allegedly worked by *dowsing*. But McCormick and the Iraqi military leaders who purchased the ADE 651 didn't care enough about the readily available facts on dowsing. Apparently, no one put the ADE 651 through a simple diagnostic test that would have surely revealed its lousy performance.[22] Major General Jihad al-Jabiri, head of Iraq's bomb squad, said, "Whether it's magic or scientific, what I care about is it detects bombs." If only Jabiri had cared more about the evidence he could have saved his country millions of pounds. McCormick and Iraqi military leaders successfully promoted the belief that the tracker could find explosives.

One group that was concerned about the truth behind the ADE 651 was the FBI. In fact, in 1996, the FBI had already permanently barred dowsing devices from being manufactured or sold as bomb detectors, declaring them to be fakes.[23] The FBI had already tested several devices like the ADE 651, and none had ever performed better than random chance. But the evidence wasn't enough. By 2009, nearly every police checkpoint and many Iraqi military checkpoints had their own ADE 651.

Because of the military's reliance on the ADE 651, suicide bombers managed to smuggle two tons of explosives into downtown Baghdad on October 25, 2009, and killed 155 people and destroyed three ministries. Video surveillance proved that the bombers would have had to pass at least one ADE checkpoint. Unfortunately, the lives lost that day were among hundreds of lives lost that could have been prevented had it not been for the investments in bullshit.[24]

When the dust settled, McCormick was convicted of three counts of fraud, sentenced to ten years of imprisonment, and ordered to forfeit cash and assets worth nearly £8 million. But the cost of McCormick's bullshit was much greater. People lost their lives because his bomb-detection devices didn't work. And for this reason, I believe endorsements of dowsing and the ADE 651 warrant three flies on the Bullshit Flies Index.

Yet there remains widespread belief in dowsing. Why do people persist in believing that dowsing works and pay big money for dowsers to work their "magic"?

People tend to find meaningful patterns in meaningless noise.[25] Combined with a willingness to pay attention to the hits while ignoring the misses, people see only what they wish to see. In the case of dowsing, what believers "see" can be characterized by the illusion known as the Texas sharpshooter fallacy.[26] The Texas sharpshooter fallacy refers to a man with a gun, but with no shooting skill. He fires a large number of bullets into the wall of a barn, proceeds to paint a bull's-eye around a cluster of bullet holes, and declares himself a sharp-shooter. Viewing data through this lens is seductive because large clusters of cases in a relatively small area create the illusion of a causal connection. Any correlations that could occur purely by chance can appear significant.

Both dowsers and non-dowsers are duped by dowsing because they fail to ask critical questions. They fail to clarify how dowsing might work. They fail to identify standards of comparison to accurately evaluate dowsing methods. And they fail to appropriately test extraordinary claims that, quite frankly, signal bullshit.

LIFE WITHOUT BULLSHIT

Better Detection, Better Disposal, Better Decisions

Whereof one cannot speak, thereof one must be silent.

—LUDWIG WITTGENSTEIN

The science of detecting bullshit may not change society—but it can have a life-changing impact on you personally. By adopting a critical posture and the power of inquisitive questioning, you awaken the natural scientist and critical thinker inside yourself.

If enough people join the collective stand against bullshit, our world will become a very different place. We won't have to listen to people talk about things they know nothing about. We won't be exposed to baseless arguments. We won't have to rely on incompetent people trying to do important jobs. Rather, we will collectively replace bullshit with evidence-based communication and reasoning, making more rational decisions based on facts, evidence, and reality.

Current research suggests that being duped by bullshit is

a result of thinking superficially rather than an inability to think. Essentially, we fail to ask the right questions when presented with bullshit. When people claim that a Moon landing was faked, that a used car will likely get us another 100,000 miles, that essential oils will calm us and provide more restful sleep, that a politician can solve all of our problems, or a Pollyannaish TED Talk speaker will save the world in only 15 minutes, it will be much easier to dispel the bullshit if everyone is asking critical questions. What agenda does the speaker have? Who is providing the evidence? How credible is the speaker? To get people to stop spreading bullshit, misinformation, fake news, and the like, we will have to get comfortable asking bullshitters, How do you know this to be true? To the best of your knowledge, is the claim accurate? What sort of evidence supports your conclusion?[1] If we do not, bullshit will only continue to pile around us while we waste precious opportunities to encourage optimal decision-making by refocusing on reality and evidence.

A MANIFESTO FOR A
NEW COMMUNICATIVE CLIMATE

Only recently has public interest in the social science of detecting bullshit intensified. With the emergence of social media, fake news, and an explosion of misinformation and disinformation, many worry that we now live in a world where opinions outweigh facts.[2]

How do we know when to reject false information that

feels true? Does a camel's hump really store water? No, it doesn't; it stores fat. Did Albert Einstein really fail math in school? No, he didn't; he excelled in math. Do suicide rates actually peak during the holidays? No, they don't; suicide rates rise in the spring. And how do we know when to accept factual information that feels false? Does an octopus really have three hearts? Yes, it does. Were Anne Frank and Martin Luther King Jr. born in the same year? Yes, they were. Is the unicorn really Scotland's national animal? Yes, it is.

Effective disposal of bullshit will take a collective effort, but it begins with each of us. As such, it's important to always keep in mind the following principles.

Bullshit Isn't a Bad Word

Some people find the word *bullshit* to be offensive. Other people find *bullshit* to be a fun word to say—but it is no laughing matter. If we collectively decide to stop being so uptight about the word and stop laughing, it would be a whole lot easier to call bullshit when we see it. We need to begin feeling comfortable using the word *bullshit* if we are going to start calling it out.

Besides, you are really missing out on a lot of fun if you're not already calling bullshit when you see it. Try calling bullshit at least once or twice a day—I assure you, there is more than enough bullshit to satisfy the need.

Rules for Calling Bullshit

Bullshitters are not our only targets. We can call bullshit on bullshit, but we can also call bullshit on lies, treachery, trickery, gossip, or injustice. In doing so, there are some rules we should follow to call bullshit respectfully and effectively.[3]

Rule #1: Don't call bullshit unless you are sure it is bullshit.

Rule #2: Be considerate. Consider the possibility that you are the one who is confused. When someone bullshits me, I've found that acting a bit confused can prompt bullshitters to clarify their claims and nudge the bullshitter toward critical thinking. It is better to allow the bullshitter him- or herself to recognize that their lack of concern for truth and evidence isn't going very far than to point out that they are wrong.

Rule #3: If the bullshitter doesn't self-correct, attack the claim, not the person.

Rule #4: Permit the bullshitter to restate their claim or to reduce their bullshit to an understandable error in reasoning resulting from an accidental failure to consider genuine evidence. Doing so is more forgiving and a more subtle pill for the bullshitter to swallow.

Rule #5: When you find yourself guilty of bullshitting, admit it. Don't double down on it. It only makes things worse. Admitting one's bullshit takes a bit of humility. When I began writing this book, I often requested that my wife scratch my back while I wrote, explaining that the wonderful sensation created by her nails on my back released endorphins that helped me to relax and focus. I know that endorphins are chemicals produced by the body and they are believed to relieve stress and pain. But the reality is, I have absolutely no idea what I'm talking about. Nor does it matter. The truth is, I wanted her company while I worked. I didn't need to frame it with bullshit to admit that her gentle caress calmed me enough to focus on the book. Perhaps I framed it with bullshit to cover my guilt for asking her to do me this favor. But she didn't comply because she believed in my endorphin argument. She complied because we support one another. When I came clean, she didn't act surprised; she already knew it was bullshit.

Rule #6: Be prepared and willing to offer evidence-based reasoning yourself when combatting bullshit. In other words, don't fight bullshit with more bullshit! Explain how available evidence leads you to a different conclusion.

CAUTION: Because calling bullshit can be a real conversation killer (people don't necessarily enjoy being called on their bullshit), you may lose some friends along the way. But you wouldn't care for "friends" who always lied to you, would you? If bullshit is more insidious than lies, then you shouldn't be accepting of people who always bullshit you.

Treat Bullshit Like Lies

Lies have consequences. Often, bullshit does not. It's time we change that. It can feel uncomfortable to confront people when they are bullshitting us. Yet we indirectly encourage bullshit when we fail to hold people accountable to the standards of genuine evidence and critical reasoning.

In my Bullshit Studies Lab at Wake Forest University, my students and I took a closer look at social perceptions of and reactions to bullshitters and liars. We wanted to know: Do people evaluate bullshitters differently than liars? Our study was a simple one. Participants read a brief scenario about Tom the bullshitter or Jim the liar. Without ever using the words *bullshitter* or *liar*, both scenarios held the very same content; both were described as talking with other people about the advantages and disadvantages of daycare for pre-kindergarten children. The difference was that the bullshitter (Tom) communicated something he *didn't know to be true or false*, nor did he care to know, whereas the liar (Jim) communicated what *he knew to be false*. What did we find?

Although the bullshitter was rated negatively, respondents rated the liar significantly more harshly than they did the bullshitter. Overall, respondents did not perceive the bullshitter and liar to differ with respect to a lack of concern for their listeners or their attempts to maintain positive impressions. When we accounted for all of the reasons why bullshitters might be viewed less negatively than liars, only three factors were predictive of respondents' evaluations: ignorance, dishonesty, and expressing opinions. Specifically, the bullshitter was rated as more ignorant and more likely to be simply expressing an opinion than the liar, whereas the liar was rated as being more dishonest than the bullshitter. People are sensitive to the qualitative differences between bullshitting and lying. Ignorance is not desirable, but it is significantly more tolerable than outright lies. Both are deceptive in disguising their disinterest in the truth, but we don't see them the same way. Herein lies a major problem with bullshit: our reactions to bullshit leave our thinking vulnerable to distortions that our reactions to lies do not.

Suppose I told you that Frazier is the last name of the boxer who later became known as Muhammad Ali, a full house is the poker hand in which all of the cards are of the same suit, or that St. Peter's ceiling was painted by Michelangelo. All of these statements sound feasible and they could all pass as bullshit or lies—but they are all false. Yet you are more likely to misremember them as true simply because your brain has just processed them. Even highly knowledgeable people misremember such falsehoods as true after a single suggestion that the falsehood is legitimate.[4]

What if you later learned that everything I just said about Muhammad Ali, a full house in poker, and St. Peter's ceiling were in fact lies—that I knew the truth but I tried to deceive you? Not only would you probably feel negatively about me, but you would also think differently about the information. You would know that all of the information was unequivocally false. On the other hand, what if you later learned that everything I said about Muhammad Ali, a full house in poker, and St. Peter's ceiling was bullshit—that I didn't actually know if what I said was true or false, and that I didn't really care to know? Now it isn't clear to you if the information is true or false. With bullshit, some or all of it could be true and some or all of it could be false. Of course, something that is treated as true will have a different effect on judgment and decision-making than something that is treated as false. The best defense is to treat bullshit like we do lies—as false—until we obtain evidence to conclude otherwise.

Peer Pressure and Behavioral Contagion

To develop a culture that promotes calling out bullshit when it is needed, calling bullshit must become a contagious behavior. This can be accomplished by changing the unwritten rules of which behaviors are considered acceptable in society—our *social norms*.[5] To understand how this can work, it is important to understand how social norms drive our behavior.

There are two ways in which people are influenced by others. The first is called *normative social influence*. It is a result of our social desire to be liked and accepted by other people, which stems from our human identities as social beings with affiliation and companionship needs. We go along with what other people do in order to be liked and accepted by them. We often conform to a group's beliefs and behaviors publicly without necessarily believing what other people are doing or saying. The second is called *informational social influence*. Our need for information and our tendency to believe what others tell us results in conformity to what others are doing or saying. These pressures of conformity drive the widespread acceptance and use of bullshit as an acceptable form of communication. However, we can use them to help us reverse the process.

Although people are generally guided by their personal values and norms, in social settings they are motivated to do the right thing. When motivated to do the right thing, behavior is most frequently guided by one's perception of how people typically behave in the setting (i.e., the *descriptive norm*), as well as one's perception of what is acceptable and socially valued in the setting (i.e., the *injunctive norm*). As such, descriptive norms represent what we think most people *actually do* in a particular situation, whereas *injunctive norms* represent what we think we *should do* in that situation.[6]

Overall, social behavior tends to be guided more by descriptive than injunctive norms, especially when injunctive norms may be unclear or when people believe that injunctive norms are typically ignored in the situation. People do behave in accordance with injunctive norms if they are particularly strong norms or prompted by things within the situation (for example, NO SMOKING signs).[7]

Calling bullshit is currently an injunctive norm—it is what we should do when we are exposed to bullshit. For calling bullshit to become more commonplace, calling bullshit will either need to transform from an injunctive norm to a descriptive norm or the injunctive norm must become a more salient feature of our society.

Research conducted by social psychologists Robert Cialdini and his colleagues provides an example of how descriptive norms can be replaced by injunctive norms to affect littering behavior. In one study, they manipulated the environment by either clearing a city library parking lot of any and all litter, such as paper cups and cigarette stubs, or spreading the litter throughout the parking lot.[8] When a patron exited the library and walked to the parking lot, an experimenter hurried ahead of the patron to model a behavior. In some cases, the experimenter just walked by and did nothing out of the ordinary. In some other cases, the experimenter modeled the descriptive norm by dropping an empty fast-food bag on the ground, subtly communicating that *this is what people do in this situation*. In other cases, the experimenter modeled the injunctive norm by picking up a littered fast-food bag from the ground, subtly communicating that *littering is wrong*.

How were the littering behaviors of the library patrons affected? When patrons returned to their cars, they found a large flyer slipped under the driver's side of their vehicle's windshield. The flyer appeared on all the other cars too (the experimenters put them there). The patrons could litter by throwing the flyer on the ground or dispose of it later by placing the flyer inside their car.

The baseline percentage of littering when the experimenter had modeled neither the descriptive nor injunctive norm was about 38%. It didn't matter if the area was clean (37%) or a mess (38%). When the descriptive norm was modeled by the experimenter littering, it communicated two different messages, depending on the state of the parking lot. When the parking lot was littered, the experimenter's behavior reminded patrons that *people often litter here*. The experimenter served as just one more example of the type of behavior that leads to a messy parking lot in the first place. In this situation, patrons littered about 30% of the time. In the clean parking lot, however, the experimenter's littering behavior communicated a different message. Now the behavior stood out as unusual, by reminding patrons that most people don't litter in this area—which is why it looked so clean. In this situation, patrons littered 11% of the time. However, when the injunctive norm was made salient by seeing the experimenter picking up someone else's litter—suggesting that littering is wrong—littering among patrons was substantially reduced to about 5% in both the clean (7%) and littered (4%) parking lots.

In another study of prosocial behavior, Cialdini and his colleagues made residents of a California neighborhood more aware of energy usage levels in their community.[9] Neighborhood households were first identified as consuming energy either above or below the average for the neighborhood. Some households were mailed a basic postcard highlighting the descriptive norm by detailing how much energy they had used that week and how much energy the average household in their neighborhood had used. Other households were mailed a more detailed postcard highlighting both the descriptive and injunctive norms by including a smiley face if they had consumed less energy than the average household or a sad face if they had consumed more energy than the average household.

Weeks later, Cialdini and his colleagues measured energy usage again. Households mailed the basic postcard significantly cut back and conserved energy if they had been consuming more energy than average, but significantly increased usage if they had been consuming less energy than average. However, households mailed the more detailed postcard, which also highlighted the injunctive norm, significantly cut back and conserved energy if their usage had been above average and did not significantly increase their usage if it was already below average. A simple smiley face reminded people to either join the rest of the neighborhood in conserving energy or that they were already doing the right thing and to keep on doing it.[10]

Cialdini's research demonstrates that what we think we should do (injunctive norms) can become more powerful than what we usually do (descriptive norms) and produce more desirable behavior. It shouldn't be too surprising, given that injunctive norms tap conformity and that seeing someone demonstrate injunctive behavior reminds us what our society approves and disapproves of. If other people see us litter, we will feel embarrassed, looking like selfish slobs. While we know that littering is bad, other injunctive norms—like calling bullshit—are not always present or salient to us. In order to promote socially beneficial communication behaviors, we need to draw attention to relevant norms. Anything that makes anti-bullshit injunctive norms more salient can be harnessed to create positive communication changes.[11]

If increasing the salience of injunctive norms can stop people from littering, get people to clean up others' litter, and get people to reduce their energy usage, surely it can be used to promote calling bullshit. If we can get the ball rolling, *behavioral contagion*, the pervasive tendency of people to unconsciously copy others' behavior, should take care of the rest. Behavioral contagion can occur when a single person displays novel behavior worthy of copying. If people see you calling bullshit and witness the outcome, they may think about it for the very first time. They might ask you about it. They might consider trying it out themselves. And before you know it, everyone is calling bullshit.[12]

Behavioral contagion encourages adopting risky behaviors, joining social movements and protests, experimenting with avant garde fashions, or adopting new technologies when we see any of these things modeled.[13] Likewise, making calling bullshit commonplace will require social modeling and encouragement.

Failure to call bullshit only permits bullshit to proliferate. But it's not inevitable, or, shall I say, it is within our power to not be victims of bullshit. By refusing to accept bullshit, we can promote critical thinking and evidence-based communication. When bullshitters no longer have influence, we can force bullshitters to do some critical thinking before engaging with us. When they comply, we need to further promote critical thinking and evidence-based communication by rewarding their good character and decision to be smarter.

Assess the Need for Evidence

Don't be fooled into assuming, as I once did, that all that is needed to correct misinformed bullshitters is evidence. Studies show that overwhelming people with compelling evidence does very little to change minds.[14]

I once debated a pro-gun friend about the benefits of better gun control. I did my homework. I found empirical evidence suggesting violence may be triggered by other acts of violence, but guns make the violence worse.[15] I found Leonard Berkowitz and Anthony LePage's studies conducted over 50 years ago, which showed that the presence of a gun sitting on a table, relative to an object not associated with violence (like a badminton racquet), elicits stronger aggressive responses from participants.[16] I found that more than 32,000 people die and over 67,000 people are injured by firearms each year in the United States. I found that firearm injuries result in over $48 billion in medical and work-loss costs annually.[17] I believe attitudes about firearms should be scientifically driven and evidence-based, but none of these facts mattered to my pro-gun friend! Low-need-for-evidence individuals may portray themselves as concerned with or conveying evidence, but evidence is not actually important to them. Only high-need-for-evidence individuals care about evidence.

Many beliefs are based on bullshit. Evidence—a snapshot of reality——is necessary to understand the risks associated with decision alternatives and identify effective solutions to problems. People who advocate for unfounded ideas usually mean well and truly believe their stance is correct and benefits society. The problem is, they don't care about the implications of their views, much less the actual data. As the saying goes, the road to hell is paved with good intentions.

Yet providing relevant evidence and encouraging critical thinking is at the heart of public campaigns to address bias and correct misinformed beliefs.[18] Unfortunately, these attempts sometimes fail to improve judgment and decision-making, even when people are motivated to employ rational judgment, because people have already made up their minds.[19]

In fact, in some cases, presenting a litany of facts can backfire. The *backfire effect* occurs when people respond to evidence that refutes their misinformed beliefs by doubling down on their original beliefs.[20]

So if presenting bullshitters with evidence and encouraging them to think critically is unlikely to improve their judgment or decision-making, what will work? Bullshitters usually know enough to think they are right, but not enough to know why they are wrong. An effective way to persuade a low-need-for-evidence bullshitter to engage in critical thinking and seek out new evidence is to model the behavior ourselves. If we can get low-need-for-evidence individuals to begin asking, "What am I really saying?" and "How do I know this to be true?," we can nudge them to replace bullshit with evidence-based reasoning. Getting bullshitters to find inconsistencies themselves will be a much more potent motivator than our best counterarguments would ever be.

Define the Problem Accurately

A great challenge with bullshit is that it makes even simple problems difficult to comprehend and the solutions to those problems more difficult to see. Because they are not concerned with truth and evidence, bullshitters tend to make things unnecessarily more difficult than they need to be.[21] With a lack of regard for truth and evidence, bullshitters are likely to problem-solve by imposing unnecessary limitations and rules or ignoring evidence and facts that would otherwise lead to viable solutions. Bullshitters block themselves and us from creative thinking by their reliance on anecdotal evidence, past experiences, and unwarranted assumptions. When people begin to critically analyze and recognize bullshit for what it is, solutions quickly and easily emerge.

Take for instance the response to COVID-19 in the United States. The collective goal was to slow the spread of the virus until a vaccine could be discovered and distributed on a mass scale. The only available prescription was to wear a mask, wash your hands frequently, and physically distance. But amid the 2020 presidential election, things like wearing masks and social distancing became political issues. As simple and banal as these guidelines were, the choice not to wear a mask and physically distance represented for some a rejection of oppression and a fight for freedom. It was peak bullshit, but that didn't stop millions of Americans from supporting bullshit claims that mask-wearing and physical distancing were no longer necessary, which resulted in actions that increased the spread of the virus several times over.[22] Had individual judgment and decision-making not been clouded by bullshit, stricter mask-wearing and physical distancing would surely have slowed the virus and fewer lives would have been lost. Disposing of unnecessary bullshit makes every problem, including health crises, easier to solve.

Intellectual Humility

Of course, no one can always be right or aware of everything. To be intellectually humble is to protect yourself against the inevitable tug of bullshit when you're trying to prove you know something about everything. An attitude of *intellectual humility* involves recognizing that our knowledge is limited and that our beliefs might be wrong. By the same token, you will do well to be wary of perennial know-it-alls.[23]

Intellectual humility is a great starting point for bullshit detection and reduction for two very important reasons: First, when we are not expected by others and ourselves to have an opinion about everything or to be the authority on everything, there is a lot less pressure to have all of the answers. It is when we work outside of the confines of our knowledge or abilities that we tend to bullshit.

Second, considering the possibility that we are wrong protects against bullshit reasoning by letting us entertain alternatives to our conclusions. Someone who thinks they can speak knowledgably about everything tends to endorse the very first things that come to mind, despite the fact that the very first things that come to mind are rarely correct. Humbly recognizing you don't know everything and holding a passionate commitment to the truth can help you avoid bullshit reasoning.

↳ *recognize you don't know everything*

The hallmark of the educated thinker and competent communicator is to counter the pull of bullshit reasoning with critical thinking and evidence-based reasoning. Practicing data-driven, rational decision-making requires being aware of and certain about the real world as much as possible. Doing so will involve giving up fantasies about how the world works that may be comforting but ultimately distort our perceptions of reality. It will require coming to grips with the reality that wanting and wishing things to be true does not make them so. It will require recognizing that it is our nature to be biased, and that science is our only systematic safeguard against such bias. Failing to meet these requirements, and continuing onward with a bullshit mindset, will have dire consequences.

If we assume that we "know everything," we cannot learn. If it becomes okay to admit to ourselves and others that we don't know everything, we place ourselves in a position to learn. If we collectively buy into the notion that we and everyone around us doesn't "know everything," there will be little obligation to provide uninformed opinions and baseless arguments. In other words, there will be less motivation to engage in bullshitting.

Because bullshit often leads decision makers away from reality, the compunction to bullshit should puzzle and disturb us. Our attitudes and beliefs ought to be sacred to us because they are fundamental to our decisions.[24] Humans have beliefs about who we are, our past, our present, our future; beliefs about where we've been, where we're going, our families and friends; beliefs about our neighborhoods, the society we live in, and about the way things are and the way they should be; beliefs about politics, religion, medicine, law, energy, the environment, and our workplace. Our beliefs and attitudes shape our identities and guide our behaviors and reactions. Beliefs and attitudes guide our interpersonal relationships and motivate our decisions. We respond not to the world as it actually is, but to the world as we believe it to be.

It is my hope that you are motivated to lock arms with allies interested in evidence and truth and in joining the great

struggle against bullshit. The truth is, a world with less bullshit won't happen without a collective effort. We must make
calling bullshit part of our communication culture. It is the
responsibility of each of us to search for the truth, discern fact
from fiction, and communicate what we know to be true, not
just what we want or hope to be true. Fighting bullshit on an
individual level contributes to the collective struggle to rid our
culture of bullshit. I can assure you, the benefits are worth the
effort.

Even when conformity is at its strongest, it only takes one
person to call bullshit for what it is and stop its unwanted effects. We know that under the right circumstances, what people think they *should do* can outweigh the influence of what
people *tend to do*.[25] Armed with evidence and perhaps a few
allies, you can play an important role in the struggle against
bullshit. And, don't forget, calling bullshit can be great fun!
Disposing of it entirely is even better. In a future without so
much bullshit, better judgment and decision-making await us.

Legend has it that at the door of the academy he founded
in Athens, Plato engraved, "Let no one ignorant of geometry
enter." Presumably, not as an end in itself but as a prerequisite,
understanding geometry indicated that the student already had
the ability to go beyond their level of sensible experience to
reason about the world in a thoughtful way. By the same token, I propose that students shouldn't be permitted to exit the
gates of their schools unless they've learned how to think critically and scientifically. Critical and scientific thinking skills
are essential for citizens to have. Giving people information
and facts and hoping they will figure everything out on their

own is insufficient. Giving people the skills to weigh things like conflicting evidence and understand the inner workings of their own minds enlarges their vision and can advance our society far beyond that which bullshit reasoning can. My hope is that *The Life-Changing Science of Detecting Bullshit* will help more of us travel farther down that road of rationality.

rationality
critical-thinking skills

ACKNOWLEDGMENTS

There are many people I wish to thank. Foremost among these are my stunning wife, Lina, and my indomitable daughter, Sydney (my first readers). Their patience and understanding have afforded me the necessary time to indulge in this project. They have also taught me that it doesn't take a PhD in psychology to digest the ideas discussed within *The Life-Changing Science of Detecting Bullshit*.

The Life-Changing Science of Detecting Bullshit had its beginning after I read analytic philosopher Harry Frankfurt's most wonderful essay, "On Bullshit," a third time. The 20-page essay-turned-book not only changed the direction of my research, but it changed my life. I am eternally grateful to Harry Frankfurt.

Special thanks are extended to Robbie M. Sutton, an editor for the *Journal of Experimental Social Psychology*, for taking my research on bullshitting seriously when so many other editors desk-rejected my work for no apparent reason. Special thanks are also extended to Bret L. Simmons and Tiffany A. Brown, for liking that very first article and nudging me (twice) to do a TEDx Talk at the University of Nevada, Reno. And, of course, I could never forget the unstoppable David Burkus for connecting me to my most brilliant literary agent, Giles Anderson. I am indebted to Giles Anderson's fine literary sense, timeliness, and pinpoint accuracy. Special thanks also go to Kate Adams for her editing of an earlier version of this project.

The plain truth is *The Life-Changing Science of Detecting Bullshit* would have never been completed without my incredible editor, Pronoy Sarkar at St. Martin's Press. Pronoy Sarkar treated me with far more patience, confidence, and lack of ridicule than I deserved through the journey of the writing process, and has given me textual and substantive criticism of incalculable value. When he writes his own book someday, I will be the very first to read it.

I could not have hoped for a more killer book cover than that designed by Jonathan Bush, nor could I have hoped for better managing and copy editors than Alan Bradshaw and Katherine Haigler.

Special thanks are extended to my prodigious colleagues in the Department of Psychology at Wake Forest University—most especially the remarkable Catherine E. Seta and John J. Seta—they provided much-needed support in the early challenges of the empirical work that supports this project.

Through the long journey of my formal and informal education, I have had the privilege of meeting many special people who have taught me most everything I know about bullshit and its detection. I am grateful for all of them—I offer my sincere thanks to Jeffrey M. Bates, Constance A. Beatty, Danielle L. Beatty, Thomas J. Beatty, Eric R. Buzard, W. Keith Campbell, Jim Cox, Patty Cox, Ryan J. Frickanish, Earl J. Ginter, Alan G. Gittis, Brian A. Glaser, David B. Gray, Steve Grossman, Sherry E. Haggins, Daisy I. Hayden, Michael A. Hayden, Edward R. Hirt, Sonya S. Hissem, Natasha M. Howard, Darwin Huey, Anna Kuntz, Fred Kuntz, Gary Lagana, Robert T. Lewis, Mary Lytle, Mark T. Mangino, B. Eugene Nicholson, Sean C. O'Shea, Sharon A. Petrocelli, Walter S. Petrocelli, Annette Petrocelly, Celeste Y. Petrocelly, Kenneth L. Petrocelly, Nancy L. Ritsko, Julio I. Rojas, Kenneth Rutto, Wesley "Kippy" Rutto, Steven J. Sherman, Donald A. Strano, Alma S. Taubensee, Tom H. Taubensee, Alexi "Chebet" Towett, Beatrice C. Towett, Catherine C. Towett, Martha C. Towett, William C. Towett, Rick "Connors" Venezie, Sandra K. Webster, Karen Williams, and Maxie F. Williams.

The Life-Changing Science of Detecting Bullshit covers much ground, but it can be no more satisfactory than the experimental studies upon which I relied. My endnotes indicate, I hope, where my gratitude rests, but they doubtlessly fall short of acknowledging the full weight of my indebtedness to contemporary experimental social psychology. In addition to their everyday use, the words *bullshit* and *bullshitting* are now technical terms as used here and in psychology and philosophy. A deeper understanding of bullshitting might be one of the single most important intellectual and social issues that we face at the moment. Fostering the concern for truth, and paying attention to what is said—and how it is being said—are likely to be the most straightforward but significant means of improving the integrity and impact of empirical knowledge. I am grateful that the field of experimental social psychology will be at the forefront of that movement.

APPENDIX

Problems in Thinking

Affect Heuristic. Making snap judgments and decisions on the basis of feelings rather than facts (i.e., going with your gut).

For example, "I want to go camping—it reminds me of cozy campfires and roasted marshmallows." "I don't—camping reminds me of being chased by a bear and running for my life."

All-or-Nothing Thinking. Endorsing a dichotomous, black-and-white style of thinking by viewing situations categorically and ignoring other possibilities.

For example, "If this investment for the future isn't a total success, it's a complete failure."

Anchoring and Insufficient Adjustment. Estimating frequencies or likelihoods based on incomplete computations or insufficient adjustments from arbitrary initial values.

For example, if asked, "Are the calories in this one serving of chocolate cake more or less than 90? How many calories do you think it contains?" A person might guess 200, failing to sufficiently adjust upward due to the low anchor (90 calories) provided in the original question. A slice of chocolate cake contains about 500 calories.

Anecdotal Fallacy. Broad generalization using only anecdotal evidence or vivid examples.

For example, "My uncle smoked a pack of cigarettes every day and chewed tobacco for 50 years and he never got lung cancer. Therefore, tobacco products don't cause lung cancer."

Appeal to Authority. Using arguments made by an "authority figure" in support of an idea, even when the authority figure has no expertise in the area.

For example, "NBA star Kyrie Irving said that astrophysics is useless and the Earth is flat."

Appeal to (False) Consensus. Believing and arguing that something is true because everyone in the vicinity appears to believe or like the idea.

For example, "Most sports fans think that college athletes should be paid like salaried workers and should be permitted to use performance-enhancing drugs because everybody else is doing so anyway. Therefore, college athletes should be paid and no longer penalized for using performance-enhancing drugs."

Appeal to Ignorance. Arguing that something must be true because it can't be proven false.

For example, a friend says, "The Russians are secretly spying on our every move and putting chemicals in our water to alter our minds." When you try to point out that this is a baseless conspiracy theory, they counter, "Can you prove that it isn't happening?"

Appeal to Nature. Arguing that something is good because it is natural or that something is bad because it is artificially produced.

For example, "Natural herbs and essential oils are much better for treating diseases and ailments than are regulated pharmaceuticals because drugs are full of artificial chemicals and toxins."

Argument from Consequences and a Belief in a Just World. Basing the truth of a claim on its alignment with a dogmatic just-world ideology.

For example, "Good things come to those who are good."

Availability Heuristic. Judging the frequency of a category or the probability of an event based on the ease with which it comes to mind.

For example, many believe car accidents and homicides are leading causes of death in the United States because the media devotes more coverage to homicides and car accidents than diabetes and stomach cancer, which kill twice as many Americans annually.

Catastrophizing. Predicting negative future outcomes without considering other likely outcomes or falsely enhancing the probability that a negative event will result in a complete disaster.

For example, "I'll be so upset if the Red Sox don't win the first game of the seven-game series; they'll lose the entire series and I won't be able to function at all."

Composition Fallacy/Erroneous Induction. Suggesting that a general principle is true because some parts of it appear to be true.

For example, "I throw my dead nickel-cadmium batteries right in with the regular trash and it doesn't make any difference at all to my water or my neighbor's water. Therefore, sending nickel-cadmium batteries to the landfills are not hazardous to the environment."

Confirmation-Biased Testing. Selectively collecting data and failing to seek out objective facts, interpreting new information to support existing beliefs, recalling details that uphold one's preexisting beliefs, and ignoring any information that challenges one's beliefs.

For example, a scientist might say to their colleague, "We conducted nine experiments but only one of them supported our hypothesis. Let's submit that one experiment for publication. The other eight studies probably weren't significant because of human error."

Confusing Correlation with Causation. Assuming that because two events or variables co-occur that one causes the other. Correlation does not imply causation.

For example, "A survey shows that people who sent their children to college are more likely to report having gray hair than people who did not send their children to college. Therefore, sending your children to college causes your hair to turn gray."

Disqualifying or Discounting. Unfairly and unreasonably concluding that positive or negative evidence does not count.

For example, "He just fell flat on his face, but that doesn't mean he's clumsy or not athletic."

Division/Erroneous Deduction. Recklessly arguing that because something is a member of a group that each member of the group possesses the same characteristics the group is believed to possess.

For example, "My brother moved to California and struck it rich. Therefore, money grows on trees in California and all Californians are rich."

Emotional Reasoning. Making misguided conclusions that something is true because one "feels" it strongly while ignoring or discounting evidence to the contrary.

For example, "I just know she's the one for you—I can see it. Don't make a mistake and let her go."

Equivocation. Mistakenly equating two meanings of a word/phrase or failing to see that using a word/phrase in two different ways can make the argument invalid.

For example, "All trees have bark. Every dog has a bark. Therefore, every dog is a tree."

False Analogy. Using perceived similarities to infer additional similarities that have yet to be observed.

For example, "Bette and May both drive pickup trucks. Bette is a successful actress. Therefore, May must also be a successful actress."

False Dichotomy. Assuming there are only two sides to a claim.

For example, "I can't find my wallet! It was either stolen by aliens or I never had it. I know I had it. Therefore, it must have been stolen by aliens."

Fixed Labeling. Putting a fixed, global label on something without considering that the evidence might more reasonably lead to a much different conclusion.

For example, "He's a loser." "He's no good."

Framing Effect. Forming judgments and making decisions on whether the claims are framed negatively or positively.

For example, "This frozen yogurt has 20% fat. Nope, I don't want it. Ah, this frozen yogurt is 80% fat free. Yes, I'll take three."

Gambler's Fallacy. Falsely believing that good things will occur directly following unfavorable/undesirable outcomes.

For example, "My favorite baseball player is a .330 hitter. He's failed to reach base in his first four at bats. He is surely due to get a hit now."

Genetic Fallacy. Arguing solely based on someone's or something's history, origin, or source, overlooking any differences to be found in the present situation.

For example, "Uncle Bernard claims that the senator was taking bribes. But we all know he isn't credible. You can't trust anything Uncle Bernard says."

Hasty Overgeneralization. The practice of making sweeping generalizations on the basis of pure coincidence or a few examples.

For example, "As all babies do, my son had his first shot of hepatitis B vaccine within the first 12 hours after birth. Later, my son developed autism. Therefore, all vaccines cause autism."

Hindsight Reasoning. Perceiving events that have already occurred as having been more predictable than they actually were. One can always explain outcomes (or data) better once the results are known.

For example, "I just knew Married for Money was going to win the horse race—if only I'd gone with my gut."

Hot-Hand Fallacy. Falsely believing that good things will occur directly following favorable/desirable outcomes.

For example. "I've won three hands of poker in a row. In the next hand I'm raising the stakes. Tonight, I can't lose."

Illusory Correlation. Perceiving a relationship between two or more things where none actually exists or perceiving a stronger relationship than one that actually exists.

For example, "My phone always rings when I am in the shower."

Impossible-to-Disprove Claims. Forgetting that extraordinary claims require extraordinary evidence and equating things that cannot be effectively or entirely disproven with truth.

For example, "Surely the Red Sox would have won the 1986 World Series if only evil aliens from outer space hadn't intervened."

Mind Reading. Believing that one knows what others are thinking and failing to consider other likely possibilities.

For example, "My boss thinks I'm a complete idiot, but he's the one who doesn't know what he's doing."

Outcome Bias. Evaluating a prior decision on the basis of the outcome rather than using the probabilities and values of the decision alternatives.

For example, "At the races, Rusty placed a $10 bet on horse 13 to win or place in the race and he won $20—Rusty isn't too shabby. In the same race, Tom placed a highly improbable $10 straight superfecta bet on horses 4–13–7–8 and he won thousands—Tom is a genius."

Overconfidence and Bold Statements. Forgetting that just because someone makes a claim with confidence and conviction doesn't mean that the claim is true.

For example, "Baby, I'll love you forever."

Post-Hoc Fallacy. Illegitimately assuming that an earlier event caused a later event due to the order in which they occurred.

For example, "I really wish they wouldn't keep turning on that seat-belt sign so much. Every time they turn the seat-belt sign on, this flight gets bumpy."

Prosecutor's Fallacy. Assuming the conditional probability of A given B is the same as the conditional probability B given A.

For example, "I know lots of people play the lottery, but the chance of any one person winning the lottery is so small. Nick won the Pennsylvania lottery twice within a span of 5 years, so he must have somehow rigged the drawing."

Representativeness Heuristic. Judging the similarity or belonging-ness of one thing N to a category Z based on the degree to which N is similar to the essential properties of the category Z.

For example, "Sonia Dara is a swimsuit model who doesn't look anything like someone who went to Harvard, therefore she did not. George Clooney is a famous actor who looks like he went to Harvard, therefore he did."

Scientific Language. Automatically assuming that something is valid because it sounds science-y.

For example, "Cosmic balance is simply the way the universe transcodes the raw potential of quantum energy into unbridled happiness."

Simulation Heuristic. Judging an event based on the ease with which alternatives to reality are mentally simulated.

For example, "I played the daily pick-three lottery tonight and my ticket number was 2–5–8. If only that 8 had been a 9. I'm disgusted."

Slippery Slope Fallacy. Insisting that a relatively small first step leads to a chain of related events culminating in some significant effect.

For example, "Stop playing so many computer games! That's why you always get a cold!" "If you don't stop, don't ever complain that you can't find a job and that you ended up a drug addict, because I swear, you will never get one red cent of your inheritance because I don't have criminal children!"

Spurious Correlations from "Big Data." Believing that statistical anomalies found in large data sets after conducting a large number of random analyses reveals the true relationships between variables.

For example, "Did you know that margarine consumption is linked to divorce rates?" "The number of films Nicholas Cage appears in each year varies along with the number of female editors of the *Harvard Law Review* that year." "The rates of homicide by steam, hot vapors, and other hot objects rises and falls with the age of the winner of the Miss America beauty pageant."[1]

Straw Man Fallacy. Distorting or misrepresenting an argument in order to make it easier to dismiss/defeat.

For example, "Unlimited access to marijuana would contribute to massive increases in drug abuse. Anyone who supports legalizing marijuana wants to kill everyone."

FACT-CHECKING

There are a number of excellent fact-checking sources available online.

centerforinquiry.com	datacolada.org	debunker.club
factcheck.org	factczech.cz	fivethirtyeight.com
ncahf.org	politifact.com	poynter.org
quackwatch.org	rationalwiki.org	reporterslab.org
sciencemag.org	scientificamerican.com	sharonahill.com
skepdoc.info	skeptic.com	skepticalinquirer.org
skeptical-science.com	skeptico.blogs.com	snopes.com

These sites exist to make bullshit detection easier. When visiting these sites, take note of the quality of evidence they provide in order to support their evaluations of the evidence. Most of these sites bring together documentation and statistical evidence to support their conclusions about the truth or falsity of a claim—far more work than anyone is willing and likely to undertake on their own, but necessary for critical thinking and bullshit detection.

The very best way to find the validity and implications of scientific claims is to go straight to the source: primary articles that report the results. The large majority of articles can be found for free online. If you can't locate an article using Google Scholar, try e-mailing the author of the publication. Scientists love when people want to learn about their research.

NOTES

Introduction

1. Editors of the American heritage dictionary (2009). *The American Heritage dictionary of the English language* (4th edition). Houghton Mifflin Harcourt.

2. Frye, C., & Jefferson, R. (Producers). (2017, February 17). Kyrie Irving-DEEP in thought 30,000 feet high above (7) [Audio podcast episode]. In *Road trippin' with RJ & Channing*. https://www.nba.com/cavaliers/features/road-trip-170217

3. Nguyen, H. (2018, April 2). Most flat Earthers consider themselves very religious. YouGov. https://today.yougov.com/topics/philosophy/articles-reports/2018/04/02/most-flat-earthers-consider-themselves-religious. Also see a reanalysis of the survey reported by Branch, G., & Foster, C. A. (2018, October 24). Yes, flat-Earthers really do exist: Despite some methodological flaws, a recent poll credibly indicates that flat-Earthery persists. *Scientific American.* https://blogs.scientificamerican.com/observations/yes-flat-earthers-really-do-exist/

4. Matyszczyk, C. (2017, February 18). NBA star Kyrie Irving believes Earth is flat. *CNET.* https://www.cnet.com/news/nba-star-kyrie-irving-believes-earth-is-flat/; Ruff, R. (2017, February 17).

Kyrie Irving actually believes Earth is flat. *Bleacher Report.* https://bleacherreport.com/articles/2693635-kyrie-irving-actually-believes-earth-is-flat

5. Boghossian, P., & Lindsay, J. (2019). *How to have impossible conversations: A very practical guide.* Lifelong Books; Randi, J. (1980). *Flim-flam! The truth about unicorns, parapsychology, and other delusions.* Lippincott & Crowell Publishers; Sagan, C. (1995). *The demon-haunted world: Science as a candle in the dark.* Random House; Shermer, M. (1997). *Why people believe weird things: Pseudoscience, superstition, and other confusions of our time.* W. H. Freeman and Company.

6. Remarkably, Eratosthenes also used his calculations to determine the circumference of the entire planet to be about 25,000 miles; an impressive feat, given his methods.

7. Magellan never completed the journey, dying in the Battle of Mactan on April 27, 1521.

8. Misinformation about the Great Wall of China's visibility dates back to a 1932 *Ripley's Believe It or Not!* cartoon that claimed the wall is the only man-made structure visible to the human eye from the Moon. The belief has persisted since Neil Armstrong returned from the Moon in 1969. Armstrong consistently reported that he could see continents, lakes, and splotches of white on blue from the Moon, but that he could not make out any man-made structures from the lunar surface. Hvistendahl, M. (2008, February 21). Is China's great wall visible from space? *Scientific American.* https://www.scientificamerican.com/article/is-chinas-great-wall-visible-from-space/

9. WebMD & Flowers, A. (2019, May 20). How to figure out your dog's age. Fetch by WebMD. https://pets.webmd.com/dogs/how-to-calculate-your-dogs-age; Purina (2017, June 14). Dog age calculator: Dog years to human years. https://www.purina.com/dog-age-calculator

10. O'Connor, A. (2004, October 26). The claim: You lose most of your body heat through your head. *New York Times.* https://www.nytimes.com/2004/10/26/health/the-claim-you-lose-most-of-your-body-heat-through-your-head.html; Pretorius, T., Bristow, G. K., Steinman, A. M., & Giesbrecht, G. G. (2006). Thermal effects of whole head submersion in cold water on non-shivering humans. *Journal of Applied Physiology, 101,* 669–675.

11. Hoover, D. W., & Milich, R. (1994). Effects of sugar ingestion expectancies on mother-child interactions. *Journal of Abnormal Child*

Psychology, 22, 501–15; Kinsbourne, M. (1994). Sugar and the hyperactive child. *New England Journal of Medicine, 330,* 355–356; Krummel, D. A., Seligson, F. H., & Guthrie, H. A. (1996). Hyperactivity: Is candy causal? *Critical Reviews in Food Science and Nutrition, 36,* 31–47.

12. Hemilä, H., & Chalker, E. (2013). Vitamin C for preventing and treating the common cold. *Cochrane Database of Systematic Reviews, 1,* CD000980.

13. Edevane, G. (2018, June 9). Kyrie Irving flat Earth theory: Celtics point guard says he's happy to start a conversation. *Newsweek.* https://www.newsweek.com/kyrie-irving-flat-earth-theory-967934

14. McIntyre, L. (2019). *The scientific attitude: Defending science from denial, fraud, and pseudoscience.* MIT Press.

15. Oreskes, N. (2019). *Why trust science.* Princeton University Press. For a concise summary, see Oreskes, N. (2019). Put your faith in science. *TIME Magazine, 194*(21), 23–24.

16. Frankfurt, H. J. (2005). *On bullshit.* Princeton University Press. https://bookauthority.org/book/On-Bullshit/0691122946

17. Bullshit as a study topic began with Frankfurt's 20-page article "On Bullshit" in 1986, now a cult classic, in which he gave the word "bullshit" the definition that we use today; Frankfurt, H. (1986). On bullshit. *Raritan Quarterly Review, 6,* 81–100; Petrocelli, J. V. (2018). Antecedents of bullshitting. *Journal of Experimental Social Psychology, 76,* 249–258.

18. Although one's own beliefs or opinions may, in fact, be based on bullshit, simply stating one's own beliefs or opinions (for example, "In my opinion, Americo's Pizzeria pizza is the best!") is not bullshit because the fact that this statement reflects one's beliefs and opinions is self-evident. Making a declaration (for example, "There is no other pizza on Earth better than Americo's Pizzeria pizza") or offering an argument, while simultaneously having little to no concern for verifiable evidence, is by definition bullshitting. If you say, "This book I am currently reading should be read by everyone because it is the best book ever written," it may be your opinion. But not only are there many ways to test your claim's validity, people will want to know how many books, and what kinds of books you have read to judge the validity of your claim. In this case, you are not lying; the statement could be true. If one is explaining their belief based on verifiable evidence, then they are not bullshitting. People frequently trust in argument (and clear bullshit), and that may not be a bad thing when verifiable evidence is hard to come by. On the

other hand, when making claims, argument does not count as evidence. Evidence is held to a higher standard to avoid bullshit claims and conclusions. Bullshit is also distinct from *mere nonsense*, as bullshit implies, but does not contain, adequate meaning or truth.

- Bullshitting is also distinct from propaganda and spin. Propaganda and spin are forms of communication, often used by political campaigners, sales agents, advertisers, and others who aim to influence the attitude of a population. Used to further an agenda, propaganda often plays to people's emotions by appealing to fears, popular desires, prejudices, and irrational hopes, rather than using rational argument, creating a rather distorted vision of the world. Similar to the liar, the propagandist is aware of the truth and frames or distorts the truth to further their agenda by influencing the attitudes of others. The bullshitter, on the other hand, is not concerned with truth and is not using it as a tool of mass persuasion. In fact, as Frankfurt surmised, sometimes one is compelled to bullshit in order to test out the reactions of those around them or to feel what it is like to say such bullshit. Although propaganda could conceivably involve bullshit, not all bullshit is propaganda. Petty, R. E., Wells, G. L., & Brock, T. C. (1976). Distraction can enhance or reduce yielding to propaganda: Thought disruption versus effort justification. *Journal of Personality and Social Psychology, 34*, 874–884; Pratkanis, A., & Aronson, E. (2001). *Age of propaganda: The everyday use and abuse of persuasion* (Rev. edition). W. H. Freeman; Sussman, G. (2011). Introduction: The propaganda society. In G. Sussman (Ed.), *The propaganda society: Promotional culture and politics in global context* (pp. 1–21). Peter Lang.

- Bullshit is also sometimes referred to as "baloney" by Carl Sagan. However, bullshit is distinct from other commonly used synonyms, including *misinformation*, *pseudo-profundity*, and *nonsense*. See Sagan, C. (1995). *The demon-haunted world: Science as a candle in the dark.* Random House.

- The disregard for evidence, characteristic of the bullshitter, should not be confused with sociopathic behavior. The sociopath behaves without regard for society in general, its rules and laws, and the rights of others. He or she also fails to feel remorse or guilt and has a tendency to display violent behavior. While it is quite likely that sociopathic behavior involves some degree of bullshitting, bullshitting in and of itself is not sociopathic. Mealey, L. (1995). The sociobiology of sociopathy: An integrated evolutionary model. *Behavioral and Brain Sciences, 18*, 523–599; Pemment, J.

(2013). Psychopathy versus sociopathy: Why the distinction has become crucial. *Aggression and Violent Behavior, 18*, 458–461.

19. Morgan, M., & Grube, J. W. (1991). Closeness and peer group influence. *British Journal of Social Psychology, 30*, 159–169; Reis, H. T., Collins, W. A., & Berscheid, E. (2000). The relationship context of human behavior and development. *Psychological Bulletin, 126*, 844–872; Smith, E. R., & Mackie, D. M. (2016). Representation and incorporation of close others' responses: The RICOR model of social influence. *Personality and Social Psychology Review, 20*, 311–331.

20. WhiteHouse.gov. (2017, January 21). Remarks by President Trump and Vice President Pence at CIA headquarters. *WhiteHouse.gov.* https://www.whitehouse.gov/briefings-statements/remarks-president -trump-vice-president-pence-cia-headquarters/

21. Dale, D. (2019, June 2). The first 5,276 false things Donald Trump said as U.S. president. *Toronto Star.* https://projects.thestar.com /donald-trump-fact-check/

22. WhiteHouse.gov. (2017, January 21). Remarks by President Trump and Vice President Pence at CIA headquarters. *WhiteHouse.gov.* https://www.whitehouse.gov/briefings-statements/remarks-president -trump-vice-president-pence-cia-headquarters/

23. ABC News. (2017, January 25). Transcript: ABC News anchor David Muir interviews President Trump. David Muir's interview with President Trump on Jan. 25, 2017. *ABC News.* https://abcnews.go .com/Politics/transcript-abc-news-anchor-david-muir-interviews -president/story?id=45047602

24. After Trump's press secretary Sean Spicer rebuked the media for accurately reporting the relatively small crowds at Trump's inauguration, US Counselor to the President Kellyanne Conway told NBC's *Meet the Press* that Spicer wasn't lying; he was simply using "alternative facts."

25. Dale, D. (2019, June 2). The first 5,276 false things Donald Trump said as U.S. president. *Toronto Star.* https://projects.thestar.com /donald-trump-fact-check/; see also Wikipedia. Inauguration of Donald Trump: Crowd size. https://en.wikipedia.org/wiki/Inauguration _of_Donald_Trump#Crowd_size

26. WhiteHouse.gov. (2020, April 23). Remarks by President Trump, Vice President Pence, and members of the Coronavirus Task Force in press briefing. *WhiteHouse.gov.* https://www.whitehouse.gov /briefings-statements/remarks-president-trump-vice-president-pence -members-coronavirus-task-force-press-briefing-31/

27. Glatter, R. (2020, April 25). Calls to poison centers spike after the president's comments about using disinfectants to treat coronavirus. *Forbes.com*. https://www.forbes.com/sites/robertglatter/2020/04/25/calls-to-poison-centers-spike-after-the-presidents-comments-about-using-disinfectants-to-treat-coronavirus/?sh=29ec84021157; Kluger, J. (2020, May 12). Accidental poisonings increased after President Trump's disinfectant comments. *Time.com*. https://time.com/5835244/accidental-poisonings-trump/; Slotkin, J. (2020, April 25). NYC Poison Control sees uptick in calls after Trump's disinfectant comments. *NPR.org*. https://www.npr.org/sections/coronavirus-live-updates/2020/04/25/845015236/nyc-poison-control-sees-uptick-in-calls-after-trumps-disinfectant-comments; see also Islam, S., et al. (2020). COVID-19–related infodemic and its impact on public health: A global social media analysis. *American Journal of Tropical Medicine and Hygiene*, *103*, 1621–1629.

28. WhiteHouse.gov. (2020, April 24). Remarks by President Trump at a signing ceremony for H.R. 266, Paycheck Protection Program and Health Care Enhancement Act. *WhiteHouse.gov*. https://www.whitehouse.gov/briefings-statements/remarks-president-trump-signing-ceremony-h-r-266-paycheck-protection-program-health-care-enhancement-act/

29. Ross, M., McFarland, C., & Fletcher, G. J. (1981). The effect of attitude on the recall of personal histories. *Journal of Personality and Social Psychology*, *40*, 627–634.

30. McGuire, W. (1964). Inducing resistance to persuasion: Some contemporary approaches. In L. Berkowitz (Ed.), *Advances in Experimental Social Psychology, Vol. 1* (pp. 191–229). Academic Press.

1: Costs of Bullshit

1. Boone, V. (2017, March 1). Jarvis 2012 Estate Grown Cave Fermented Reserve Merlot (Napa Valley). *Wine Enthusiast*. https://www.winemag.com/buying-guide/jarvis-2012-estate-grown-cave-fermented-reserve-merlot-napa-valley/

2. Krebiehl, A. (2020, March 1). Pleil 2015 Ried Gerichtsberg Merlot (Niederösterreich). *Wine Enthusiast*. https://www.winemag.com/buying-guide/pleil-2015-ried-gerichtsberg-merlot-niederosterreich/

3. Boiling, C. (2019, October 8). A simple way to boost wine sales. InternationalWineChallenge.com.https://www.internationalwinechallenge .com/Canopy-Articles/a-simple-way-to-boost-wine-sales.html; Caputo, T. (2007, October 1). Marketing matters: Wine competitions that help you sell. WinesVinesAnalytics.com. https:// winesvinesanalytics.com/columns/section/23/article/50637/Wine -Competitions-That-Help-You-Sell; USA Wine Ratings. (2018, September 14). How to market your wine awards. *USA Wine Ratings.* https://usawineratings.com/en/blog/insights-1/how-to-market-your -wine-awards-112.htm

4. Hodgson, R. T. (2008). An examination of judge reliability at a major U.S. wine competition. *Journal of Wine Economics, 3,* 105–113.

5. Morrot, G., Brochet, F., and Dubourdieu, D. (2001). The color of odors. *Brain and Language, 79,* 309–320.

6. Quandt, R. E. (2007). On wine bullshit: Some new software? *Journal of Wine Economics, 2,* 129–135.

7. Krumme, C. (2009, June 18–20). *A nose by any other name: Descriptors as signals for wine price.* Paper presented at the 3rd Annual Conference of the American Association of Wine Economists in Reims, France. Similar results were reported by Ramirez, C. D. (2010). Do tasting notes add value? Evidence from Napa Wines. *Journal of Wine Economics, 5,* 143–163.

8. ((Retail Price—Wholesale Price) / Wholesale Price) × 100%. The retail price is the selling price paid by the consumer and the wholesale price is the total cost to seller to provide the good or service.

9. Bond, R. L. (2008, May 25). Finding the right price for your retail products. *Entrepreneur.com.* https://www.entrepreneur.com/article/193986. Greeting cards carry a 200% markup, printer ink 300%, furniture 400%, hotel minibar 400%, phone charger 672%, movie popcorn 900%, that obviously overpriced cap and gown you bought for commencement 1,011%, eyeglass frames 1,329%, seat ticket at a New York Yankees game 1,567%, HDMI cable 1,900%, coffee shop coffee 2,900%, bottled water 4,000%, Prozac 4,451%, psychic phone call 9,186%, and crystal healing 2,493,828%; Cetron, A. (2019, August 25). 16 of the most outrageously overpriced products. Money Talks News. https:// www.moneytalksnews.com/19-of-the-most-outrageously-overpriced -products/; Zhang, M. (2014, July 17). 37 products with crazy-high

markups. Business Insider. https://www.businessinsider.com/personal
-finance/products-high-markups-2014-7

10. Federal Bureau of Investigation Internet Crime Complaint Center.
(2014, December 31). 2014 Internet Crime Report. https://www.fbi
.gov/news/news_blog/2014-ic3-annual-report

11. Miller, R. L., & Balcetis, E. (2005). Palm readers, stargazers, and scientists. *Skeptical Inquirer*, *29*(5), 44–49.

12. Gilbert, D. T. (1991). How mental systems believe. *American Psychologist*, *46*, 107; Gilbert, D. T., Krull, D. S., & Malone, P. S. (1990).
Unbelieving the unbelievable: Some problems in the rejection of false
information. *Journal of Personality and Social Psychology*, *59*, 601–613;
Levine, T. R. (2014). Truth-default theory (TDT): A theory of human
deception and deception detection. *Journal of Language and Social Psychology*, *33*, 378–392; Levine, T. R. (2019). *Duped: Truth-default theory
and the social science of lying and deception*. University Alabama Press.

13. Gilbert, D. T., Tafarodi, R. W., & Malone, P. S. (1993). You can't not
believe everything you read. *Journal of Personality and Social Psychology*,
65, 221–233.

14. Dawes, R. M. (1975). The mind, the model, and the task. In F. Restle,
R. M. Shiffrin, N. J. Castellan, H. R. Lindman, & D. B. Pisoni (Eds.),
Cognitive theory, Vol. 1 (pp. 119–129). Erlbaum.

15. Nickerson, R. S. (1998). Confirmation bias: A ubiquitous phenome-
non in many guises. *Review of General Psychology*, *2*, 175–220; Wason,
P. C. (1960). On the failure to eliminate hypotheses in a conceptual task. *Quarterly Journal of Experimental Psychology*, *12*, 129–140;
Wason, P. C. (1968). Reasoning about a rule. *Quarterly Journal of Experimental Psychology*, *20*, 273–281; Wason, P. C., & Johnson-Laird,
P. N. (1972). *Psychology of reasoning: Structure and content*. Harvard
University Press. For interesting exceptions, see Cosmides, L. (1989).
The logic of social exchange: Has natural selection shaped how humans reason? Studies with the Wason selection task. *Cognition*, *31*,
187–276; Cox, J. R., & Griggs, R. A. (1982). The effects of experience
on performance in Wason's selection task. *Memory and Cognition*, *10*,
496–502; Gigerenzer, G., & Hug, K. (1992). Domain-specific reasoning: Social contracts, cheating and perspective change. *Cognition*, *43*,
127–171; Griggs, R. A., & Cox, J. R. (1982). The elusive thematic-
materials effect in Wason's selection task. *British Journal of Psychology*,
73, 407–420; Kirby, K. N. (1994). Probabilities and utilities of fictional

outcomes in Wason's four-card selection task. *Cognition, 51*, 1–28; Manktelow, K. I., & Over, D. E. (1991). Social roles and utilities in reasoning with deontic conditionals. *Cognition, 39*, 85–105; Wagner-Egger, P. (2007). Conditional reasoning and the Wason selection task: Biconditional interpretation instead of reasoning bias. *Thinking and Reasoning, 13*, 484–505.

16. Petrocelli, J. V., Martin, J. L., & Li, W. Y. (2010). Shaping behavior through malleable self-perceptions: A test of the forced-agreement scale effect (FASE). *Journal of Research in Personality, 44*, 213–221; Ross, L., Lepper, M. R., & Hubbard, M. (1975). Perseverance in self-perception and social perception: Biased attribution processes in the debriefing paradigm. *Journal of Personality and Social Psychology, 32*, 880–892.

17. Bargh, J. A. (1994). The four horsemen of automaticity: Awareness, efficiency, intention, and control in social cognition. In R. S. Wyer & T. K. Srull (Eds.), *Handbook of social cognition* (2nd ed., pp. 1–40). Erlbaum; Bargh, J. A., & Chartrand, T. L. (1999). The unbearable automaticity of being. *American Psychologist, 54*, 462–479; Bargh, J. A., & Ferguson, M. J. (2000). Beyond behaviorism: On the automaticity of higher mental processes. *Psychological Bulletin, 126*, 925–945; Greenwald, A. G., & Banaji, M. R. (1995). Implicit social cognition: Attitudes, self-esteem, and stereotypes. *Psychological Review, 102*, 4–27.

18. Haidt, J. (2001). The emotional dog and its rational tail: A social intuitionist approach to moral judgment. *Psychological Review, 108*, 814–834; Haidt, J. (2004). The emotional dog gets mistaken for a possum. *Review of General Psychology, 8*, 283–290.

19. Sloman, S., & Fernbach, P. (2017). *The knowledge illusion: Why we never think alone.* Riverhead Books. See also Hemmatian, B., & Sloman, S. A. (2018). Community appeal: Explanation without information. *Journal of Experimental Psychology: General, 147*, 1677–1712; Lawson, R. (2006). The science of cycology: Failures to understand how everyday objects work. *Memory and Cognition, 34*, 1667–1675; Rabb, N., Fernbach, P. M., & Sloman, S. A. (2019). Individual representation in a community of knowledge. *Trends in Cognitive Sciences, 23*, 891–902; Rozenblit, L., & Keil, F. (2002). The misunderstood limits of folk science: An illusion of explanatory depth. *Cognitive Science, 26*, 521–562.

20. Nisbett, R. E., & Wilson, T. D. (1977). Telling more than we can know: Verbal reports on mental processes. *Psychological Review, 84*, 231–259.

21. Kuhn, D. (1991). *The skills of argument.* Cambridge University Press; Kunda, Z. (1990). The case for motivated reasoning. *Psychological Bulletin, 108*, 480–498; Nisbett, R. E., & Wilson, T. D. (1977). Telling more than we can know: Verbal reports on mental processes. *Psychological Review, 84*, 231–259; Perkins, D. N., Farady, M., & Bushey, B. (1991). Everyday reasoning and the roots of intelligence. In J. F. Voss, D. N. Perkins, & J. W. Segal (Eds.), *Informal reasoning and education* (pp. 83–105). Erlbaum.

22. Rapaille, C. (2006). *The culture code: An ingenious way to understand why people around the world buy and live as they do.* Broadway Books; Wilson, T. D., Lisle, D. J., Schooler, J. W., Hodges, S. D., Klaaren, K. J., & Lafleur, S. J. (1993). Introspecting about reasons can reduce post-choice satisfaction. *Personality and Social Psychology Bulletin, 19*, 331–339. In another study conducted by Wilson, college students involved in relationships were given a questionnaire and asked to "list all the reasons you can think of why your relationship with your dating partner is going the way it is" and instructed to try to "fill up the page" with their analysis. Doing this caused participants to change their minds about how their relationship was going. If participants wrote down positive reasons, they tended to feel more positively, but if they wrote down negative reasons, they tended to feel more negatively. Bringing to mind thoughts that are inconsistent with one's initial feelings (probably some bullshit) tends to change one's attitudes. Apparently, answering detailed questions about one's relationship or thinking about reasons for the relationship in the first place can change the way people construe their relationships, leading to attitude change. Once again, however, the effects of analyzing reasons tended to wear off over time. People's original "hard to explain" attitudes return. Thus, if people make important decisions right after analyzing reasons—such as deciding whether to break up with their boyfriend or girlfriend—they might make a decision they later regret. This is because right after analyzing reasons people tend to focus on the things that are easy to put into words (for example, "I really like his hair") and ignore feelings that are hard to explain (for example, that special chemistry). But it isn't bullshit that matters in the long run. Rather, it's

those harder-to-explain feelings that reemerge or were never really absent in the first place. Wilson, T. D., & Kraft, D. (1993). Why do I love thee?: Effects of repeated introspections about a dating relationship on attitudes toward the relationship. *Personality and Social Psychology Bulletin, 19*, 409–418.

23. The Myers-Briggs Company. (2020, May 16). ISTJ: MBTI® personality profile. https://eu.themyersbriggs.com/en/tools/MBTI/MBTI-personality-Types/ISTJ

24. Grant, A. (2013). Goodbye to MBTI, the fad that won't die. *Psychology Today*. https://www. https://www.psychologytoday.com/us/blog/give-and-take/201309/goodbye-mbti-the-fad-won-t-die

25. Fleeson, W. (2004). Moving personality beyond the person-situation debate: The challenge and the opportunity of within-person variability. *Current Directions in Psychological Science, 13*, 83–87; Sherman, S. J., & Fazio, R. H. (1983). Parallels between attitudes and traits as predictors of behavior. *Journal of Personality, 51*, 308–345.

26. Liberman, V., Samuels, S. M., & Ross, L. (2004). The name of the game: Predictive power of reputations versus situational labels in determining prisoner's dilemma game moves. *Personality and Social Psychology Bulletin, 30*, 1175–1185.

27. Paul, A. M. (2004). *The cult of personality: How personality tests are leading us to miseducate our children, mismanage our companies, and misunderstand ourselves*. Free Press.

28. The inequalities in the effort necessary to produce, detect, and dispose of bullshit are more affectionately known as *Brandolini's Law*, or as Alberto Brandolini (an Italian independent software development consultant) suggests, the *Bullshit Asymmetry Principle*: "The amount of energy needed to refute bullshit is an order of magnitude bigger than to produce it." Brandolini, A. (@ziobrando). (2013, January 11). The bullshit asimmetry [*sic*]. Twitter. https://twitter.com/ziobrando/status/289635060758507521.

29. Fazio, L. K., Brashier, N. M., Payne, B. K., & Marsh, E. J. (2015). Knowledge does not protect against illusory truth. *Journal of Experimental Psychology: General, 144*, 993–1002.

30. Alcock, J. E. (2018). *Belief: What it means to believe and why our convictions are so compelling*. Prometheus Books.

31. Cook, T. D., & Flay, B. R. (1978). The temporal persistence of experimentally induced attitude change: An evaluative review. In L.

Berkowitz (Ed.), *Advances in experimental social psychology* (Vol. 11). Academic Press; Cook, T. D., Gruder, C. L., Hennigan, K. M., & Flay, B. R. (1979). History of the sleeper effect: Some logical pitfalls in accepting the null hypothesis. *Psychological Bulletin, 86,* 662–679; Gruder, C. L., Cook, T. D., Hennigan, K. M., Flay, B. R., Alessis, C., & Halamaj, J. (1978). Empirical tests of the absolute sleeper effect predicted from the discounting cue hypothesis. *Journal of Personality and Social Psychology, 36,* 1061–1074; Priester, J., Wegener, D., Petty, R., & Fabrigar, L. (1999). Examining the psychological process underlying the sleeper effect: The elaboration likelihood model explanation. *Media Psychology, 1,* 27–48.

32. Petrocelli, J. V., Seta, C. E., & Seta, J. J. (2021). When bullshitters are more persuasive than liars: Using the sleeper effect to test the insidious bullshit hypothesis. Unpublished raw data.

33. Petty, R. E., & Cacioppo, J. T. (1986). *Communication and persuasion: Central and peripheral routes to attitude change.* Springer-Verlag.

34. Petrocelli, J. V. (2021). Bullshitting and persuasion: The persuasiveness of a disregard for the truth. *British Journal of Social Psychology, 60;* also see Petrocelli, J. V., Watson, H. F., & Hirt, E. R. (2020). Self-regulatory aspects of bullshitting and bullshit detection. *Social Psychology, 51,* 239–253.

35. Between 1941 and 1945, Nazi Germany and its collaborators systematically murdered some 6 million Jews, around two-thirds of Europe's Jewish population.

36. Dali, L. Y. (1996). *Calamity and reform in China: State, rural society, and institutional change since the Great Leap Famine.* Stanford University Press; Dikötter, F. (2018). *Mao's great famine: The history of China's most devastating catastrophe, 1958–62.* Bloomsbury; Jisheng, Y. (2013). *Tombstone: The Great Chinese Famine, 1958–1962.* Farrar, Straus and Giroux; Shapiro, J. R. (2001). *Mao's war against nature: Politics and the environment in revolutionary China.* Cambridge University Press; Thaxton, R. A. (2008). *Catastrophe and contention in rural China: Mao's Great Leap Forward famine and the origins of righteous resistance in Da Fo Village.* Cambridge University Press.

37. *Time Magazine.* (1958). Death to sparrows. *Time Magazine, 71*(18), 28.

38. Pantsov, A. V., & Levine, S. I. (2012). *Mao: The real story.* Simon & Schuster.

2: Bullibility

1. Greenspan, S. (2009). *Annals of gullibility: Why we get duped and how to avoid it*. Praeger; Greenspan, S. (2009). Foolish action in adults with intellectual disabilities: The forgotten problem of risk-unawareness. In L. M. Glidden (Ed.), *International review of research in mental retardation* (Vol. 36, pp. 145–194). Elsevier; Greenspan, S., Loughlin, G., & Black, R. (2001). Credulity and gullibility in people with developmental disorders: A framework for future research. *International Review of Research in Mental Retardation, 24*, 101–135.

2. Rotter, J. B. (1980). Interpersonal trust, trustworthiness, and gullibility. *American Psychologist, 35*, 1–7; Teunisse, A. K., Case, T. I., Fitness, J., & Sweller, N. (2020). I should have known better: Development of a self-report measure of gullibility. *Personality and Social Psychology Bulletin, 46*, 408–423.

3. Markopolos, H. (2010). *No one would listen: A true financial thriller*. John Wiley & Sons.

4. Gregoriou, G. N., & Lhabitant, F.-S. (2009). Madoff: A flock of red flags. *Journal of Wealth Management, 12*, 89–97.

5. The long list includes Fairfield Sentry-Fairfield Greenwich Group, Banco Santander, Kingate Management, Rye Investment Management-Tremont Group, Bank Medici of Austria, Ascot Partners, Access International Advisors, Fortis Bank Nederland, Thema International Fund, HSBC, Genevalor Benbassat & Cie, Aurelia Finance, Union Bancaire Privée, Natixis, Royal Bank of Scotland, Sterling Equities, Elie Wiesel, and the Elie Wiesel Foundation for Humanity.

6. Greenspan, S. (2009). Fooled by Ponzi: How Bernard Madoff made off with my money, or why even an expert on gullibility can get gulled. *Skeptic, 14*(4), 20–25.

7. Chew, R. (2008, December 15). How I got screwed by Bernie Madoff. *Time*. http://content.time.com/time/business/article/0,8599,1866398,00.html

8. Forer, B. R. (1949). The fallacy of personal validation: A classroom demonstration of gullibility. *Journal of Abnormal and Social Psychology, 44*, 118–123; Petty, R. E., & Brock, T. C. (1979). Effects of Barnum personality assessments on cognitive behavior. *Journal of Consulting and Clinical Psychology, 47*, 201–203; Stajano, F., & Wilson, P. (2011). Understanding scam victims. *Communications of the ACM, 54*, 70.

9. Many sources conclude that P. T. Barnum never actually said this.

10. Petrocelli, J. V., Martin, J. L., & Li, W. Y. (2010). Shaping behavior through malleable self-perceptions: A test of the forced-agreement scale effect (FASE). *Journal of Research in Personality, 44,* 213–221; Sherman, S. J. (1980). On the self-erasing nature of errors of prediction. *Journal of Personality and Social Psychology, 39,* 211–221.

11. Costa, P. T., & McCrae, R. R. (1991). Facet scales for agreeableness and conscientiousness: A revision of the NEO personality inventory. *Personality and Individual Differences, 12,* 887–898; Lee, K., & Ashton, M. C. (2004). Psychometric properties of the HEXACO Personality Inventory. *Multivariate Behavioral Research, 39,* 329–358.

12. Bègue, L., Beauvois, J.-L., Courbet, D., Oberlé, D., Lepage, J., & Duke, A. A. (2015). Personality predicts obedience in a Milgram Paradigm. *Journal of Personality, 83,* 299–306.

13. Milgram, S. (1963). Behavioral study of obedience. *Journal of Abnormal and Social Psychology, 67,* 371–378; Milgram, S. (1974). *Obedience to authority: An experimental view.* Harper & Row.

14. Carter, N. L., & Weber, J. M. (2010). Not Pollyannas: Higher generalized trust predicts lie detection ability. *Social Psychological and Personality Science, 1,* 274–279.

15. Yamagishi, T., Kikuchi, M., & Kosugi, M. (1999). Trust, gullibility, and social intelligence. *Asian Journal of Social Psychology, 2,* 145–161; Yamagishi, T., & Yamagishi, M. (1994). Trust and commitment in the United States and Japan. *Motivation and Emotion, 18,* 129–166.

16. Haney, C., & Zimbardo, P. G. (1998). The past and future of U.S. prison policy: Twenty-five years after the Stanford Prison Experiment. *American Psychologist, 53,* 709–727; Zimbardo, P. G. (1971, October 25). The power and pathology of imprisonment [Congressional record] (Serial No. 15). Hearings before Subcommittee No. 3 of the Committee on the Judiciary, House of Representatives, Ninety-Second Congress, First Session on Corrections, Part II, Prisons, Prison Reform and Prisoner's Rights: California. US Government Printing Office.

17. Some discussions of Zimbardo's Stanford Prison Experiment have used strong verbiage in attempt to "debunk" the conclusions, suggesting that the cruelty on the part of the guards was not a result of playing the role and was instead due to experimenter goading and prodding. The best discussions can be found here: Haslam, S. A., Reicher, S. D.,

& Van Bavel, J. J. (2019). Rethinking the nature of cruelty: The role of identity leadership in the Stanford Prison Experiment. *American Psychologist, 74,* 809–822; Reicher, S., & Haslam, S. A. (2006). Rethinking the psychology of tyranny: The BBC Prison Study. *British Journal of Social Psychology, 45,* 1–40; Zimbardo, P. G., & Haney, C. (2020). Continuing to acknowledge the power of dehumanizing environments: Comment on Haslam et al. (2019) and Le Texier (2019). *American Psychologist, 75,* 400–402.

18. Nisbett, R. E., & Wilson, T. D. (1977). Telling more than we can know: Verbal reports on mental processes. *Psychological Review, 84,* 231–259.

19. Langer, E. J., Blank, A., & Chanowitz, B. (1978). The mindlessness of ostensibly thoughtful action: The role of "placebic" information in interpersonal interaction. *Journal of Personality and Social Psychology, 36,* 635–642.

20. Cialdini, R. B. (2006). *Influence: The psychology of persuasion.* New York: Harper Business.

21. Kuhn, D. (1991). *The skills of argument.* Cambridge: Cambridge University Press.

22. Glassner, A., Weinstock, M., & Neuman, Y. (2005). Pupils' evaluation and generation of evidence and explanation in argumentation. *British Journal of Educational Psychology, 75,* 105–118.

23. Borgida, E., & Nisbett, R. E. (1977). The differential impact of abstract vs. concrete information on decisions. *Journal of Applied Social Psychology, 7,* 258–271; Reyes, R. M., Thompson, W. C, & Bower, G. H. (1980). Judgmental biases resulting from differing availabilities of arguments. *Journal of Personality and Social Psychology, 39,* 2–12.

24. Tootsie Roll Inc. FAQs. https://tootsie.com/faqs; Aaseng, N. (2005). *Business builders in sweets & treats.* Oliver Press.

25. Jacoby, L. L., Kelley, C., Brown, J., & Jasechko, J. (1989). Becoming famous overnight: Limits on the ability to avoid unconscious influences of the past. *Journal of Personality and Social Psychology, 56,* 326–338; Jacoby, L. L., Woloshyn, V., & Kelley, C. (1989). Becoming famous without being recognized: Unconscious influences of memory produced by dividing attention. *Journal of Experimental Psychology: General, 118,* 115–125.

26. Frederick, S. (2005). Cognitive reflection and decision making. *Journal of Economic Perspectives, 19,* 25–42.

27. Bronstein, M. V., Pennycook, G., Bear, A., Rand, D. G., & Cannon, T. D. (2019). Belief in fake news is associated with delusionality, dogmatism, religious fundamentalism, and reduced analytic thinking. *Journal of Applied Research in Memory and Cognition, 8*, 108–117; Pennycook, G., Cannon, T. D., & Rand, D. G. (2018). Prior exposure increases perceived accuracy of fake news. *Journal of Experimental Psychology: General, 147*, 1865–1880; Pennycook, G., & Rand, D. G. (2020). Who falls for fake news? The roles of bullshit receptivity, overclaiming, familiarity, and analytic thinking. *Journal of Personality, 88*, 185–200.

28. Pennycook, G., & Rand, D. G. (2019). Lazy, not biased: Susceptibility to partisan fake news is better explained by lack of reasoning than by motivated reasoning. *Cognition, 188*, 39–50.

29. Gigerenzer, G., Hertwig, R., & Pachur, T. (2011). *Heuristics: The foundations of adaptive behavior.* Oxford University Press; Gigerenzer, G., & Todd, P. M. (1999). *Simple heuristics that make us smart.* Oxford University Press; Kahneman, D., Slovic, P., & Tversky, A. (Eds.). (1982). *Judgment under uncertainty: Heuristics and biases.* Cambridge University Press.

30. Shermer, M. (1997). *Why people believe weird things: Pseudoscience, superstition, and other confusions of our time.* W. H. Freeman and Company.

31. Kahneman, D. (2011). *Thinking, fast and slow.* Farrar, Straus and Giroux.

32. Allen, S. (1989). *Dumbth and 81 ways to make Americans smarter.* Prometheus Books; Beck, J. S. (1995). *Cognitive therapy: Basics and beyond.* Guilford Press; Morrow, D. R. (2017). *Giving reasons: An extremely short introduction to critical thinking.* Hackett Publishing Company; Shermer, M. (1997). *Why people believe weird things: Pseudoscience, superstition, and other confusions of our time.* W. H. Freeman and Company.

33. Erickson, T. D., & Mattson, M. E. (1981). From words to meaning: A semantic illusion. *Journal of Verbal Learning and Verbal Behavior, 20*, 540–551; Song, H., & Schwarz, N. (2008). Fluency and the detection of misleading questions: Low processing fluency attenuates the Moses illusion. *Social Cognition, 26*, 791–799.

34. Seta, J. J., Seta, C. E., & McCormick, M. (2017). Commonalities and differences among frames: A unification model. *Journal of Behavioral Decision Making, 30*, 1113–1130.

35. Tversky, A., & Kahneman, D. (1981). The framing of decisions and the psychology of choice. *Science, 211*, 453–458.

36. Kühberger, A. (1995). The framing of decisions: A new look at old problems. *Organizational Behavior and Human Decision Processes, 62*,

230–240; Kühberger, A., & Gradl, P. (2013). Choice, rating, and rank-ing: Framing effects with different response modes. *Journal of Behav-ioral Decision Making, 26*, 109–117; Kühberger, A., & Tanner, C. (2010). Risky choice framing: Task versions and a comparison of prospect the-ory and fuzzy-trace theory. *Journal of Behavioral Decision Making, 23*, 314–329; Mandel, D. R. (2001). Gain-loss framing and choice: Sepa-rating outcome formulations from descriptor formulations. *Organiza-tional Behavior and Human Decision Processes, 85*, 56–76; Mandel, D. R. (2014). Do framing effects reveal irrational choice? *Journal of Exper-imental Psychology: General, 143*, 1185–1198; Seta, J. J., Seta, C. E., & McCormick, M. (2017). Commonalities and differences among frames: A unification model. *Journal of Behavioral Decision Making, 30*, 1113–1130; Tombu, M., & Mandel, D. R. (2015). When does framing influence preferences, risk perceptions, and risk attitudes? The explicated valence account. *Journal of Behavioral Decision Making, 28*, 464–476.

37. Forgas, J. P., & East, R. (2008). On being happy and gullible: Mood effects on skepticism and the detection of deception. *Journal of Exper-imental Social Psychology, 44*, 1362–1367.

38. Baron, J., & Hershey, J. C. (1988). Outcome bias in decision evalua-tion. *Journal of Personality and Social Psychology, 54*, 569–579; Seta, C. E., Seta, J. J., Petrocelli, J. V., & McCormick, M. (2015). Even better than the real thing: Alternative outcome bias affects decision judgements and decision regret. *Thinking and Reasoning, 21*, 446–472.

39. Kindleberger, C. P. (1978). *Manias, panics, and crashes: A history of fi-nancial crises.* Macmillan.

40. Aronson, E. (2018). *The social animal* (12th ed.). Worth.

41. Shiller, R. J. (2000). *Irrational exuberance.* Princeton University Press.

42. Asch, S. E. (1951). Effects of group pressure upon the modification and distortion of judgment. In H. Guetzkow (Ed.), *Groups, leadership, and men* (pp. 76–92). Carnegie Press.

43. Ibid.

44. Batson, C. D. (1975). Rational processing or rationalization? The ef-fect of disconfirming information on a stated religious belief. *Journal of Personality and Social Psychology, 32*, 176–184; Lord, C. G., Ross, L., & Lepper, M. R. (1979). Biased assimilation and attitude polar-ization: The effects of prior theories on subsequently considered ev-idence. *Journal of Personality and Social Psychology, 37*, 2098–2109; Knowles, E. S., & Linn, J. A. (Eds.) (2004). *Resistance and persuasion.*

Erlbaum; Nyhan, B., & Reifler, J. (2010). When corrections fail: The persistence of political misperceptions. *Political Behavior, 32,* 303–330. The backfire effect may not be as potent as once believed: see Chan, M. S., Jones, C. R., Jamieson, K. H., & Albarracin, D. (2017). Debunking: A meta-analysis of the psychological efficacy of messages countering misinformation. *Psychological Science, 28,* 1531–1546; Douglas, K. M., Uscinski, J. E., Sutton, R. M., Cichocka, A., Nefes, T., Ang, C. S., & Deravi, F. (2019). Understanding conspiracy theories. *Political Psychology, 40*(Suppl 1), 3–35; Wood, T., & Porter, E. (2019). The elusive backfire effect: Mass attitudes' steadfast factual adherence. *Political Behavior, 41,* 135–163.

45. Boghossian, P., & Lindsay, J. (2019). *How to have impossible conversations: A very practical guide.* Lifelong Books; Haidt, J. (2001). The emotional dog and its rational tail: A social intuitionist approach to moral judgment. *Psychological Review, 108,* 814–834; Shermer, M. (2011). *The believing brain: From ghosts and gods to politics and conspiracies—How we construct beliefs and reinforce them as truths.* Times Books, Henry Holt and Company; Tappin, B. M., van der Leer, L., & McKay, R. T. (2017). The heart trumps the head: Desirability bias in political belief revision. *Journal of Experimental Psychology: General, 146,* 1143–1149.

46. Kunda, Z. (1990). The case for motivated reasoning. *Psychological Bulletin, 108,* 480–498.

47. Festinger, L. (1957). *A theory of cognitive dissonance.* Stanford University Press.

48. Shermer, M. (2020). Why people believe conspiracy theories. *Skeptic, 25*(1), 12–17.

49. Ritchie, H. (2016, December 30). Read all about it: The biggest fake news stories of 2016. CNBC. https://www.cnbc.com/2016/12/30/read-all-about-it-the-biggest-fake-news-stories-of-2016.html; Schaedel, S. (2016, October 24). Did the Pope endorse Trump? FactCheck.org. https://www.factcheck.org/2016/10/did-the-pope-endorse-trump/; Samuelson, K. (2016, December 5). What to know about Pizzagate: The fake news story with real consequences. *Time.* https://time.com/4590255/pizzagate-fake-news-what-to-know/. And apparently the possibility that it could be true is enough for many people: Effron, D. A. (2018). It could have been true: How counterfactual thoughts reduce condemnation of falsehoods and increase political polarization. *Personality and Social Psychology Bulletin, 44,* 729–745; Manjoo, F.

(2008). *True enough: Learning to live in a post-fact society.* John Wiley & Sons.

3: When and Why People Bullshit

1. Bever, L., & Phillips, K. (2017, October 13). The mother jailed for refusing to vaccinate her son says she would "do it all over again." *Washington Post.* https://www.washingtonpost.com/news/to-your-health/wp/2017/10/12/a-mother-was-jailed-for-refusing-to-vaccinate-her-son-now-shes-outraged-hes-been-immunized/?noredirect=on&utm_term=.f4e6c1378476

2. McKee, C., & Bohannon, K. (2016). Exploring the reasons behind parental refusal of vaccines. *Journal of Pediatric Pharmacology and Therapeutics, 21,* 104–109.

3. Lyall, K., Croen, L., Daniels, J., Fallin, M. D., Ladd-Acosta, C., Lee, B. K., Park, B. Y., Snyder, N. W., Schendel, D., Volk, H., Windham, G. C., & Newschaffer, C. (2017). The changing epidemiology of autism spectrum disorders. *Annual Review of Public Health, 38,* 81–102.

4. Wakefield, A. J., Murch, S. H., Anthony, A., Linnell, J., Casson, D. M., Malik, M., Berelowitz, M., Dhillon, A. P., Thomson, M. A., Harvey, P., Valentine, A., Davies, S. E., & Walker-Smith, J. A. (1998). RETRACTED: Ileal-lymphoid-nodular hyperplasia, non-specific colitis, and pervasive developmental disorder in children. *The Lancet, 351,* 637-641.

5. Deer, B. (2010). Reflections of investigating Wakefield. *British Medical Journal, 340,* 295; Deer, B. (2010). Wakefield's "autistic enterocolitis" under the microscope. *British Medical Journal, 340,* c1127; Deer, B. (2011). How the case against the MMR vaccine was fixed. *British Medical Journal, 342,* 77–82; Deer, B. (2011). How the vaccine crisis was meant to make money. *British Medical Journal, 342,* 136–142; Deer, B. (2011). *The Lancet's* two days to bury bad news. *British Medical Journal, 342,* 200–204; Deer, B. (2011). Pathology reports solve "new bowel disease" riddle. *British Medical Journal, 343,* 985–989; Deer, B. (2011). Who saw the "histological findings"? *British Medical Journal, 343,* 1205.

6. Like many scientific journals, *The Lancet* requires that authors state conflicts of interest. Failure to do so is usually considered fraud.

7. Jain, A., Marshall. J., Buikema, A., Bancroft, T., Kelly, J. P., Newschaffer, C. J. (2015) Autism occurrence by MMR vaccine status among US children with older siblings with and without autism. *Journal of the American Medical Association, 313*, 1534–1540.

8. Hviid, A., Hansen, J. V, Frisch, M., & Melbye, M. (2019). Measles, mumps, rubella vaccination and autism: A nationwide cohort study. *Annals of Internal Medicine, 170,* 513–520.

9. Rao, T. S., & Andrade, C. (2011). The MMR vaccine and autism: Sensation, refutation, retraction, and fraud. *Indian Journal of Psychiatry, 53,* 95–96.

10. Korownyk, C., Kolber, M. R., Mccormack, J., Lam, V., Overbo, K., Cotton, C., Finley, C., Turgeon, R. D., Garrison, S., Linblad, A. J., Banh, H. L., Campbell-Scherer, D., Vandermeer, B., & Allan, G. M. (2014). Televised medical talk shows—what they recommend and the evidence to support their recommendations: A prospective observational study. *British Medical Journal, 349,* g7346.

11. Mutnick, A. (2014, June 17). Senators scold Dr. Oz for weight-loss scams. *USA Today.* https://www.usatoday.com/story/life/people/2014/06/17/dr-oz-senate-panel-weight-scams/10701067/

12. Frankfurt, H. (1986). On bullshit. *Raritan Quarterly Review, 6,* 81–100.

13. It is worth noting that survey respondents are not obligated to do anything. In fact, our participants were reminded multiple times that they could withdraw from the experiment at any time without any loss of benefits already agreed upon. Furthermore, half of our participants were reminded that they had no obligation to provide their opinions. The fact that these participants still provided bullshit suggests that social cues of obligation need not be very strong to cue bullshit as an acceptable form of communication.

14. Gigerenzer, G., Gaissmaier, W., Kurz-Milcke, E., Schwartz, L. M., & Woloshin, S. (2007). Helping doctors and patients make sense of health statistics. *Psychological Science in the Public Interest, 8,* 53–96; Hoffrage, U., & Gigerenzer, G. (1998). Using natural frequencies to improve diagnostic inferences. *Academic Medicine, 73,* 538–540. In the United States alone, approximately 250,000 people die each year from decision errors made by medical professionals, making it the third-most common cause of death (after heart disease and cancer, but before strokes, suicides, and diabetes). See Makary, M. A., & Daniel,

M. (2016). Medical error: The third leading cause of death in the US. *British Medical Journal, 353*, i2139-i2141. According to autopsy reports, 5% of these deaths are due to misdiagnoses that, if corrected and treated, would not have led to deaths: Newman-Toker, D. E., & Pronovost, P. J. (2009). Diagnostic errors: The next frontier for patient safety. *Journal of the American Medical Association, 301*, 1060–1062. These statistics are particularly disturbing in light of the fact that such mistakes are made by trained experts in medical decision making.

15. Casscells, W., Schoenberger, A., & Grayboys, T. B. (1978). Interpretation by physicians of clinical laboratory results. *New England Journal of Medicine, 299*, 999–1000; Brush, J. E., Lee, M., Sherbino, J., Taylor-Fishwick, J. C., Norman, G. (2019). Effect of teaching Bayesian methods using learning by concept vs learning by example on medical students' ability to estimate probability of a diagnosis: A randomized clinical trial. *Journal of the American Medical Association, Network Open, 2*(12): e1918023; Eddy, D. M. (1982). Probabilistic reasoning in clinical medicine: Problems and opportunities. In D. Kahneman, P. Slovic, & A. Tversky (Eds.), *Judgment under uncertainty: Heuristics and biases* (pp. 249–267). Cambridge University Press; Hammerton, M. (1973). A case of radical probability estimation. *Journal of Experimental Psychology, 101*, 252–254; Kerlikowske, K., Grady, D., Barclay, J., Sickles, E. A., & Ernster, V. (1996). Effect of age, breast density, and family history on the sensitivity of first screening mammography. *Journal of the American Medical Association, 276*, 33–38; Kerlikowske, K., Grady, D., Barclay, J., Sickles, E. A., & Ernster, V. (1996). Likelihood ratios for modern screening mammography: Risk of breast cancer based on age and mammographic interpretation. *Journal of the American Medical Association, 276*, 39–43; Molinaro, A. M. (2015). Diagnostic tests: How to estimate the positive predictive value. *Neuro-oncology Practice, 2*, 162–166.

16. Buys, S. S., et al. (2011). Effect of screening on ovarian cancer mortality: The Prostate, Lung, Colorectal and Ovarian (PLCO) Cancer Screening Randomized Controlled Trial. *Journal of the American Medical Association, 305*, 2295–2303.

17. Wegwarth, O., & Gigerenzer, G. (2018). US gynecologists' estimates and beliefs regarding ovarian cancer screening's effectiveness 5 years after release of the PLCO evidence. *Scientific Reports, 8*(1): 17181.

18. Simonson, I., & Nye, P. (1992). The effect of accountability on susceptibility to decision errors. *Organizational Behavior and Human Decision Processes, 51,* 416–446.

19. Kahneman, D. (2011). *Thinking, fast and slow.* Farrar, Straus and Giroux.

20. Frankfurt, H. (1986). On bullshit. *Raritan Quarterly Review, 6,* 81–100.

21. Craig, D. (2017). *How to become a human bullshit detector: Learn to spot fake news, fake people, and absolute lies.* Racehorse Publishing; Ekman, P. (2009). *Telling lies: Clues to deceit in the marketplace, politics, and marriage.* W.W. Norton & Company; Meibauer, J. (2019). *The Oxford handbook of lying.* Oxford University Press.

22. WhiteHouse.gov. (2017, January 20). The inaugural address. https://www.whitehouse.gov/briefings-statements/the-inaugural-address/

23. WhiteHouse.gov. (2020, November 20). Press briefing by Press Secretary Kayleigh McEnany, 11/20/2020. https://www.whitehouse.gov/briefings-statements/press-briefing-press-secretary-kayleigh-mcenany-11-20-2020/

24. Petrocelli, J. V. (2021). Politically-oriented bullshit detection: Attitudinally conditional bullshit receptivity and bullshit sensitivity. *Group Processes and Intergroup Relations, 24.*

25. Brem, S. K., & Rips, L. J. (2000). Explanation and evidence in informal argument. *Cognitive Science, 24,* 573–604.

26. Petrocelli, J. V. (2018). Antecedents of bullshitting. *Journal of Experimental Social Psychology, 76,* 249–258.

27. Psychologists Delroy Paulhus and his colleagues have even found that people are willing to claim knowledge about things that do not exist! Paulhus, D. L., Harms, P. D., Bruce, M. N., & Lysy, D. C. (2003). The over-claiming technique: Measuring self-enhancement independent of ability. *Journal of Personality and Social Psychology, 84,* 890–904.

28. Fuocco, M. A. (1996, March 21). Trial and error: They had larceny in their hearts, but little in their heads. *Pittsburgh Post-Gazette,* p. Dl.

29. Kruger, J., & Dunning, D. (1999). Unskilled and unaware of it: How difficulties in recognizing one's own incompetence lead to inflated self-assessments. *Journal of Personality and Social Psychology, 77,* 1121–1134.

30. Yet another example of so-called cognitive-training software programs is Fast ForWord, which is marketed to help children with learning disabilities. It is no surprise that a systematic meta-analytic review found no conclusive evidence that Fast ForWord is an effective treatment for children's oral language or reading difficulties.

Many cognitive-training software programs are no more effective at improving the abilities of children with learning disabilities than Head Start programs designed to boost reading ability in prenatals to two-year-olds; Strong, G. K., Torgerson, C. J., Torgerson, D., & Hulme, C. (2011). A systematic meta-analytic review of evidence for the effectiveness of the "Fast ForWord" language intervention program. *Journal of Child Psychology and Psychiatry, and Allied Disciplines, 52*, 224–235.

31. Shepherd, R. (2017). 10 ways to sell your product even when there's no evidence that it works: The Arrowsmith Program of cognitive exercises. *Myndplan*. https://medium.com/myndplan/myndplan-9961a084f750

32. Baumeister, R. F., & Leary, M. R. (1995). The need to belong: Desire for interpersonal attachments as a fundamental human motivation. *Psychological Bulletin, 117*, 497–529.

33. Gonsalkorale, K., & Williams, K. D. (2007). The KKK won't let me play: Ostracism even by a despised outgroup hurts. *European Journal of Social Psychology, 37*, 1176–1186; Williams, K. D. (2007). Ostracism. *Annual Review of Psychology, 58*, 425–452; Zadro, L., Williams, K. D., & Richardson, R. (2004). How low can you go? Ostracism by a computer is sufficient to lower self-reported levels of belonging, control, self-esteem, and meaningful existence. *Journal of Experimental Social Psychology, 40*, 560–567.

34. Interestingly, Williams's confederates didn't even need to be in the room for the negative effects of ostracism to occur. A clever version of the ostracism game is Cyberball, essentially a computerized simulation of playing catch. Here, the participant sits at a computer in a private cubicle and is led to believe that she has been matched with two participants in two other private cubicles in the lab. The other two participants are nothing more than programmed algorithms, but the participant still feels sadness and rejection when exclusion begins.

35. Van Beest, I., & Williams, K. D. (2006). When inclusion costs and ostracism pays, ostracism still hurts. *Journal of Personality and Social Psychology, 91*, 918–928.

4: Bullshit Artists

1. Rosenblatt, A. I., & Carbone, P. S. (2019). *Autism spectrum disorder: What every parent needs to know.* American Academy of Pediatrics.

2. Biklen, D. (1990). Communication unbound: Autism and praxis. *Harvard Educational Review, 60*, 291–315.

3. Beck, A. R., & Pirovano, C. (1996). Facilitated communicators' performance on a task of receptive language. *Journal of Autism and Developmental Disorders, 26*(5), 497–512; Green, G., & Shane, H. C. (1993). Facilitated communication: The claims vs. the evidence. *Harvard Mental Health Letter, 10*, 4–5; Montee, B. B., Miltenberger, R. G., & Wittrock, D. (1995). An experimental analysis of facilitated communication. *Journal of Applied Behavior Analysis, 28*, 189–200; Moore, S., Donovan, B., Hudson, A., Dykstra, J., & Lawrence, J. (1993). Evaluation of facilitated communication: Eight case studies. *Journal of Autism and Developmental Disorders, 23*, 531–539; Mostert, M. P. (2001). Facilitated communication since 1995: A review of published studies. *Journal of Autism and Developmental Disorders, 31*, 287–313; Szempruch, J., & Jacobson, J. W. (1993). Evaluating the facilitated communications of people with developmental disabilities. *Research in Developmental Disabilities, 14*, 253–264.

4. Palfreman, J. (Producer). (1993, October 19). *Frontline: Prisoners of silence*. WGBH Public Television.

5. See Dismay over Syracuse appointment of dean: Statement of disapproval of the research and teacher education communities in special education of the appointment of Douglas Biklen as Dean of Education at Syracuse University. *SpedPro*. https://web.archive.org/web/20070311014306/http://spedpro.org/2005/10/31/dismay-over-syracuse-appointment-of-dean/; Riggott, J. (2005). Pseudoscience in autism treatment: Are the news and entertainment media helping or hurting? *Scientific Review of Mental Health Practice, 4*(1). https://web.archive.org/web/20131112175428/http://www.srmhp.org/0401/media-watch.html. Also see Herbert, J. D., Sharp, I. R., & Gaudiano, B. A. (2002). Separating fact from fiction in the etiology and treatment of autism: A scientific review of the evidence. *Scientific Review of Mental Health Practice, 1*(1), 23–43.

6. Five additional tactics are less commonly used, but useful to bullshit artists nonetheless: (1) Using feelings like anger and fear to motivate people to adopt their causes: Leventhal, H., Watts, J. C., & Pagano, F. (1967). Effects of fear and instructions on how to cope with danger. *Journal of Personality and Social Psychology, 6*, 313–321; Feinberg, M., & Willer, R. (2011). Apocalypse soon? Dire messages reduce belief in

global warming by contradicting just-world beliefs. *Psychological Science*, *22*, 34–38; Liberman, A., & Chaiken, S. (1992). Defensive processing of personally relevant health messages. *Personality and Social Psychology Bulletin*, *18*, 669–679. (2) The principle of reciprocity (for example, I'll scratch your back if you scratch mine): Cialdini, R. B., Green, B. L., & Rusch, A. J. (1992). When tactical pronouncements of change become real change: The case of reciprocal persuasion. *Journal of Personality and Social Psychology*, *63*, 30–40; Strohmetz, D. B., Rind, B., Fisher, R., & Lynn, M. (2002). Sweetening the till: The use of candy to increase restaurant tipping. *Journal of Applied Social Psychology*, *32*, 300–309; Seiter, J. S. (2007). Ingratiation and gratuity: The effect of complimenting customers on tipping behavior in restaurants. *Journal of Applied Social Psychology*, *37*, 478–485. (3) The illusion of scarcity: Ruge, D. W. (2015). *The top 20% in the modern digital age: Why 80% of small businesses fail at sales and marketing and how you can succeed.* The Successful Sales Manager. (4) Consensus information: Economist and Nobel laureate Robert Shiller describes this mechanism as a social feedback pressure known as *irrational exuberance* and *feedback loop investor bubbles* (terms often attributed to former Federal Reserve chairman Alan Greenspan, but actually coined by Shiller, who later wrote a book with that title): Shiller, R. J. (2000). *Irrational exuberance.* Princeton University Press. (5) The principles of commitment and consistency: Sherman, S. J. (1980). On the self-erasing nature of errors of prediction. *Journal of Personality and Social Psychology*, *39*, 211–221; Cialdini, R. B., & Sagarin, B. J. (2005). Interpersonal influence. In T. Brock & M. Green (Eds.), *Persuasion: Psychological insights and perspectives* (pp. 143–169). Sage; Guéguen, N., Joule, R. V., Courbet, D., Halimi-Falkowicz, S., & Marchand, M. (2013). Repeating "yes" in a first request and compliance with a later request: The four walls technique. *Social Behavior and Personality*, *41*, 199–202.

7. Lilienfeld, S. O., Marshall, J., Todd, J. T., & Shane, H. C. (2014). The persistence of fad interventions in the face of negative scientific evidence: Facilitated communication for autism as a case example. *Evidence-Based Communication Assessment and Intervention*, *8*, 62–101.

8. Failure to recognize the importance of disconfirming evidence against facilitated communication is illustrated by the story of Clever Hans.

Clever Hans was a horse whose owner claimed that he was able to do lots of difficult mathematical sums and solve complicated problems. Conducting a formal investigation in 1907, psychologist Oskar Pfungst demonstrated that the horse was not actually performing these mental tasks. Clever Hans was picking up on subtle cues from the owner and watching the reactions of the people who were watching him to provide the correct answer. Heinzen, T. E., Lilienfeld, S. O., & Nolan, S. A. (2015). Clever Hans: What a horse can teach us about self deception. *Skeptic*, *20*(1), 10–17; Pfungst, O. (1907). *Clever Hans: The horse of Mr. Van Osten*. New York: Holt, Rinehart and Winston. All accounts of facilitated communication have been debunked. See Gorman, B. J. (1998). Facilitated communication in America: Eight years and counting. *Skeptic*, *6*(3), 64–71. A well-produced and compelling visual demonstration of the basic method used to debunk facilitated communication can be found in an episode of *Frontline*: Palfreman, J. (Producer). (1993, October 19). *Frontline: Prisoners of silence*. WGBH Public Television; Sobel, S. (2018). Facilitated communication redux: Persistence of a discredited technique. *Skeptic*, *23*(3), 6–9.

9. Bausell, R. B. (2007). *Snake oil science: The truth about complementary and alternative medicine*. Oxford University Press; Ernst, E. (2018). *SCAM: So-called alternative medicine*. Imprint Academic.

10. Choy, E. (2018, December 2). How two leaders use hidden storytelling techniques to inform and influence. *Forbes*. https://www.forbes.com/sites/estherchoy/2018/12/02/how-leaders-use-storytelling/#1ee6507a5703; Dunlop, W. L., & Tracy, J. L. (2013). Sobering stories: Narratives of self-redemption predict behavioral change and improved health among recovering alcoholics. *Journal of Personality and Social Psychology*, *104*, 576–590; Krippendorff, K. (2010, September 23). Storytelling and influence: Learn how to get what you want. *Fast Company*. https://www.fastcompany.com/1680723/storytelling-and-influence-learn-how-get-what-you-want; Krippendorff, K. (2012). *Outthink the competition: How a new generation of strategists sees options others ignore*. John Wiley & Sons; McGregor, I., & Holmes, J. G. (1999). How storytelling shapes memory and impressions of relationship events over time. *Journal of Personality and Social Psychology*, *76*, 403–419; Merchant, A., Ford, J. B., & Sargeant, A. (2010). Charitable organizations' storytelling influence on donors' emotions and intentions. *Journal of Business Research*, *63*, 754–762; Petrocelli, J. V., &

Sherman, S. J. (2010). Event detail and confidence in gambling: The role of counterfactual thought reactions. *Journal of Experimental Social Psychology*, *46*, 61–72; Valsesia, F., Diehl, K., & Nunes, J. C. (2017). Based on a true story: Making people believe the unbelievable. *Journal of Experimental Social Psychology*, *71*, 105–110.

11. Jenni, K. E., & Loewenstein, G. (1997). Explaining the "Identifiable Victim Effect." *Journal of Risk and Uncertainty*, *14*, 235–257; Schelling, T. C. (1968). The life you save may be your own. In S. B. Chase (Ed.), *Problems in public expenditure analysis*. The Brookings Institute; Small, D. A., & Loewenstein, G. (2003). Helping a victim or helping the victim: Altruism and identifiability. *Journal of Risk and Uncertainty*, *26*, 5–16.

12. Shermer, M. (1997). *Why people believe weird things: Pseudoscience, superstition, and other confusions of our time*. W. H. Freeman.

13. Nisbett R. E., & Ross, L. (1980). *Human inference: Strategies and shortcomings of social judgment*. Prentice-Hall; Sagan, C. (1995). *The demon-haunted world: Science as a candle in the dark*. Random House; Kahneman, D., Slovic, P., & Tversky, A. (Eds.). (1982). *Judgment under uncertainty: Heuristics and biases*. Cambridge University Press; Tversky, A., & Kahneman, D. (1971). Belief in the law of small numbers. *Psychological Bulletin*, *76*, 105–110.

14. Chopra, D. [@DeepakChopra] (2020, May 16). Twitter. https://twitter.com/DeepakChopra

15. Baer, H. A. (2003). The work of Andrew Weil and Deepak Chopra—Two holistic health/new age gurus: A critique of the holistic health/new age movements. *Medical Anthropology Quarterly*, *17*, 240–241; Chopra, D. (1989). *Quantum healing: Exploring the frontiers of mind/body medicine*. Bantam Books; Chopra, D. (1995). *Boundless energy: The complete mind/body program for overcoming chronic fatigue*. Harmony Books; Chopra, D. (1997). *Ageless body, timeless mind: The quantum alternative to growing old*. Random House; Chopra, D. (2007). *Perfect health: The complete mind body guide*. Three Rivers Press.

16. Pennycook, G., Cheyne, J. A., Barr, N., Koehler, D. J., & Fugelsang, J. A. (2015). On the reception and detection of pseudo-profound bullshit. *Judgment and Decision Making*, *10*, 549–563.

17. Chopra, D. (2020, October 1). [Tweet]. Twitter. https://twitter.com/DeepakChopra.

18. Cohen, G. A. (2002). Deeper into bullshit. In S. Buss & L. Overton (Eds.). *Contours of agency: Essays on themes from Harry Frankfurt* (pp. 321–339). MIT Press.

19. Brafman, O., & Beckstrom, R. A. (2006). *The starfish and the spider: The unstoppable power of leaderless organizations.* Penguin Books.

20. A great example of this is found in Redding, D., & Whitmire, T. (2014). *Freed to lead: F3 and the unshackling of the modern-day warrior.* The Iron Project. Also see F3Nation. Lexicon. https://f3nation.com /lexicon/. "4E" short for "Fourth Estate (The Media)" and the complete bullshit idea of "10/90" for the "general premise that 10% of the people in any community or organization will account for 90% of its impact."

21. Orwell, G. (1949). *Nineteen eight-four: A novel.* Harcourt, Brace and Company.

22. Law, S. (2011). *Believing bullshit: How not to get sucked into an intellectual black hole.* Prometheus Books.

23. The Chopra Center (2018, August 31). 10 tips on how to live your best life. https://chopra.com/articles/how-to-live-your-best-life. Deepak's approach to the good life may sound fantastic, but the reality is that very little of it is supported by empirical evidence. If Deepak instead relied on scientific evidence, he might have included things that are well supported by the literature on subjective well-being and life satisfaction, such as trying to see others' points of view, understanding that people—not things—make us happy, putting life before work, using conscious reasoning to slowly make the changes we want, and dealing with stress by first determining a stressor's importance and whether anything can be done about it. See Bakker, G. M. (2019). Nine evidence-based guidelines for a good life. *Skeptic, 43*(6), 34–39.

24. And a lot of people apparently buy it. See Dalton, C. (2016). Bullshit for you; transcendence for me. A commentary on "On the reception and detection of pseudo-profound bullshit."*Judgment and Decision Making, 11,* 121–122; Pennycook, G., Cheyne, J. A., Barr, N., Koehler, D. J., & Fugelsang, J. A. (2016). It's still bullshit: Reply to Dalton (2016). *Judgment and Decision Making, 11,* 123–125.

25. Barnes, R. (Producer). (2007, August 13). *The enemies of reason.* IWC Media. See also Molé, P. (1998). Deepak's dangerous dogmas. *Skeptic, 6*(2), 38–45; Shermer, M. (2007). The great afterlife debate: Michael Shermer v. Deepak Chopra. *Skeptic, 13*(4), 52–55.

26. Sokal, A. D. (1996). Transgressing the boundaries: Toward a transformative hermeneutics of quantum gravity. *Social Text, 14,* 217–252; Sokal, A., & Bricmont, J. (1998). *Intellectual impostures.* Profile Books.

27. Sokal, A. (1996, May 1). A physicist experiments with cultural studies. *Lingua Franca.* http://linguafranca.mirror.theinfo.org/9605/sokal.html

28. Heap, M. (2002). Ideomotor effect (the "Ouija Board" effect). In M. Shermer (Ed.), *The skeptic encyclopedia of pseudoscience* (pp. 127–129). ABC-CLIO.

29. Simpkins, A. M., & Simpkins, C. A. (2016). *Core principles of meditation for therapy: Improving the outcome of psychotherapeutic treatments.* John Wiley & Sons.

30. Even theoretical physicist and Nobel laureate Richard Feynman said, "I think I can safely say that nobody understands quantum mechanics."

31. Bausell, R. B. (2007). *Snake oil science: The truth about complementary and alternative medicine.* Oxford University Press; Buekens, F., & Boudry, M. (2015). The dark side of the loon: Explaining the temptations of obscurantism. *Theoria, 81,* 126–142; Ernst, E. (2018). *SCAM: So-called alternative medicine.* Imprint Academic; Lindeman, M. (2011). Biases in intuitive reasoning and belief in complementary and alternative medicine. *Psychology and Health, 26,* 371–382; Sperber, D. (2010). The guru effect. *Review of Philosophy and Psychology, 1,* 583–592.

32. Enron Annual Report (2000). https://picker.uchicago.edu/Enron/EnronAnnualReport2000.pdf

33. Corporate Gibberish Generator provided by Andrew Davidson.

34. Fugere, B., Hardaway, C., & Warshawsky, J. (2005). *Why business people speak like idiots: A bullfighter's guide.* Free Press.

35. We now have several dictionaries devoted to bullshit to keep us straight on the what-what of the corporate, legal, and political worlds. Beckwith, L. (2006). *The dictionary of corporate bullshit: An a to z lexicon of empty, enraging, and just plain stupid office talk.* Broadway Books; Duncan, K. (2016). *The business bullshit book: The world's most comprehensive dictionary.* LID Publishing; Fugere, B., Hardaway, C., & Warshawsky, J. (2005). *Why business people speak like idiots: A bullfighter's guide.* Free Press; Law, D. (2008). *A dictionary of bull****: A lexicon of corporate and office-speak.* Constable and Robinson; Webb, N. (2010). *The dictionary of political bullshit.* JR Books; Webb, N. (2006). *The dictionary of (bull–shit): A shamelessly opinionated guide to all that is*

absurd, misleading and insincere. Sourcebooks; Young, R. (2007). *The dictionary of legal bullshit.* Sphinx Publishing.

36. Kelley, H. H. (1967). Attribution theory in social psychology. In D. Levine (Ed.), *Nebraska Symposium on Motivation* (Vol. 15, pp. 192–238). University of Nebraska Press; Kelley, H. H. (1973). The process of causal attribution. *American Psychologist, 28*, 107–128.

37. Mallet, M., Nelson, B., & Steiner, C. (2012, January 26). The most annoying, pretentious and useless business jargon. *Forbes.* https://www.forbes.com/sites/groupthink/2012/01/26/the-most-annoying -pretentious-and-useless-business-jargon/#66f9fb982eea

38. Emre, M. (2018). *The personality brokers: The strange history of Myers-Briggs and the birth of personality testing.* Doubleday.

39. Anthropologist David Graeber offers compelling arguments for this notion: Graeber, D. (2018). *Bullshit jobs: A theory.* Simon & Schuster.

40. https://arrowsmithschool.org/arrowsmith-schoolonline/

41. Weber, R. C., Denyer, R., Yeganeh, N. M., Maja, R., Murphy, M., Martin, S., Chiu, L., Nguy, V., White, K., & Boyd, L. (2019). Interpreting the preliminary outcomes of the Arrowsmith Programme: A neuroimaging and behavioural study. *Learning: Research and Practice, 5,* 126–148.

42. Hovland, C. I., & Weiss, W. (1951). The influence of source credibility on communication effectiveness. *Public Opinion Quarterly, 15,* 635–650; Kelman, H. C., & Hovland, C. I. (1953). "Reinstatement" of the communicator in delayed measurement of opinion change. *Journal of Abnormal and Social Psychology, 48,* 327–335; Mills, J., & Jellison, J. M. (1967). Effect on opinion change of how desirable the communication is to the audience the communicator addressed. *Journal of Personality and Social Psychology, 6,* 98101; Petty, R. E., & Wegener, D. T. (1998). Attitude change: Multiple roles for persuasion variables. In D. T. Gilbert, S. T. Fiske, & G. Lindzey (Eds.), *The handbook of social psychology* (Vol. 1, pp. 323–390). McGraw-Hill; Rhine, R., & Severance, L. (1970). Ego-involvement, discrepancy, source credibility, and attitude change. *Journal of Personality and Social Psychology, 16,* 175–190.

43. Dorlo, T. P., Betz, W., & Renckens, C. N. (2015). WHO's strategy on traditional and complementary medicine: A disgraceful contempt for evidence-based medicine. *Skeptical Inquirer, 39*(3), 42–45; Gorski, D. H. (2015). *Science* sells out: Advertising traditional Chinese medicine in three supplements. *Skeptical Inquirer, 39*(3), 46–48; Nickell,

J. (2012). Traditional Chinese medicine: Views East and West. *Skeptical Inquirer, 36*(2), 18–20; Renckens, C. N., & Dorlo, T. P. (2019). Quackery at WHO: A Chinese affair. *Skeptical Inquirer, 43*(5), 39–43; Novella, S. (2011). What is acupuncture? *Skeptical Inquirer, 35*(4), 28–29; Point, S. (2019). Laser acupuncture: High-tech placebo. *Skeptical Inquirer, 43*(5), 50–51; Ulett, G. A. (1997). Acupuncture's secrets revealed. *Skeptic, 5*(4), 46–51; Ulett, G. A. (2003). Acupuncture, magic, and make-believe. *Skeptical Inquirer, 27*(2), 47–50.

44. Deepak Chopra: Never eat with people you don't like. *The Oprah Winfrey Show*, Oprah Winfrey Network. https://www.youtube.com/watch ?v=55nTtwpIPro

45. Bleske-Rechek, A., Paulich, K., & Jorgensen, K. (2019). Therapeutic touch redux: Twenty years after the "Emily Event," energy therapies live on through bad science. *Skeptic, 24*(2), 26–31; Rosa, L., Rosa, E., Sarner, L., & Barrett, S. (1998). A close look at therapeutic touch. *Journal of the American Medical Association, 279,* 1005–1010.

46. McCarthy, T. (2017, August 18). A year in Trump's orbit: A timeline of Steve Bannon's political career. https://www.theguardian.com /us-news/2017/aug/18/a-year-in-trumps-orbit-a-timeline-of-steve -bannons-political-career. On February 2, 2017, Bannon was branded "the Great Manipulator" and "second most powerful man in the world" on the cover of *Time* magazine. President Trump reportedly became unhappy with his lieutenant's prominence in the media. By April 4, 2017, Trump concurred with reports that Bannon had fallen out of favor by telling the *New York Post*, "I am my own strategist," and telling the *Wall Street Journal* that Bannon was just "a guy who works for me."

47. Kelsey, A., & Stracqualursi, V. (2016, November 15). Why Trump's appointment of Steve Bannon has raised so many alarms. *ABC News.* https://abcnews.go.com/Politics/trumps-appointment-steve-bannon -raised-alarms/story?id=43554212

48. Graham, D. A. (2018, January 3). Why Trump turned on Steve Bannon. *The Atlantic.* https://www.theatlantic.com/politics/archive/2018 /01/the-president-vs-steve-bannon/549617/

49. Bump, P. (2019, January 29). Bolton joins a select group: Those once praised and now derided by the president. *Washington Post.* https:// www.washingtonpost.com/politics/2020/01/29/bolton-joins-select -group-those-once-praised-now-derided-by-president/; Malloy, A. (2020, January 29). Trump slams Bolton as Senate considers calling

him as a witness. *CNN Politics*. https://www.cnn.com/2020/01/29 /politics/donald-trump-john-bolton/index.html

50. Frazin, R. (2019, August 31). Trump renews attacks on Omarosa, slamming her as "disgusting and foul mouthed." *The Hill*. https://thehill .com/homenews/administration/459522-trump-slams-omarosa-as -disgusting-and-foul-mouthed

51. Underberg, J. E., Gollwitzer, A., Oettingen, G., & Gollwitzer, P. M. (2020). The best words: Linguistic indicators of grandiose narcissism in politics. *Journal of Language and Social Psychology*, *39*, 271–281.

52. Hamblin, C. (1970). *Fallacies*. Methuen; Lewiński, M., & Oswald, S. (2013). When and how do we deal with straw men? A normative and cognitive pragmatic account. *Journal of Pragmatics*, *59*, 164–177.

53. Cooper, H. (2009, May 23). Some Obama enemies are made totally of straw. *New York Times*. https://www.nytimes.com/2009/05/24/us /politics/24straw.html

54. Bizer, G. Y., Kozak, S. M., & Holterman, L. A. (2009). The persuasiveness of the straw man rhetorical technique. *Social Influence*, *4*, 216–230.

55. Lance Murphy's story is universal and emblematic of pharmaceutical salespeople the world over. However, in the interest of protecting his identity, Lance Murphy's name, position, and the companies he has worked for are fictitious. All other elements of Murphy's story remain true.

56. O'Connor, C., & Weatherall, J. O. (2019). *The misinformation age: How false beliefs spread*. Yale University Press; O'Connor, C., & Weatherall, J. O. (2019). Why we trust lies: The most effective misinformation starts with seeds of truth. *Scientific American*, *321*(3), 54–61.

5: Bullshit Detection Wheelhouse

1. A wonderful parody of TED Talks can be found in *Last Week Tonight with John Oliver* (season 3, episode 11, aired May 8, 2016). Oliver mocked misleading scientific studies with fake TED Talks known as TODD Talks. The parody exaggerates the misleading information typically shared in TED Talks, but not by much.

2. Thurlow, C. (2019, May 15). *Intermittent fasting: Transformational technique*. TedxGreenville. https://www.youtube.com/watch?v =A6Dkt7zyImk

3. Bhutani, S., Klempel, M. C., Kroeger, C. M., Aggour, E., Calvo, Y., Trepanowski, J. F., Hoddy, K. K., Varady, K. A. (2013). Effect of exercising

while fasting on eating behaviors and food intake. *Journal of the International Society of Sports Nutrition*, *10*, 50; Byrne, N. M., Sainsbury, A., King, N. A., Hills, A. P., & Wood, R. E. (2017). Intermittent energy restriction improves weight loss efficiency in obese men: The MATADOR study. *International Journal of Obesity*, *42*, 129; Hoddy, K. K., Gibbons, C., Kroeger, C. M., Trepanowski, J. F., Barnosky, A., Bhutani, S., & Varady, K. A. (2016). Changes in hunger and fullness in relation to gut peptides before and after 8 weeks of alternate day fasting. *Clinical Nutrition*, *35*, 1380–1385; Klempel, M. C., Bhutani, S., Fitzgibbon, M., Freels, S., & Varady, K. A. (2010). Dietary and physical activity adaptations to alternate day modified fasting: Implications for optimal weight loss. *Nutrition Journal*, *9*, 35; Varady, K. A., & Hellerstein, M. K. (2007). Alternate-day fasting and chronic disease prevention: a review of human and animal trials. *American Journal of Clinical Nutrition*, *86*, 7–13.

4. Rabinowitz, J. D., & White, E. (2010). Autophagy and metabolism. *Science*, *330*, 1344–1348.

5. Stockman, M. C., Thomas, D., Burke, J., & Apovian, C. M. (2018). Intermittent fasting: Is the wait worth the weight? *Current Obesity Reports*, *7*, 172–185.

6. As you might expect, the more conditional the claim, the less likely it is to be true. Researchers in judgment and decision-making refer to outcomes with multiple conditions as *conjunctions*. Sports books and casinos thrive on conjunctive bets because the outcomes/payouts are so unlikely. The more conjunctions there are to making something true, the more likely the claim is bullshit.

7. Liberman, N., Trope, Y., McCrea, S. M., & Sherman, S. J. (2007). The effect of level of construal on the temporal distance of activity enactment. *Journal of Experimental Social Psychology*, *43*, 143–149; McCrea, S. M., Liberman, N., Trope, Y., & Sherman, S. J. (2008). Construal level and procrastination. *Psychological Science*, *19*, 1308–1314.

8. Alcock, J. E. (2018). *Belief: What it means to believe and why our convictions are so compelling*. Prometheus Books; Boghossian, P., & Lindsay, J. (2019). *How to have impossible conversations: A very practical guide*. Lifelong Books; Haidt, J. (2001). The emotional dog and its rational tail: A social intuitionist approach to moral judgment. *Psychological Review*, *108*, 814–834; Shermer, M. (2011). *The believing brain: From ghosts and gods to politics and conspiracies—How we construct beliefs and reinforce them as truths*. Times Books, Henry Holt.

9. The New York Yankees did beat the Pittsburgh Pirates in the 1927 World Series. However, the Pirates beat the Yankees in the "more recent" 1960 World Series.

10. Schwartz, N. (1999). Self-reports: How the questions shape the answers. *American Psychologist, 54*, 93–105.

11. Bellos, A. (2016, March 28). Did you solve it? The logic question almost everyone gets wrong. *The Guardian*. https://www.theguardian.com/science/2016/mar/28/did-you-solve-it-the-logic-question-almost-everyone-gets-wrong; Robson, D. (2019). *The intelligence trap: Why smart people make dumb mistakes*. W. W. Norton.

12. Of course, this advice holds only when it is safe to assume that Monty will always offer contestants the chance to switch, regardless of their initial choice in doors. If the game-show host was mischievous by nature, she would make the offer to stick or switch only if contestants initially picked the door with the grand prize behind it. Switching would then always lead to a goat and the game-show host could keep the big prize for the next show.

13. Petrocelli, J. V., & Harris, A. K. (2011). Learning inhibition in the Monty Hall Problem: The role of dysfunctional counterfactual prescriptions. *Personality and Social Psychology Bulletin, 37*, 1297–1311; Rosenhouse, J. (2009). *The Monty Hall problem: The remarkable story of math's most contentious brain teaser*. Oxford University Press.

14. The distance from Washington, DC, to San Francisco is almost 3,000 miles and covers three time zones. Neither city is near the equator, but it is reasonable to estimate that at the equator the four time zones in the USA (Eastern, Central, Mountain, and Pacific) cover about 4,000 miles; approximately 1,000 miles per time zone. There are 24 time zones. A reasonable estimate of the circumference of the Earth is approximately 24,000 miles. The actual circumference of the Earth is approximately 24,900 miles. Folding a piece of paper in half 100 times is impossible. 1 fold = .2mm; 2 folds = .4mm; 5 folds = 3.2mm; 30 folds = 1 mile; 42 folds = 275,000 miles (more than the distance from the Earth to the Moon); 100 folds = radius of the known universe, 1 billion light-years, or 850 trillion times the distance from the Earth to the Sun! (93 million miles).

15. Fox News. (2016, December 27). Food stamp fraud at an all-time high: Is it time to end the program? https://video.foxnews.com/v/5262528761001#sp=show-clips

16. United States Department of Agriculture. (2017, September 1). Food and Nutrition Service: Supplemental Nutrition Assistance Program, Program Accountability and Administration Division. State activity report. Fiscal Year 2016. https://fns-prod.azureedge.net/sites/default /files/snap/FY16-State-Activity-Report.pdf. The total loss to fraud in 2016 was $592.7 million, not $70 million (no one knows where *Fox & Friends* got $70 million). The total cost of SNAP in 2016 was $66,539,000,000, making the percent lost to fraud .009, still less than 1%. In 2016, the US population was 323 million and 44.2 million were SNAP recipients (13.6%). The average aid received monthly by SNAP recipients was $125.40 ($1,504.80 for the year). In 2016, the number of recipients disqualified following investigations was 55,930 (less than 1% of the total recipients).

17. Wemple, E. (2016, December 29). Agriculture Department seeks correction from Fox News on food-stamp fraud report. *Washington Post*. https://www.washingtonpost.com/blogs/erik-wemple/wp/2016 /12/29/agriculture-department-seeks-correction-from-fox-news-on -food-stamp-fraud-report/. This total was still incorrect, but close to the actual total of $858 million: United States Department of Agriculture. (2013, August 1). The extent of trafficking in the Supplemental Nutrition Assistance Program: 2009–2011 (Summary). https://fns -prod.azureedge.net/sites/default/files/Trafficking2009_Summary .pdf; Wemple, E. (2016, December 30). Fox News runs incorrect correction of food-stamp fraud report, then corrects correction. *Washington Post*. https://www.washingtonpost.com/blogs/erik-wemple /wp/2016/12/30/fox-news-runs-incorrect-correction-of-food-stamp -fraud-report-then-corrects-correction/

18. Hancock, J. T., Curry, L. E., Goorha, S., & Woodworth, M. (2008). On lying and being lied to: A linguistic analysis of deception in computer-mediated communication. *Discourse Processes*, *45*, 1–23; Niederhoffer, K. G., & Pennebaker, J. W. (2002). Linguistic style matching in social interaction. *Journal of Language and Social Psychology*, *21*, 337–360; Newman, M. L., Pennebaker, J. W., Berry, D. S., & Richards, J. M. (2003). Lying words: Predicting deception from linguistic styles. *Personality and Social Psychology Bulletin*, *29*, 665–675.

19. Lee, M. S., Choi, J., Posadzki, P., & Ernst, E. (2012). Aromatherapy for healthcare: An overview of systematic reviews. *Maturitas*, *71*, 257–260.

20. Le Trionnaire, S., Perry, A., Szczesny, B., Szabo, C., Winyard, P. G., Whatmore, J. L., Wood, M. E., & Whiteman, M. (2014). The synthesis and functional evaluation of a mitochondria-targeted hydrogen sulfide donor, (10-oxo-10-(4-(3-thioxo-3H-1,2-dithiol-5-yl)-phenoxy)decyl)triphenylphosphonium bromide (AP39). *Medical Chemistry Communication, 5,* 728–736.

21. ScienceDaily.com. (2014, July 9). Rotten egg gas holds key to healthcare therapies. *ScienceDaily.com.* https://www.sciencedaily.com/releases/2014/07/140709115455.htm

22. Many of these articles were retracted after it was discovered that they incorrectly summarized the findings and implications of the Le Trionnaire et al. (2014) report. See Stampler, L. (2014, July 11). A stinky compound may protect against cell damage, study finds. *Time.* https://time.com/2976464/rotten-eggs-hydrogen-sulfide-mitochondria/; Downey, A. (2017, October 27). Sniffing your partners' farts could help ward off disease. *New York Post.* https://nypost.com/2017/10/27/sniffing-your-partners-farts-could-help-ward-off-disease/

6: Expert Bullshit Detectors

1. Fisher, R., Ury, W., & Patton, B. (1981). *Getting to yes: Negotiating agreement without giving in.* Penguin Books.

2. Epstein, E. J. (1982) Have you ever tried to sell a diamond? *Atlantic Monthly, 249*(2), 23–34.

3. Crockett, Z., Dhar, R., & Mayyasi, A. (2014). *Everything is bullshit.* Priceonomics.

4. Christina Pryce's story is universal and emblematic of real estate agents the world over. However, in the interest of protecting her identity, Christina Pryce's name is fictitious. All other elements of Pryce's story remain true.

5. Turpin, M. H., Walker, A. C., Kara-Yakoubian, M., Gabert, N. N., Fugelsang, J. A., & Stolz, J. A. (2019). Bullshit makes the art grow profounder. *Judgment and Decision Making, 14,* 658–670.

6. Rule, A., & Levine, D. (2012). International art English: On the rise, and the space, of the art world press release. *Triple Canopy, 16,* 7–30.

7. Dawes, R. M. (1979). The robust beauty of improper linear models in decision making. *American Psychologist, 34,* 571–582; Hardman, D. (2009). *Judgment and decision making: Psychological perspectives.*

BPS-Blackwell; Harte, J. M., & Koele, P. (2001). Modelling and describing human judgement processes: The multiattribute evaluation case. *Thinking and Reasoning, 7,* 29–49; Kim, N. S. (2018). *Judgment and decision making: In the lab and the world.* Palgrave; Payne, J. W., Bettman, J. R., & Johnson, E. J. (1988). Adaptive strategy selection in decision making. *Journal of Experimental Psychology: Learning, Memory, and Cognition, 14,* 534–552; Svenson, O. (1979). Process descriptions of decision making. *Organizational Behavior and Human Performance, 23,* 86–112.

8. Newell, A., & Simon, H. A. (1972). *Human problem solving.* Prentice-Hall.

9. Hirt, E. R., & Castellan, N. J. (1988). Probability and category redefinition in the fault tree paradigm. *Journal of Experimental Psychology: Human Perception and Performance, 14,* 122–131.

10. Facione, P. A., Facione, N. C., & Giancarlo, C. A. (2014). *User manual: The California Critical Thinking Disposition Inventory.* California Academic Press; Facione, P. A., Giancarlo, C. A., Facione, N. C., & Gainen, J. (1995). The disposition toward critical thinking. *Journal of General Education, 44,* 1–25.

11. Stone, E. R., Yates, J. F., & Parker, A. M. (1994). Risk communication: Absolute versus relative expressions of low-probability risks. *Organizational Behavior and Human Decision Processes, 60,* 387–408.

12. Kahneman, D., & Thaler, R. (2006). Utility maximization and experienced utility. *Journal of Economic Perspectives, 20,* 221–234.

13. Stanovich, K. E. (2016). The comprehensive assessment of rational thinking. *Educational Psychologist, 51,* 23–34; Stanovich, K. E., & West, R. F. (1997). Reasoning independently of prior belief and individual differences in actively open-minded thinking. *Journal of Educational Psychology, 89,* 342–357; Toplak, M. E., West, R. F., & Stanovich, K. E. (2014). Rational thinking and cognitive sophistication: Development, cognitive abilities, and thinking dispositions. *Developmental Psychology, 50,* 1037–1048. See also McElroy, T., & Dowd, K. (2007). Susceptibility to anchoring effects: How openness-to-experience influences responses to anchoring cues. *Judgment and Decision Making, 2,* 48–53. But also see Furnham, A., Boo, H. C., & McClelland, A. (2012). Individual differences and the susceptibility to the influence of anchoring cues. *Journal of Individual Differences, 33,* 89–93.

14. Pennycook, G., Cheyne, J. A., Barr, N., Koehler, D. J., & Fugelsang, J. A. (2015). On the reception and detection of pseudo-profound bullshit. *Judgment and Decision Making, 10*, 549–563.

15. Facione, P. A. (1990). *Critical thinking: A statement of expert consensus for purposes of educational assessment and instruction.* California Academic Press. The Delphi Method is a qualitative research methodology involving an interactive panel of experts that works toward consensus on defining and outlining a particular topic. Experts participate in several rounds of questions that require thoughtful and detailed responses. Panelists work toward consensus by sharing reasoned opinions and reconsidering their opinions with regard to comments, objections, and arguments offered by other experts. A total of 46 scholars, educators, and leading figures in critical-thinking theory and critical-thinking assessment research were gathered for the panel meetings. About half of the panelists were primarily affiliated with philosophy departments; the others were affiliated with education, social sciences, or physical sciences. Recommendations resulting from the discussions addressed the cognitive dimensions of critical thinking, the dispositional dimensions of critical thinking, and specific recommendations on critical-thinking instruction and assessment, including development of a critical-thinking curriculum.

16. Novella, S., & DeAngelis, P. (2002). Dowsing. In M. Shermer (Ed.), *The skeptic encyclopedia of pseudoscience* (pp. 93–94).: ABC-CLIO.

17. United States Geological Survey. (2020, October). General facts and concepts about ground water. https://pubs.usgs.gov/circ/circ1186/html/gen_facts.html

18. Enright, J. T. (1999). The failure of the Munich experiments. *Skeptical Inquirer, 23*(1), 39–46. Also see CoolGuy23423 (2009, January 30). *Dawkins debunks dowsing, from part one of* The Enemies of Reason [Video]. YouTube. https://www.youtube.com/watch?v=_VAasVXtCOI

19. National Consortium for the Study of Terrorism and Responses to Terrorism. (2017). *Global terrorism database.* https://www.start.umd.edu/research-projects/global-terrorism-database-gtd; Ritchie, H., Hasell, J., Appel, C., & Roser, M. (2019). *Terrorism: Our world in data.* https://ourworldindata.org/terrorism#how-many-people-are-killed-by-terrorists-worldwide

20. The cost to make one of the devices was no more than $60. Norland, R. (2009, November 3). Iraq swears by bomb detector U.S. sees as

useless. *New York Times*. https://www.nytimes.com/2009/11/04/world/middleeast/04sensors.html

21. Hawley, C., & Jones, M. (January 22, 2010). Useless bomb detector sold worldwide risks lives. *BBC News*. http://news.bbc.co.uk/2/hi/programmes/newsnight/8471187.stm; Mohammed, R., & Nordland, R. (January 23, 2010). British man held for fraud in Iraq bomb detectors. *New York Times*. https://www.nytimes.com/2010/01/24/world/europe/24scanner.html

22. French, C. (2013, April 27). The unseen force that drives Ouija boards and fake bomb detectors. *The Guardian*. https://www.theguardian.com/science/2013/apr/27/ouija-boards-dowsing-rods-bomb-detectors

23. Doherty, B. (1996, November 11). Box of dreams. *Reason*. https://reason.com/1996/11/01/box-of-dreams/; Higginbotham, A. (2013, July 11). In Iraq, the bomb-detecting device that didn't work, except to make money. *Bloomberg Businessweek*. https://www.bloomberg.com/news/articles/2013-07-11/in-iraq-the-bomb-detecting-device-that-didnt-work-except-to-make-money

24. Hussain, M. (2015, November, 23). This fake bomb detector is blamed for hundreds of deaths. It's still in use. *TheIntercept.com*. https://theintercept.com/2015/11/23/this-fake-bomb-detector-is-blamed-for-hundreds-of-deaths-its-still-in-use/

25. Shermer, M. (2011). *The believing brain: From ghosts and gods to politics and conspiracies—How we construct beliefs and reinforce them as truths.* Times Books, Henry Holt and Company.

26. Gilovich, T., Vallone, R., & Tversky, A. (1985). The hot hand in basketball: On the misperception of random sequences. *Cognitive Psychology*, *17*, 295–314; Kahneman, D., & Tversky, A. (1971). Belief in the law of small numbers. *Psychological Bulletin*, *76*, 105–110; Thompson, W. C. (2009). Painting the target around the matching profile: The Texas sharpshooter fallacy in forensic DNA interpretation. *Law, Probability and Risk*, 8, 257–276.

Conclusion

1. Fazio, L. (2020). Pausing to consider why a headline is true or false can help reduce the sharing of false news. *Harvard Kennedy School Misinformation Review*, *1*(2), 1–8; Pennycook, G., McPhetres, J., Zhang, Y., Lu, J. G., & Rand, D. G. (2020). Fighting COVID-19

misinformation on social media: Experimental evidence for a scalable accuracy nudge intervention. *Psychological Science, 31*(7), 770–780.

2. Lewandowsky, S., Ecker, U. K. H., & Cook, J. (2017). Beyond misinformation: Understanding and coping with the "post-truth" era. *Journal of Applied Research in Memory and Cognition, 6,* 353–369.

3. Carl Bergstrom was the first to recommended rules 1–5 for calling bullshit. I find them perfect and succinct. Bergstrom, C. Calling bullshit: Data in a reasonable digital world. https://callingbullshit.org/index.html

4. Arkes, H. R., Hackett, C., & Boehm, L. (1989). The generality of the relation between familiarity and judged validity. *Journal of Behavioral Decision Making, 2,* 81–94; Bacon, F. T. (1979). Credibility of repeated statements: Memory for trivia. *Journal of Experimental Psychology: Human Learning and Memory, 5,* 241–252; Fazio, L. K., Brashier, N. M., Payne, B. K., & Marsh, E. J. (2015). Knowledge does not protect against illusory truth. *Journal of Experimental Psychology: General, 144,* 993–1002; Hasher, L., Goldstein, D., & Toppino, T. (1977). Frequency and the conference of referential validity. *Journal of Verbal Learning and Verbal Behavior, 16,* 107–112; Hawkins, S. A., & Hoch, S. J. (1992). Low-involvement learning: Memory without evaluation. *Journal of Consumer Research, 19,* 212–225; Johar, G. V., & Roggeveen, A. L. (2007). Changing false beliefs from repeated advertising: The role of claim-refutation alignment. *Journal of Consumer Psychology, 17,* 118–127.

5. Asch, S. E. (1951). Effects of group pressure upon the modification and distortion of judgment. In H. Guetzkow (Ed.), *Groups, leadership, and men* (pp. 76–92). Carnegie Press; Asch, S. E. (1956). Studies of independence and conformity: A minority of one against a unanimous majority. *Psychological Monographs, 7* (9), 1–70; Deutsch, M., & Gerard, H. G. (1955). A study of normative and informational social influence upon individual judgment. *Journal of Abnormal and Social Psychology, 51,* 629–636.

6. Berkowitz, A. D. (2005). An overview of the social norms approach. In L. Lederman, L. Stewart, F. Goodhart, & L. Laitman (Eds.), *Changing the culture of college drinking: A social situated prevention campaign* (pp. 187–208). Hampton Press; Borsari, B., & Carey, K. B. (2003). Descriptive and injunctive norms in college drinking: A meta-analytic integration. *Journal of Studies on Alcohol, 64,* 331–341; Cialdini, R. B., Reno, R. R., & Kallgren, C. A. (1990). A focus theory of normative conduct: Recycling

the concept of norms to reduce littering in public places. *Journal of Personality and Social Psychology, 58,* 1015–1026; Lapinski, M. K., & Rimal, R. N. (2005). An explication of social norms. *Communication Theory, 15,* 127–147; Rimal, R. N., & Lapinski, M. K. (2015). A re-explication of social norms, ten years later. *Communication Theory, 25,* 393–409.

7. Rimal, R. N. (2008). Modeling the relationship between descriptive norms and behaviors: A test and extension of the theory of normative social behavior (TNSB). *Health Communication, 23,* 103–116.

8. Reno, R. R., Cialdini, R. B., & Kallgren, C. A. (1993). The trans-situational influence of social norms. *Journal of Personality and Social Psychology, 64,* 104–112.

9. Schultz, P. W., Nolan, J. M., Cialdini, R. B., Goldstein, N. J., & Griskevicius, V. (2007). The constructive, destructive, and reconstructive power of social norms. *Psychological Science, 18,* 429–434.

10. Accordingly, the use of smiley and sad faces to give injunctive norm feedback, combined with descriptive norm energy-usage information, is now used by utility companies in various major metropolitan areas. Kaufman, L. (2009, January 30). Utilities turn their customers green with envy. *New York Times.* https://www.nytimes.com/2009/01/31/science/earth/31compete.html

11. Bodimeade, H., Anderson, E., La Macchia, S., Smith, J. R., Terry, D. J., & Louis, W. R. (2014). Testing the direct, indirect, and interactive roles of referent group injunctive and descriptive norms for sun protection in relation to the theory of planned behavior. *Journal of Applied Social Psychology, 44,* 739–750.

12. Glad, W., & Adesso, V. J. (1976). The relative importance of socially induced tension and behavioral contagion for smoking behavior. *Journal of Abnormal Psychology, 85,* 119–121; Grosser, D., Polansky, N., & Lippitt, R. (1951). A laboratory study of behavioral contagion. *Human Relations, 4,* 115–142; Krassa, M. A. (1988). Social groups, selective perception, and behavioral contagion in public opinion. *Social Networks, 10,* 109–136; Polansky, N., Lippitt, R., & Redl, F. (1950). An investigation of behavioral contagion in groups. *Human Relations, 3,* 319–348; Polansky, N. A. (1952). On the dynamics of behavioral contagion. *Group, 14,* 3–8; Ritter, E. H., & Holmes, D. S. (1969). Behavioral contagion: Its occurrence as a function of differential restraint reduction. *Journal of Experimental Research in Personality, 3,* 242–246; Suzuki, S., Jensen, E. L. S., Bossaerts, P., & O'Doherty, J. P. (2016).

Behavioral contagion during learning about another agent's risk-preferences acts on the neural representation of decision-risk. *PNAS Proceedings of the National Academy of Sciences, 113*, 3755–3760; Watanabe, K. (2008). Behavioral speed contagion: Automatic modulation of movement timing by observation of body movements. *Cognition, 106*, 1514–1524; Wheeler, L. (1966). Toward a theory of behavioral contagion. *Psychological Review, 73*, 179–192; Wheeler, L., Smith, S., & Murphy, D. B. (1964). Behavioral contagion. *Psychological Reports, 15*, 159–173.

13. Centola, D., & Macy, M. (2007). Complex contagions and the weakness of long ties. *American Journal of Sociology, 113*, 702–734.

14. Nyhan, B., & Reifler, J. (2010). When corrections fail: The persistence of political misperceptions. *Political Behavior, 32*, 303–330. Also see Wood, T., & Porter, E. (2019). The elusive backfire effect: Mass attitudes' steadfast factual adherence. *Political Behavior, 41*, 135–163.

15. Moyer, M. W. (2017). Journey to gunland. *Scientific American, 317*(4), 54–63.

16. Berkowitz, L., & LePage, A. (1967). Weapons as aggression-eliciting stimuli. *Journal of Personality and Social Psychology, 7*, 202–207. In this study, male college students agreed to participate in a study they believed examined physiological reactions to stress induced by mild electric shocks. Each participant was paired with another alleged participant who was actually an assistant to the experimenters. Participants were told that they would have to solve a problem and they knew that their performance would be evaluated by their partner. The participant and his partner were placed in separate but adjacent rooms. Shock electrodes were placed on the participant's forearm, and galvanic skin response electrodes were attached to the participant's fingers, with wires trailing from the electrodes to the next room. During the evaluation task, all participants received either a single shock or they received seven shocks. As soon as the first "evaluation" was completed, the participant was taken to the room holding the shock machine operating key and was informed that it was his turn to evaluate his partner's work on a different problem. In one condition, a 12-gauge shotgun and a .38-caliber revolver were lying on a table near the desk that was equipped with the shock-delivery key. In two control conditions, there was either nothing at all on the table near the shock key or there were two badminton racquets lying on the table. All other aspects of the

experiment were the same. When it was the participant's turn to deliver electric shocks to his partner, he tended to deliver a *greater number of shocks* and *more enduring shocks* when he had earlier received seven shocks than when he received only one shock. Importantly, what was lying on the table mattered. When guns were on the table, the frequency and duration of the electric shocks were greater than when a set of badminton racquets and/or nothing was on the table. In addition to a greater frequency and duration of electric shocks, other aggression studies have shown that the very same procedures can also result in delivering a *greater intensity of electric shocks*. These studies don't suggest that "guns kill people," but they do suggest that the presence of guns elicits stronger aggressive responses. After all, what is more strongly associated with violence than a gun?

17. Fowler, K. A., Dahlberg, L. L., Haileyesus, T., & Annest, J. L. (2015). Firearm injuries in the United States. *Preventive Medicine, 79*, 5–14; Hemenway, D., & Solnick, S. J., (2015). The epidemiology of self-defense gun use: Evidence from the National Crime Victimization Surveys 2007–2011. *Preventive Medicine, 79*, 22–27.

18. Rice, R., & Atkin, C. (Eds.) (2001). *Public communication campaigns* (3rd ed.). Sage.

19. Schwarz, N., Sanna, L. J., Skurnik, I., & Yoon, C. (2007). Metacognitive experiences and the intricacies of setting people straight: Implications for debiasing and public information campaigns. In M. P. Zanna (Ed.), *Advances in experimental social psychology* (Vol. 39; pp. 127–161). Academic Press.

20. Boghossian, P., & Lindsay, J. (2019). *How to have impossible conversations: A very practical guide*. Lifelong Books; Lord, C. G., Ross, L., & Lepper, M. R. (1979). Biased assimilation and attitude polarization: The effects of prior theories on subsequently considered evidence. *Journal of Personality and Social Psychology, 37*, 2098–2109; Washburn, A. N., & Skitka, L. J. (2017). Science denial across the political divide: Liberals and conservatives are similarly motivated to deny attitude-inconsistent science. *Social Psychological and Personality Science, 9*, 972–980; Chan, M. S., Jones, C. R., Jamieson, K. H., & Albarracin, D. (2017). Debunking: A meta-analysis of the psychological efficacy of messages countering misinformation. *Psychological Science, 28*, 1531–1546; Nyhan, B., & Reifler, J. (2010). When corrections fail: The persistence of political misperceptions. *Political Behavior, 32*, 303–330. Also see Wood, T., &

Porter, E. (2019). The elusive backfire effect: Mass attitudes' steadfast factual adherence. *Political Behavior*, *41*, 135–163.

21. For several interesting and unfortunate examples, see Hofstadter, R. (1962). *Anti-intellectualism in American life*. Vintage Books; Watzlawick, P. (Ed.). (1984). *The invented reality: How do we know what we believe we know?* W. W. Norton; Watzlawick, P., Weakland, J. H., & Fisch, R. (1974). *Change: Principles of problem formation and problem resolution*. W. W. Norton.

22. Chu, D. K., et al. (2020). Physical distancing, face masks, and eye protection to prevent person-to-person transmission of SARS-CoV-2 and COVID-19: A systematic review and meta-analysis. *The Lancet*, *395*, P1973–1987. See also Centers for Disease Control and Prevention. (2020, November 20). Scientific brief: Community use of cloth masks to control the spread of SARS-CoV-2. https://www.cdc.gov/coronavirus/2019-ncov/more/masking-science-sars-cov2.html

23. Lynch, M. P. (2019). *Know-it-all society: Truth and arrogance in political culture*. Liveright Publishing.

24. Alcock, J. E. (2018). *Belief: What it means to believe and why our convictions are so compelling*. Prometheus Books.

25. Cialdini, R. B., Reno, R. R., & Kallgren, C. A. (1990). A focus theory of normative conduct: Recycling the concept of norms to reduce littering in public places. *Journal of Personality and Social Psychology*, *58*, 1015–1026; Goldstein, N. J., Cialdini, R. B., & Griskevicius, V. (2008). A room with a viewpoint: Using social norms to motivate environmental conservation in hotels. *Journal of Consumer Research*, *35*, 472–482; Jacobson, R. P., Mortensen, C. R., & Cialdini, R. B. (2011). Bodies obliged and unbound: Differentiated response tendencies for injunctive and descriptive social norms. *Journal of Personality and Social Psychology*, *100*, 433–448; Jacobson, R. P., Mortensen, C. R., Jacobson, K. J. L., & Cialdini, R. B. (2015). Self-control moderates the effectiveness of influence attempts highlighting injunctive social norms. *Social Psychological and Personality Science*, *6*, 718–726; Kallgren, C. A., Reno, R. R., & Cialdini, R. B. (2000). A focus theory of normative conduct: When norms do and do not affect behavior. *Personality and Social Psychology Bulletin*, *26*, 1002–1012; Reno, R. R., Cialdini, R. B., & Kallgren, C. A. (1993). The transsituational influence of social norms. *Journal of Personality and Social Psychology*, *64*, 104–112.

Appendix

1. Today, we have greater access to more data than we've ever had before. The things discovered by scientists, statisticians, data crunchers and miners, and anyone who knows how to test a correlation or multiple regression model are quite remarkable—so they seem. Their failure to recognize correlations as spurious bullshit is often grounded in mistaken notions of probability and confusing model and test data. Too much irrelevant data can be a problem in that it makes us think there are true relationships between things that are actually nothing but chance occurrences. If a data set has thousands of variables, you will be sure to find several statistically significant correlations. And the more data you give to a prediction model, the more it will discover random, arbitrary, and spurious correlations. No amount of data will identify causal underpinnings of spurious correlations. When I was a budding statistician in graduate school, I discovered that I could design incredibly accurate statistical models to predict the outcomes of NBA basketball game scores with fewer than two dozen variables, all of which were readily available on ESPN.com. The problem was my statistical models were only successful at identifying the idiosyncratic patterns of data that the models were built on and were never able to predict new outcomes. So, when a hotshot statistician tells you he's going to be the next sport-betting champion or that he can reliably predict sophisticated fluctuations in the stock market, ask him if the performance of his prediction models has been tested on new cases not used to build the parameters of the models in the first place. Both correlational and experimental data are often used in the development of prediction models. Statisticians use data to basically fit parameters of a prediction model to the model data. Essentially, prediction models designed from preexisting data "cheat" because they have knowledge of both the predictor variables (for example, home team turnover percentage, away team rebound percentage, home team foul-shot percentage, etc.) and the outcome variable (for example, final score of an NBA basketball game). New test data are needed to assess the real predictive performance of the model. Fletcher, J. (2014, May 26). Spurious correlations: Margarine linked to divorce? *BBC News*. https://www.bbc.com/news/magazine-27537142.

The very same idea is central to machine learning. An algorithm is programmed or "trained" with data to recognize patterns in the data. Only once the algorithm is fine-tuned for accuracy and efficiency can it be tested. But the performance of the algorithm is not tested with the data used to train it. Rather, the algorithm is tested with new cases (i.e., test data) to determine how well the machine can predict new answers based on its training. Before Orville and Wilbur Wright tested the world's first successful motor-operated airplane, they used lots of data to fine-tune their design. However, they didn't use their pre-existing data to conclude that their design of the airplane flies and call it a day. Rather, they proved that the airplane flew by testing their design on subsequent trials. This is why having access to "big data" (i.e., a lot of data on lots of different variables) to learn from can make it paradoxically worse rather than better. In other words, when someone has way too much information, they can begin to behave like they have very little information. The fundamental goal of science is not to search for statistical correlations in large data sets and then build sensible narratives around them. That is a misguided fishing expedition masquerading as science. Science's goal is to find causal relationships, which often requires the development of new measurement instruments and materials to make new observations guided by new insights and new ideas. See Calude, C. S., & Longo, G. (2017). The deluge of spurious correlations in big data. *Foundations of Science*, *22*, 595–612; Kassan, P. (2018). I've got algorithm. Who could ask for anything more? *Skeptical Inquirer*, *42*(5), 48–51; O'Neil, C. (2016). *Weapons of math destruction: How big data increases inequality and threatens democracy*. Crown Publishers.

INDEX